Perennial Garden Color
FOR TEXAS AND THE SOUTH

William C. Welch

Foreword by Neil Sperry

TAYLOR PUBLISHING COMPANY
Dallas, Texas

Designed by Bonnie Baumann

Copyright 1989 by William C. Welch

Published by TAYLOR PUBLISHING COMPANY
1550 West Mockingbird Lane
Dallas, Texas 75235

Library of Congress Cataloging-in-Publication Data

Welch, William C. (William Carlisle), 1939–
    Perennial garden color.

    Bibliography: p.
    Includes index.
    1. Perennials—Texas.   2. Perennials—Southern
States.   3. Old roses—Texas.   4. Old roses—Southern
States.   5. Color in gardening—Texas.   6. Color in
gardening—Southern States.   I. Title.
SB434.W45   1989   635.9'32'09764   88-24820
ISBN 0-87833-628-1

Printed in the United States of America

10 9 8 7 6 5 4 3 2 1

To my wife, Diane,
for her encouragement and support

Acknowledgments

Contributions and encouragement from old and new gardening friends have been a continuing source of inspiration during the preparation of this book. Sharing knowledge, experiences and plants is a tradition among gardeners that is not only alive and well, but thrives as an almost instant bond and basis for communication, sometimes even among total strangers.

Some of my most cherished relationships began when I noticed an unusual plant and stopped to ask the gardener about his experiences with it. More often than not, I have left the gardens of strangers not only with valuable information, but also cuttings, seedlings or plants, and a new friendship. It is in this spirit that the information has been gathered and is given to those who read these pages.

Primary source historical research on early Texas gardens and plants is a special interest of Miss Pamela Ashworth Puryear of Navasota, Texas. Her scholarly approach and her knowledge of library resources contributed greatly to the sections on garden history and old garden roses.

A. Scott Ogden of New Braunfels provided much of the information on bulbs. His vast knowledge, coupled with his enthusiasm for sharing, added valuable depth to the information on naturalized Narcissus, Hymenocallis, Crinum, Sedum and Zephyranthes, among many others. Scott, along with Thad Howard, D.V.M., also provided many of the beautiful photographs of flowering bulbs.

The assistance of Greg Grant, Bexar County Extension Horticulturist, has been a real asset in providing information on the identity and history of roses and perennials. Mrs. Paul Kane was most helpful with the gingers and unusual perennials. Charles A. Walker, Jr., president of the Heritage Rose Foundation, served as special editor for the section on old garden roses. His research abilities and organizational skills are making a major impact on the future of old garden roses.

I sincerely appreciate the enthusiastic support from the American Iris Society. Mrs. Jeane Stayer, Secretary, introduced me to Mrs. Olive Rice, the Chairman for Public Relations, who provided photographs and basic information that greatly enriched the section on irises. Marie Caillet, of Little Elm, Texas, a noted authority and author on Louisiana Irises provided significant input and most of the beautiful illustrations in the iris section. Chris Corby, Publisher of *Texas Gardener Magazine* graciously allowed the use of a major article on irises by Marie Caillet for source material.

The American Daffodil Society assisted my efforts by providing information, photographs and encouragement for the section on daffodils. Dr. Theodore E. Snazelle, the Society's current president, furnished suggestions on culture, while Mrs. James Kerr from Dallas and Mrs. Kelly Shryoc from Ft. Worth provided useful information on recommended varieties and photographs for the section.

Mrs. Nell C. Crandall of Houston cheerfully and carefully guided me through the Daylilies. Her beautiful photographs and enthusiastic editorial input has me ready to fill my garden with these wonderful plants. Mrs. Peggy Hammell added suggestions for landscape use of specific varieties adapted to North Texas and similar climates.

Marvin Yarotsky from Houston and James Sterling from Dallas, both members of the Chrysanthemum Society of America, gave freely of information and photographs of this genus. Sterling Cornelius and Steve Moore, of Houston, edited the section on Chinese Hibiscus and provided many of the photographs.

Neil Sperry, whose *Complete Guide to Texas Gardening* has become a fixture in the homes of thousands of Texas gardeners, provided valuable advice and encouragement on the publication process. I also wish to thank Neil Sperry and Rita Miller Atkins for permission to use material from articles I wrote for Neil's *Gardens and More* Magazine.

Arnie Hanson, Mary Kelly, and the entire staff at Taylor have been patient and helpful throughout the writing and publishing processes. Working with Tom Christopher as he provided editorial assistance for the manuscript was a joy.

I want to thank my colleagues in Extension Horticulture at Texas A & M University and the Texas Agricultural Extension Service for their encouragement and help with the text. Last, but certainly not least I want to thank my wife Diane and son William, as well as my entire family, for understanding how important this book is to me.

The following individuals provided valued assistance with the book and are gratefully acknowledged by the author.

William D. Adams
Peter Adkins
Robert Basye
John Begnaud
Allen Bush
Flora Ann Bynum
Roberta Churchin
Dr. Sam Cotner
Paul Cox
Hugh Dargan
James David
S.J. Derby
Dr. Severn Doughty
R. Gordon Echols
Edith Eddelman
John Fairey
Ted L. Fisher
Manuel Flores
Dwight S. Hall
Bluefford G. Hancock
Keith Hansen
Madelene Hill
William Lanier Hunt
Everett E. Janne

Mary Palmer Kelley
Josephine Kennedy
John Koros
Thomas R. LeRoy
Dr. Jeff Lewis
Tom Longbrake
Dr. Calvin Lyons
Hazel McCoy
Dr. Ed McWilliams
Vincent J. Mannino
Cynthia Mueller
Peggy Newcomb
Dean Norton
Suzanne O'Connell
Dr. Neil G. Odenwald
Henry Painter
Dr. Jerry Parsons
Judy Patterson
Dr. Brent Pemberton
Catina Perkins
Sue Rowan Pittman
Dr. Tom Pope
Dr. J.C. Raulston
Dr. Robert S. Reich

Dr. Roland E. Roberts
Mattie Rosprim
Susan Schmidtke
Mark J. Schusler
Margaret Sharpe
Holly Shimizu
G. Michael Shoup, Jr.
Brenda Beust Smith
John Snowden
Sally McQueen Squire
Dr. Richard Stadtherr
Quentin Steitz
Lee Ann Toles
Suzanne L. Turner
Janice Vilegi
Nancy Volkman
Bob Webster
Douglas F. Welsh
Dr. Joe White
John M. White
Dr. Don Wilkerson
Joe Woodard

CONTENTS

PART I: THE PERENNIAL GARDEN

PART II: PERENNIALS FOR THE GARDEN

PART III: OLD GARDEN ROSES AND COMPANION PLANTS

Foreword

When Bill Welch told me he planned to write a book on perennials for the South, I knew it would be a masterpiece destined for the library of every true Southern plantperson. I knew I'd be standing in line for one of the very first copies. Now that I've read it, I know I'm right!

In your hands is the work of one of the South's most outstanding gardening authorities. Bill has been a close friend of mine for 18 years and those years have only deepened our friendship and my respect for his knowledge. He's a patient teacher, as thousands already know. He has worked with gardeners at all levels—from nurserymen and landscape architects to dedicated hobbyists and rank newcomers throughout the gardening South. At every level Bill has received awards and accolades for his dedicated service to gardening. Having worked alongside him in the Extension Horticulture ranks for seven years, I can also say he has the utmost respect of his peers.

On many nights during the growing season, I fall asleep planning changes in the Sperry perennial garden. True, there are some outstanding references on the bookshelves, but they're too often for other parts of the country. This book changes all that. Enjoy this book about a wonderful group of plants! Pick it up often. Use it as the tool it's intended to be—to help make our perennial gardens here in the South as great as those in our dreams.

Look especially to the detailed information on cottage gardening and how it relates both to our past and current landscapes. There is also invaluable information on old garden roses, one of Bill's favorite plant groups.

Bill Welch has my appreciation for taking the time to share his great knowledge of an exciting topic with all of us. May this book be as successful as it deserves to be.

Best wishes, Bill. Thanks for the great job!

Neil Sperry

PART ONE

The Perennial Garden

1
The Roots of Our Gardens

EARLY GARDEN DESIGN IN TEXAS AND THE SOUTH

A spring stroll down a Texas country lane during the Victorian period (1837–1904) was certain to take one past a flowering yard, more often than not, tended by a lady in a poke bonnet, wielding a hoe. A rambling and glorious show of color literally erupted from the dooryard. Climbing roses dripped from the fences and the front porch of the modest cottage or farmhouse; fruit trees were in full bloom, and the air was heavy with delightful scents of the garden. But the passage of time has brought near extinction to this form of gardening once handed down from mother to daughter, in spite of the dictates of fashion. The few examples one encounters today are usually bits and pieces of what was once a strong tradition.

HISTORY OF THE COTTAGE GARDEN

European Origins

A look at the history of this so-called cottage gardening concept gives insight into its application in early Texas and the South. Along with most of European culture, medieval monasteries saved gardening ideas from the wreck of the Roman Empire. In the usually peaceful cloister, the monks grew their "simples:" herbs for medicines, flavorings, and food. In separate areas they often grew lilies and roses to deck their churches during the great festivals. They saved these plants, and passed them on to the common folk, who also collected wild plants for their needs.

During the relative peace of the Tudor era, the idea of growing these "simples" and some flowers for ornament literally took root and flourished among the general

Ann Hathaway's garden at Stratford-upon-Avon, England, is world famous as an example of an authentically restored cottage garden.

This cottage garden at the remains of the C. C. Hairston house in Independence, Texas, was designed by the author.

population. The whole English people seemed to go garden crazy. Even the common folk took part in the fashion. Exotic and unusual plants were arriving from newly-discovered portions of the world and neighbors vied among themselves to show the neatest and most colorful front garden. The plants they chose were the simple, thrifty sorts—"steadfast," in the vernacular of the time. In keeping with the natural charm of the plants, the cottagers gave them imaginative common names: love-lies-bleeding, heal-all, thrift, loose-strife, bachelor's buttons, bouncing Bet, ragged robin, forget-me-not, dame's rocket, monkshood, love-in-a-mist, and baby's breath, to name a few.

Early American Gardens

Colonial America inherited the cottage gardening style from settlers as they came from the Old World. The American colonial house was supremely suited to having this sort of garden before it. In New England, for example, the tradition flourished. Alice Morse Earle, in her 1902 book *Old Time Gardens*, writes: "I cannot doubt the first gardens that our foremothers had, which were

wholly flowering plants, were front yards, little enclosures hard won from the forest" (38).

Before the American Revolution, in the older settled portions of Virginia and the Carolinas, a more formal gardening tradition held. The restored gardens at Mt. Vernon and at the Governor's Palace at Williamsburg and the residential gardens of old Charleston are prime examples of the colonial use of formal parterre, which is a garden area in which the flower beds and paths form a pattern. This gardening tradition was continued by the wealthy and cultured of the American South and was contemporary with the cottage gardens of the lower and middle classes.

In the 1830s, with the advent of Classical Revival styles of architecture, Southern garden-makers had a choice of the formal parterre gardens or the informal cottage garden design; both greatly enhanced the beautiful Classical Revival homes of the period. Once again, it was the upper classes who favored the more formal garden style. The enclosed geometric spaces and great avenues of trees of the plantation homes in the Lower South reflect this tradition. In Louisiana, Oak Alley, Belle Helene (Ashland) and Rosedown plantations are examples. The residential gardens in the older sections of New Orleans

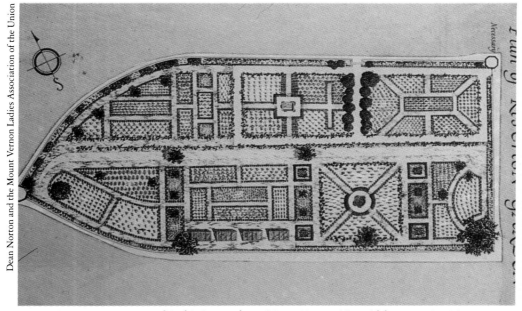

(Top) This is the lower terrace of the kitchen garden at Mount Vernon. The cold frames to the right are appropriate but their exact location during Washington's time is not known. The large building in the background is the paddock. (Bottom) The 1936 plan of the kitchen garden at Mount Vernon was researched and drawn by Morley Jeffers Williams. Washington and his gardeners usually referred to this area as the lower garden.

(Left) Note the bed designs of the lower terrace. The tending of the grass paths was often recorded in the gardener's weekly reports. (Below) The formal gardens at the Governor's Palace in Williamsburg, Virginia, illustrated the use of perennials and annuals in a formal setting.

(Below) *Parterre* in the Louisiana garden of Dr. and Mrs. Jack D. Holden relies upon clipped privet hedges to outline the beds. (Right) The Herman-Grima courtyard in New Orleans, Louisiana, features patterned beds in an enclosed court. Restoration by Suzanne L. Turner. (Bottom) The grand avenue of live oaks at Oak Alley Plantation in Vacherie, Louisiana, visually connects the house to the Mississippi River.

7

(Top) This *parterre* garden in Charleston, South Carolina, includes a front public garden planted in perennials and annuals typical of an eighteenth-century garden. A private garden in back contains a fountain, English urn, seventeenth-century sundial, and grass panel. Twelve-foot camellias provide separation between the gardens. Garden design by Hugh Dargan Associates, Inc., Columbia, South Carolina. (Bottom) The paisley design of the *parterre* is reinforced with appropriate colors of annuals and perennials.

still have a few surviving geometric parterres. Some gardens very successfully combined elements of both formal and cottage gardening styles, with the results typically including simple geometric designs for paths with masses of various perennials, herbs and annuals spilling over and softening the edges of the plantings.

Texas Pioneer Gardens

For early Texas, sources for documenting garden design are scant. The first settlers had little time for anything but maintaining the essentials of food, safety and shelter. Diaries and literature document ornamental perennials and herbs being present as the frontier was tamed. Later, with prosperity and increased population, gardens became a part of nearly every homestead.

During the 1700s the French and Spanish competed for control in the territory we now call Texas. The Spanish built missions in Eastern, Southern, Central and parts of Western Texas. These missions, enclosed by thick walls of stone in South and West Texas and heavy timbers in East Texas, share some characteristics with the monasteries of Europe. Chapels within the mission complexes were elegant and massive structures, a credit to the ingenuity and expertise of the early clergy who built them by hand, largely with unskilled labor. The Spaniards were kind to the Indians, but although the Indians liked the food prepared at the missions, few of them adopted the Christianity or lifestyle of their Spanish "hosts." The early Franciscan missionaries dedicated

themselves to raising food, and planted their cloisters with native flowering trees for shade and shrubs for color. As in Europe, the Church was active in preserving and spreading plant material.

The Spanish mission experiment was considered a failure by some at the time, but the trail was blazed for settlers who began to filter into Texas from the Eastern United States and later in waves of immigration from Europe. During the Mexican period (1821–1836) large and influential Texas landowners began settling and establishing extensive plantations that included some very interesting gardens.

Adina de Zavala, in an article published September 2, 1934, in the *San Antonio Express*, and December 16, 1934, in the *Dallas Morning News*, related her memories of conversations with her grandmother, Emily West de Zavala, and visits to her garden created in the early 1830s. The de Zavala Plantation was located at Lynchburg on the San Jacinto River near the present site of the San Jacinto Monument. Lorenzo de Zavala, Emily's husband, was an early Mexican and Texas statesman and the first vice president of the Republic of Texas. In addition to naming specific roses, which were her grandmother's favorite flower, Adina also referred to borders of violets and masses of dianthus and verbenas. Pictures of the home and garden indicate a large columned front porch of the typical East Texas house surrounded by an attractive wooden picket fence. Roses, perennials, annuals and herbs filled the inside of the garden. Occasional hedges and borders of roses added a touch of formality to what

(Right) A rendering of the De Zavala house in Lynchburg, Texas, circa 1834. (Far right) The plan of the De Zavala garden interpreted from an article by Adina De Zavala that appeared in the *San Antonio Express* on September 2, 1934. The Renderings are by Karen Benson.

could be described as an early Texas cottage garden. The de Zavala home and garden surely ranked among the finest of early Texas.

Another Texas landmark garden in the colonial period was William Wharton's Eagle Island Plantation in Brazoria County, Texas. Wharton imported an English gardener to tend a lovely, lakeshore garden that featured a several-tiered central fountain and a formal parterre surrounded by topiary. Mary Austin Holley described and sketched both the house and garden in 1837 in her diary. Eagle Island and nearby Lake Jackson Plantation both were renowned for their artificial garden islands and were considered among the finest gardens in Texas. They also reflected the formal gardening tradition of the upper class South.

A brief but interesting garden description also found in Holley's diary relates to a visit to Bolivar, brother Henry Austin's Brazos River Plantation near Columbia. On May 15, 1835, Holley wrote: "Discovered the little burying ground with roses blooming on two fresh graves—dropped there a tear—had dreaded to inquire for them. It is well chosen—a little enclosure—figs growing luxuriantly without, flowers blooming within" (22). Holley also wrote of walking and conversing in the shrubbery at Bolivar and of pruning and burning the refuse there in the autumn.

One of the best sources of information on the gardens and lifestyles of Texans and other Southerners can be found in the almanacs published by Thomas Affleck. These were produced annually from 1845 until about 1861. Affleck could be considered the consummate early American pioneer. He constantly sought new frontiers, exploited many areas of farming and business, espoused the virtues of environmental awareness, and was an early advocate of organic gardening, crop rotation and animal husbandry. His *Southern Rural Almanac* ranged in circulation from 20,000 to 56,000 copies per year which, along with his articles in the *New Orleans Picayune* and other important publications of his time, indicate that he was widely read and appreciated.

Thomas Affleck's almanacs often included articles on gardening as well as mail-order offerings from his Southern Nurseries, first located on his wife's plantation near Natchez, Mississippi, and then later including more than 3,000 acres known as Glenblythe Plantation near Gay Hill, Washington County, Texas. In her research on southern garden history at Louisiana State University, Suzanne Turner, Associate Professor of Landscape Architecture, cites an interesting and very descriptive excerpt from the *1852 Southern Rural Almanac* which describes a typical southern plantation garden of his period:

> In forming a shrubbery, the finer shrubs and evergreens should be planted at such distances, as that when the more common kinds planted between crowd too much, they may be gradually removed and the others left to occupy the ground. . . . That there may be a pleasant variety, in anything of an extensive shrubbery, one kind of a shrub, or flower should always prevail in one place: so that every turn of the walk may present something new, and

The Ferdinand Lindheimer house and garden in New Braunfels, Texas, serve as a museum and memorial to the famous German-born botanist.

yet the general character be preserved. In one turn or stretch, let the rose predominate; in another the phlox and the dahlia; here clumps of bright annuals, and here masses of verbenas, scarlet geraniums, etc. (6).

The almanacs and other writings of Thomas Affleck indicate that the people of his time were not only interested in cash crops, but aspired to and achieved landscapes that provided a well-organized and refined lifestyle in which ornamental plants played a major role.

Germanic Traditions

Texas was settled by people from a wide variety of cultural and ethnic backgrounds. Germans, Czechs, Scandinavians, English, Spanish, African and French all brought their gardening traditions to the new frontier they were to call home. Northern European gardens all shared many similarities. The practical Germans were the largest group to call the new state their home and were well known then, as today, for their success with both edible and ornamental plants. They tended to keep their plants in rows and mix many colors in the garden. Prince Carl Solms-Braunfels who was responsible for settling many of his countrymen in the Hill Country of Central Texas in the 1840s, considered the gardens of his German countrymen in Texas to be superior and scorned

what he considered laziness and lack of gardening expertise among the Anglos. He spoke glowingly of the neat dooryards of flowers he found among even the first newcomers in New Braunfels.

Mid and Late Victorian Design

There may have been some truth to Prince Carl Solms-Braunfels prejudices, but the English were masters at gardening, even in the smallest plots. As the late Victorian architectural styles of the 1870s began to dominate structures of the time, gardening trends began to favor "bedding out" displays. Another benchmark of the Victorian style was the use of randomly spaced shrubs and trees in lawn areas. This new style consisted of small geometric beds set in mowed lawns, packed with annuals, all of a similar size and shape, in bright colors. American middle classes adopted the trend, and scorned the old-fashioned cottage garden as messy and disorderly.

The humble and conservative country people in America and Northern Europe continued to garden as they always had, however, and by the turn of the century, the cottage garden style was reborn as the "herbaceous border," which was nothing more than a strip of cottage garden.

Another form to gain popularity in this period was the enclosed garden. Part of the excitement achieved by

AS IT IS.   AN UNPLEASANT HOME.
BEFORE PATRONIZING THE NURSERYMEN.

GRAPE ARBOR.
Ornamental as well as useful.
M. Brunswick & Co., Rochester, N. Y.

AS IT WILL BE.   A PLEASANT HOME.
AFTER PATRONIZING THE TREE DEALER.

(Top left) These Victorian era advertising cards were printed as an aid for nursery salesmen. Note the black smoke coming from the chimney, the broken fence, the shutter, and the pig in the yard of the "unpleasant home." (Bottom left) The "after picture" with Victorian flower beds. (Above) This Victorian nursery sales aid featured grape arbors.

many of the great gardens of Northern Europe is that the visitor cannot see the entire garden at once. The anticipation of moving from one room or area to another creates a feeling of excitement similar to touring various rooms of a great home. These "rooms" may be formed with walls of stone, brick, wood or with living materials such as evergreen hedges. Another possibility is permanent structures designed to support roses or other vines. These can take the form of walls or arches over entrances or garlands, all of which were popular during the heyday of Gertrude Jekyll, the famous English gardener of Victorian times. Jekyll is credited with perfecting the concept of the herbaceous border. Her borders could be described as strips of cottage garden. Jekyll was a great believer in roses on structures and offered some very creative ideas on how they can be incorporated into the garden in her book, *Roses for English Gardens*. She further stressed the use of species and old rambling rose varieties known

to be hardy and easily maintained. Broad walkways partially covered by wooden or iron structures were beautifully softened by roses selected for their graceful growth habits as well as the fragrance and beauty of their flowers.

Gertrude Jekyll loved the natural look of tree trunks and limbs. This was evident in the natural wood furniture and structures she popularized during her time. Her influence can be seen in some of the Southern cottage gardens remaining today. These gardens were far different from the formal "bedding out" displays typically seen with Victorian architecture of the period. Walls and overhead structures served as the "bones" of her gardens. Roses, shrubs, perennials and annuals created tapestry effects in her wide herbaceous borders. This resulted from planting "drifts" of plants having various colors, forms and textures. As she said in *Colour Schemes for the Flower Garden*, "Many years ago I came to the conclusion that in all flower borders it is better to plant

(Above) The English border at Hampton Court features "bedding out" arrangements often found in Victorian era gardens. (Right) Authentic cottage gardens may still be found in rural areas of Texas and the South. Walter Kessel tends the vegetables that are interplanted in the garden of his Paige, Texas, landscape. (Above right) White Lady Banks Rose forms an enclosure at the entrance to the Antique Rose Emporium in Independence, Texas. Garden design by Nancy Volkman and the author. (Far right) The "room effect" of the James David garden in Austin, Texas, is achieved partially by the grape arbor.

in long rather than block shaped patches. . . . The word "drift" conveniently describes the shape I have in mind. . . ." (26).

The vertical element was always strongly present in Jekyll's planting designs along with an inspiring awareness of texture and color. Her gardens created a great deal of interest. Modern gardeners are discovering that her design philosophy is timeless and as relevant today as it was during her lifetime (1843–1932).

In analyzing cottage gardening style, we see that the fences, walls, hedges and walks provided design continuity for a combination of plant materials otherwise so informal as to be confusing. Each garden tended to be a unique expression of its creator, and each season offered its own blend of colors and flower types. The more one studies this design type, the more one realizes the potential for creating unique and beautiful tapestries of materials. Spike flowers such as larkspur and salvia contrast effectively with ray flowers like daisies and coreopsis. Foliage color and texture can create contrast and interest even when plants are out of flower. Gray-foliaged plants were commonly used for accent in English cottage gardens. Ornamental grasses also offer a pleasant textural and color contrast.

(Left) Fall flowering perennials provide abundant color in the circa 1855 garden at the remains of the C. C. Hairston house in Independence, Texas. It currently serves as a cottage garden display for the Antique Rose Emporium. Garden design by the author. (Above) Running roses and picket fencing enclose the "chicken run" at a Fredericksburg, Texas, garden. A chicken run was part of nearly every nineteenth-century landscape in rural areas of Texas and the South.

Plant Materials in Texas Gardens

These early gardens were as practical as they were beautiful. Many of the plants were useful in some way; rosemary, wormwood, dill, thyme and borage often appeared along with a host of other culinary and medicinal herbs. Settlers often planted soapberry (*Sapindus drummondi*) and bouncing Bet (*Saponaria officinalis*) for the sake of convenience as well as beauty, since the soapberry's fruits and the bouncing Bet's roots furnished homegrown substitutes for soap. Various dye plants and dishrag gourds were other practical necessities common to these gardens.

Native plants were gathered from the wild and planted because they were beautiful, available and easily grown. It is well to remember that garden hoses and sprinkler systems were unknown commodities to early cottage gardeners, and plants had to be tough and thrifty if they were to survive. Any imported plants must naturalize easily and be available at low cost since survival was the first order of business, and the average settler had little extra money for luxuries.

These settlers carefully saved seeds of annuals each year after the initial purchase. Reseeding annuals such as larkspur (*Delphinium grandiflorum*), poppies (*Papaver*

A Garden of Perennials

This beautiful illustration of a perennial garden was drawn and colored by Margaret Scruggs and adorned the inside cover of *Gardening in the Southwest*. Published by Southwest Press of Dallas, Texas, in 1932, this volume featured an extensive treatment of gardening in the Southwest and included detailed descriptions of wind, weather, and soil conditions for Texas, Louisiana, Arkansas, New Mexico, and Oklahoma.

somniferum) and hollyhocks *(Alcea rosea)* were present in nearly every garden. These settlers traded and shared various colors and forms of garden plants among family and friends.

Flowering and fruiting trees were in these dooryard gardens, but large shade trees were usually relegated to spaces outside the enclosed area. Mexican plums *(Prunus mexicana),* persimmons *(Diospyros virginiana),* crepe myrtles *(Lagerstroemia indica),* native crabapple *(Malus angustifolia),* pomegranate *(Punica granatum),* and fig *(Ficus carica)* were among the most popular choices and added to the beauty and fragrance of the garden. Mulberries *(Morus spp.)* and chinaberry *(Melia azederach)* were present on most properties but usually in the chicken yard or farm lot.

Fragrance was an essential ingredient in the garden. Mothers gave their daughters favorite roses when a new home was established, while plants such as lavender and artemesias were grown and used to scent linens and repel insects. Dianthus, nicotiana, violets and paper white narcissus endeared themselves to early gardeners because of their delicious fragrances.

Vines added still another dimension to the landscape along with grapes *(Vitis spp.),* morning glories *(Ipomea spp.), Dutchman's pipe (Aristolochia durior),* coral vine *(Antigonon leptopus),* honeysuckle *(Lonicera sempervirens)* and, of course, rambling roses being favorites. Rambling roses were known as "running roses" in Texas and the South.

Perhaps the best analysis of the role vines played in the traditional cottage garden came from Andrew Jackson Downing (1815–1852), America's first landscape architect. A man of many talents, Downing also practiced as a nurseryman and architect so that he could furnish clients not only with garden plans, but also with the plants with which to plant them, and even blueprints for a residence. Through the articles and books he wrote about landscape design, Downing greatly influenced American tastes in gardens and gardening. The guidelines he set for these became very popular after his death, and many Victorian homes and residential areas in Texas and the South echo his ideas. In his book of 1850, *The Architecture of Country Houses*, Downing included a section titled "Vines for the Decoration of Cottages." There he states:

> Take almost any of those exquisite cottages in English landscapes, which charm every beholder by a wonderful beauty, found in no other land in the same perfection, and subject it to the dissecting knife of the searcher after the secrets of that beauty, and what does he find? That not one of these cottages is faultless in a strictly architectural sense— nay, that they abound with all sorts of whimsical and picturesque violations of architectural rules and proportions, and are often quite destitute of grace of form or outline. But, on the other hand, they are so bewitchingly rural . . . but mainly through the beautiful vines and shrubs that embower them, which, by partly concealing and partly adorning their walls, give them that expressive beauty of rural home and feeling which makes them so captivating to every passer-by (206–207).

GARDEN DESIGN TODAY

From this brief look at garden history emerge some concepts that appear to be timeless due to their appeal and reappearance over long periods. Several of the lessons taught by these gardeners and their memorable, although sometimes modest, creations include:

- The inclusion of adaptable, historic and naturalizing plants
- Achieving interest and character by the use of vertical elements or "rooms" to define areas of the landscape
- Massing plants for unified effects
- The contrast between formal fencing or hedging of the outlines of the garden with the informal arrangement and growth of the plants within
- Gardens created to fill the needs of families and carefully tended by them are often aesthetically pleasing.

There is a certain appropriateness in these gardens that, once experienced, make more modern landscape efforts appear out of place for older or authentically restored structures. The design of these older gardens was quite flexible; sometimes it included a touch of formality from patterns of walks and bed arrangement that contrast nicely with the informality of the plant placements.

Garden designers could make modern structures appear less stereotyped and rigid with the additions of enclosed plantings for part or all of the land area. Small land spaces adjacent to many town homes and condominiums seem an appropriate target for this type of personal and colorful garden. A handsome enclosure of picket fencing, stone or brick wall enhances most architectural styles. The addition of an appropriate walk, a few well-chosen flowering trees, old-fashioned roses, and herbs will make a good beginning; the rest can be filled in with native and adapted perennials, vines and annuals.

2 Perennials for Easy Garden Color

LANDSCAPE DESIGN POSSIBILITIES

Perennials are versatile plants that offer a variety of creative uses in the garden. Descriptive lists in Chapter 5 will help you choose from among the many species of flowering and foliage plants adapted to our area. Perennials, you'll find, offer an infinite number of exciting combinations. From tiny terrace gardens of inner city apartments, to extensive country estates, perennials can add color, form and texture, often for many years and with a minimum of maintenance. A look at some of the landscape possibilities should help to stimulate ideas for specific applications.

THE PERENNIAL BORDER

We inherited from England the perennial border style as we know it today, and it is a version of the cottage gardens that evolved during the seventeenth and eighteenth centuries. The two greatest popularizers of this planting style were Gertrude Jekyll (1843–1932) and William Robinson (1838–1935), who proposed it as a rebellion against Victorian gardens, landscapes that Robinson once described as "the ugliest gardens ever made" (27). Typically, the gardens of upper class Victorians featured rigid, geometric masses of brightly colored annuals, all maintained at a uniform height like tufts in a carpet. This style was known as "bedding out," and it had gained popularity after 1845 when the British government lifted the tax on glass. By lowering the cost of building greenhouses on residential estates, this measure made it possible to produce annuals economically and in quantity.

In the place of these monotonous floral carpets, Jekyll and Robinson beautifully articulated more natural combinations of plants, primarily perennials, both in the gardens they designed and through their writings. They extended the flower seasons from a few months in spring and summer to all year long through the use of bulbs, ornamental grasses, and old-fashioned plants and herbs collected from the simple gardens of the English cottagers. Earth and plant forms inspired the new concept of garden design as the plants' seasons, ecology and arrangement in nature created the basis for the design revolution so clearly espoused by these two pioneers.

Jekyll was an accomplished painter until her eyesight began failing in her forties, at which point she began fully devoting her talents to the garden. Taking the earth as her canvas and plants as her palette, she went to work on what she considered the ultimate expression

(Top) A shady perennial border at the Wisley headquarters for the Royal Horticulture Society near London, England. (Above) A perennial border at Hampton Court in England.

of garden art, the herbaceous border. Jekyll fashioned beautiful pictures by carefully selecting plants, and then arranging them in the long clumps of color she referred to as "drifts."

Through her selection of plants, Jekyll also varied forms, heights, colors and textures within her borders. To be successful, she believed, the designer must intimately know the growing habits and requirements as well as aesthetic qualities of the plants.

Jekyll, Robinson and their followers also recognized the great importance of the quality of light. Shadow was of equal importance to color, form and texture in their gardens. As American landscape architect of that era, Beatrix Jones, said, "Shadow is a color and must be used as one!" (10). The depth and dimension that a feeling for a balance between light and shade contributes is as essential to a well-designed garden as to a fine painting. Indeed, the difference in the quality of light is a fundamental reason that English gardens differ from our own. The relatively cool, moist climate of England is conducive to more intense flower colors than our generally bright, sunny conditions.

English herbaceous borders were almost always limited in space by constructed walls or hedges. These walls or hedges not only physically limited the garden space, but also provided a sense of continuity or organization to the composition. Strong, simple organization contrasts with the wide variety of plants, each plant displaying colors, forms and textures and reaching its peak at a different time of the year.

The design philosophies that Jekyll, Robinson, and others created and refined are as appropriate today as ever. The major challenge is for the designer to be sufficiently familiar with the palette of plants adapted to

our area so that the English herbaceous border can be successfully interpreted into our climate, topography and lifestyle. This is no small task, but when done well, is a splendid form of garden design. A final consideration to keep in mind is that to be at their best, herbaceous borders require considerable space. For small properties, the idea of a cottage garden may be more appropriate than a border. There are always exceptions, but minimum dimensions for borders should be in the range of 5'–6' wide and 20'–30' long. Wider and longer borders offer more opportunity for manipulation and gradation of color, form and texture.

This sunny perennial border at Wisley features foliage color contrasts.

THE MIXED BORDER

The mixed border is a combination of perennials, annuals and flowering shrubs. The same design concepts that apply to the herbaceous border also apply to the mixed border, although usually it requires more space, since the effect is partially dependent upon shrubs such as old roses. Reseeding annuals can also be an important part of mixed borders. As with herbaceous borders, it is important to have as little bare ground showing as possible. This not only results in a fuller and more satisfying appearance, but also provides less opportunity for weeds to grow and compete with the ornamental plants.

The section of old garden roses provides many possibilities for integrating them with perennials and annuals in this manner. Many old roses are large and handsome shrubs, but there are also a number of intermediate and smaller types that are well suited to modest sized properties. Consult the recommended use lists at the conclusion of the section on old roses for ideas on how they may be incorporated into the landscape.

Climbing roses and other flowering vines may also be trained on walls, trellises and arbors to provide a sense of vertical space, useful in developing gardens into a series of outdoor rooms. Gardens developed in this manner offer continually unfolding vistas that add to the viewer's interest by never allowing him to see the entire development at one time. This plan, dividing the garden into a series of different rooms, also allows for the design of smaller areas featuring specific color ranges, plant specialties or other garden themes.

Annuals are a good way to quickly fill in empty spaces and provide quick color in mixed borders. For the first year or two after planting, mixed borders may appear a bit sparse, since roses and other flowering shrubs require more time to develop than most annuals or perennials. During this interim, annuals can provide important filler.

(Left) These mixed border, shrubs, and perennials adorn the home of Dr. and Mrs. Jeff Lewis of Athens, Ga. (Below) This mixed border adorns the author's garden in College Station, Texas. It features Hinckley's Columbine, Yellow Lady Banks Roses, Dianthus, and Chinese Fringe tree (*Chionanthus retusas*). (Bottom) This mixed border at the author's garden in College Station, Texas, features Spuria Iris, Redbud, Centaurea, Red China Roses, and Dianthus.

A cutflower garden is a focal point at the Mordecai house in Raleigh, North Carolina.

CUTTING GARDENS

There are several advantages to creating a cutting garden. Where flowers are enjoyed and used in large volume in the home, their removal from borders and other landscaped areas may detract from the intended effect. By providing a special cut flower garden, the gardener can anticipate and plan for these needs without disturbing or diminishing landscape plantings. The well-planned cutting garden also offers another very practical advantage: Annuals and perennials may be conveniently and efficiently grown in rows where they are easily gathered and maintained.

Cutting gardens need not be unattractive, but it is a sensible plan to locate them in an area where they are not a focal point when not at their peak. Old time gardeners of Texas and the Gulf South often included cut flowers in the vegetable garden where they could tend and harvest them easily. Finer estates in our area would sometimes have a separate area devoted to producing the favorite cut flowers of the family, but annuals such as marigolds, zinnias, poppies, sweet peas, bells of Ireland, nasturtium, globe amaranth and larkspur were frequently found in vegetable and cutting gardens of our ancestors. Shasta daisies, phlox, and chrysanthemums were especially popular perennials.

THE CONTEMPORARY COTTAGE GARDEN

Today's homeowner can easily update the cottage gardening style so common in Texas and the Gulf South 50 to 150 years ago. A garden of this sort is particularly appropriate for town houses and other small properties where most modern landscaping efforts consist of a few uninteresting evergreen shrubs and groundcovers unimaginatively placed against foundations of the structure.

Traditional cottage gardens need not be extravagantly expensive, nor must they require great physical sacrifice. They are appropriate for new housing developments in the city, suburban bungalows or country homes.

There are few rules to keep in mind when planning a cottage garden. Usually, they are modest in size, often enclosed by picket fencing, walls or hedges, and contain a wide variety of plant materials selected by the owner for their beauty, emotional attachment, family favorites or real usefulness. Cottage gardens reflect one of the best aspects of America's combined North European heritage—individualism. Since they should reflect the tastes of their owners, no two cottage gardens should ever be alike. Gardeners should study the countryside and older gardens in their area. Native plants and those that have been successfully grown in local gardens for many years are often the best choices.

One writer felt it was impossible for the true cottage garden to be in poor taste, relying as it does on the natural form of the plants. Andrew Jackson Downing (1815–1852), the great American architect and probably our first professional landscape architect, thought

that the cottage garden was "perfect of its kind," and that the charm and attractiveness of these gardens made them "little gems of rural and picturesque beauty" (67).

In addition to enclosure with fences, walls and hedges, extensive collections of plants, and limitation in size, cottage gardens usually had a straight walk or path leading to the front door. Another typical feature was the separately enclosed "swept" backyard. There was no turf or groundcover in that space, and where the ground was free of plants, the cottage gardener would periodically sweep the bare earth with a broom. Backyards were often planted with small fruit trees and included outbuildings, a chicken run and chicken coop. Curving or straight walks of native stone or brick sometimes intersected the front walk near the entrance and provided access to the sides and back garden areas. Sometimes cottage gardens included touches of formality such as a parterre that may feature a sundial, birdbath or other garden ornament as well as garden benches.

Planting a Cottage Garden

In developing a new cottage garden it is important to keep in mind the design concepts concerning the arrangement of plants. Consider the cottage garden as a piece of a herbaceous or mixed border: the same principles that are important in planning borders apply to the cottage garden as well.

(Above) Privet hedge lines the left side of the walk in a Louisiana cottage garden. Ruellia and old garden roses are featured on the right. (Left) This curved stone walk leads into a Houston, Texas, cottage garden.

Cottage gardens are still occasionally found in rural areas of Texas and the South.

The best times of year to begin a cottage garden are autumn and spring, since soils usually contain sufficient moisture at that time to be workable. Such a schedule avoids the intense heat of mid-summer. Unless natural soil conditions are ideal, work the soil deeply and incorporate large quantities of organic material and recommended amounts of fertilizer. Heavy duty rototillers are ideal for loosening hard-packed soil and evenly incorporating amendments. At least 4″–6″ of compost, sphagnum peat moss, well-rotted manure or pine bark is necessary to modify heavy clay or sandy soils. The addition of organic material will improve the soil's ability to hold moisture over longer periods, and reduce summer water use. The organic material also adds air space to the soil, thus improving its drainage and providing a better root environment for plants. Remember that planting areas for shrubs and perennials are usually not disturbed for two or more years and should be especially well prepared initially.

When the soil is in good shape, lay out the path to the door and around the house to the sides or back yard. If picket fences or walls are to be added or repaired, it is ideal to complete these construction tasks before plants are added. Drip or sprinkler irrigation systems should

also be in place before planting if practical. An arch of juniper, arborvitae, yaupon, or climbing roses makes a picture frame for the entry gate.

The next step should be to plant any small flowering trees or large shrubs, since they are more permanent than annuals and perennials and provide a visual framework or "bones" for the garden. Then gradually add flowering annuals and perennials. This is your opportunity to make your garden truly original. The changes of level and texture at bloom time are what make a cottage garden unique.

After planting is complete, consider adding a top-dressing of mulch which will conserve moisture in the soil and help control weeds. Use leaves and grass clippings, bark or hay. If hay is used, try coastal Bermuda grass since it has no viable seed. Plants should be grouped in fairly close proximity to help conserve soil moisture and shade out sprouting weeds.

Although most of the decisions regarding the cottage garden are made during the initial design and installation period, there will be continuing opportunities to fill in with new materials where original ones have performed poorly or died. One of the characteristics of cottage gardens is that they are continually changing as

some plants seem to make themselves at home and others indicate, by their poor performance, a desire to be moved or replaced. Annuals will move themselves by seeding in new places every year.

Cottage gardens can add a softness to old or new structures that is timeless in appeal. When well-planned and maintained they are satisfying to viewers and owner alike. Whether in the suburbs, inner city or countryside, the well-planned cottage garden can provide an ever-changing panorama of color, form and texture while being a true expression of the gardener and the natural environment of which it is a part.

(Left) Rambling roses cover an archway over the entrance walk to a Navasota, Texas, garden. (Below) 'Alice du Pont' Mandavilla and Muscadine grapes cover an arbor in the south Louisiana garden of Dr. and Mrs. Jack D. Holden.

CONTAINER GARDENING

Container gardening is well-rooted in history as a practical way to replace lost ground space in our urban environments. By effectively selecting and placing container plants one may add formal or informal appeal to the garden. Advantages to container culture of perennials, roses and annuals include the ability to control soil quality, watering, and placement of the plants. Most containers are relatively portable and may be grouped or moved to take adavantage of seasonal displays. Another advantage of container gardening is that tropical plants such as Bougainvilleas may be used in areas outside their natural range of cold tolerance by moving them to protected locations for short periods during the winter.

Perennial plants with cascading growth habits such as *Asparagus Sprengeri*, lantana, verbena, and dianthus are particularly effective in containers where they can spill over the edge to create their special effects. Large, specimen trees and shrubs are often more attractive when the soil at their bases is covered with various flowering annual or perennial plants. Flowering bulbs may also be included to add their special effects at various seasons of the year.

Hanging containers can add still another dimension to the landscape. When used with restraint and scaled to the surroundings, hanging ferns, lantanas, and various cascading annuals and perennials can be a significant addition to courtyards, entrance areas and terraces.

Container plants usually require more maintenance, however, than those planted directly in the ground. Restricted root zones in containers require more frequent watering and fertilizing to keep plants in top condition. Plants in containers are also more susceptible to damage from extremes of cold or heat since the roots are above ground and more exposed to the elements.

Both aesthetic and practical factors will dictate the choice of containers. Unglazed clay pots generally require more watering than plastic or glazed pots since water and air actually penetrate the relatively porous clay. A drainage hole in the bottom or sides is essential for success in growing most plants in containers. If containers without drain holes must be used, consider "double potting" by simply lining the undrained container with a smaller pot that is equipped with drain holes. Since the growing area is restricted it is important that the media be of high quality. Packaged potting mixes are available in large or small quantities and a practical choice for most situations. If soil is used, it should be mixed with liberal amounts of sphagnum peat, compost or rotted pinebark.

This whiskey barrel planter with *Podocarpus macrophylla* and *Graptopetalum paraquayense* contrasts nicely in foliage color and plant form.

POCKETS OF COLOR

Although this book focuses on herbaceous borders and cottage gardens, there are other effective ways to use perennials in the landscape. Most landscapes have sufficient evergreen shrub materials to avoid a totally bleak look, but there is little seasonal change or flower color. For those who are interested in adding interest to this type of planting with perennials there are usually good opportunities.

By enlarging planting areas in front of evergreen shrubs it is often possible to prepare modest sized spaces for clumps of seasonal color. Make sure, however, to plant a suffcient quantity of the flower of your choice so

Daylilies provide pockets of color in an Athens, Georgia, shrub border.

(Left) Gaillardias lend strong color to this Fredericksburg, Texas, meadow garden. (Above) 'Campernelle' Narcissus provide pockets of color before an interestingly pruned privet hedge in central Texas.

that the effect is not just a "spot" in the overall picture. Keep in mind that shrubs and nearby trees may have so completely laced the potential planting area with their roots that sometimes they must be removed in order to be successful with flowering plants.

Possibilities that come to mind for this type of pocket-planting include masses or borders of some of the lower growing daylilies or irises in front of evergreen shrubs. Entrance areas are a logical place to provide welcoming pockets of color. For most homeowners, the amount of space they can comfortably maintain in annuals or perennials is relatively small. It seems sensible to concentrate these efforts where they will be seen and enjoyed most. Perennials generally require less maintenance than annuals, and since they do tend to return each year, they can be a wise gardening investment.

For pockets of color around outdoor living areas, swimming pools, and entrance courts, containers offer possibilities. Portability is a special asset of container plants, since they can usually be moved to a less prominent location when not at their best.

With our long growing seasons and relatively short winters landscape maintenance becomes an almost year-round affair. By selecting well-adapted perennials and placing them in the most important places, year-round color can become a practical reality.

WOODLAND GARDENS

Woodland areas offer special challenges and opportunities for gardening. "Natural gardens," Beatrix Jones wrote at the turn of the century, "are hardest to fit in [to residential gardens] because they have no artificial straight lines or ornament for emphasis" (8). If you plan to garden on a heavily wooded site, first consider removing some of the underbrush and low-lying limbs of trees.

Often, it is sensible to remove small, weak trees that are too close together to develop or contribute to the overall effect. In her book *Wood and Garden*, Gertrude Jekyll suggested tying white paper ribbon around the trunks of trees being considered for removal, then observing them for several days from various angles before removing them (8). It is much easier to remove trees than to put them back! Shade is a major challenge to succesful woodland gardening. Sometimes limbing up and thinning mature trees will not only provide more penetration of light, but will also enhance the tree's beauty by exposing its structure.

Improving the soil in woodland areas will also pose a problem since woodland soil tends to be filled with roots. Although several inches of leaf mold and leaves may cover the surface of the ground, this is rarely enough organic material in which to plant successfully. Add at least 5″–6″ of compost, rotted pine bark, peat moss, or similar material to the soil surface before spading or tilling it in. Slightly raised irregular paths of bark, mulch or natural colored gravel can add a nice touch to wooded gardens while providing pedestrian circulation and design continuity.

Since deciduous trees allow considerable sunlight to reach the ground beneath them during winter and early spring, woodland gardeners tend to rely on spring flowering plants. There are, however, numerous ferns, aspidistra, *Vinca major*, liriope, and others that can add textural variation and colors of green to such a setting. Native shrubs like black haw, dogwood, and Mexican plum also provide good fall color as well as spring bloom. Certain of the summer flowering annuals such as impatiens, wax begonias, and caladiums are dependable sources of bright color in shady gardens.

Woodland gardens are more difficult to create than cottage gardens or herbaceous borders because they rarely have well-defined boundaries and can easily fall into a stiff or unnatural appearance. Groupings of spring flowering bulbs are popular in wooded areas or near their edge because they will look natural, once established, especially if set out in "drifts" as suggested by Jekyll. Some experts even recommend pitching bulbs over one's shoulder and planting them where they land to ensure a "natural" look!

Aquilegia canadensis have naturalized and bloom beautifully in the Burton, Texas, woodland garden of Sue Rowan Pittman.

(Above) The Burton, Texas, garden of Karen and Don Lehto reflects garden design often found in the rural South around the turn of the century. Garden design by the author. (Left) This woodland garden features spring bulbs naturalized under deciduous trees. *Facing page:* (Top left) The Holden residence near Rougon, Louisiana, includes a late eighteenth-century raised cottage and a beautifully designed and maintained garden from the same period. (Top right) Vegetables, fruit trees, and cutflowers are important plants in the restored gardens of Old Salem, North Carolina. (Bottom) The woodland gardens at the Mercer Arboretum in Humble, Texas, feature drifts of annuals and perennials.

These restored gardens are at Monticello, the home of Thomas Jefferson near Charlottesville, Virginia. Accurate garden diaries written by Jefferson, combined with meticulous archaeological work, helped create this authentic garden restoration.

GARDENS FOR RESTORED STRUCTURES

There is a trend to restore country and city homes in Texas and the Gulf South, but unfortunately, the restoration rarely reaches the garden. Instead, 20th century foundation plantings of modern shrubs surround 1850s classical revival homes or 1870 frame farmhouses. Clearly, this is inappropriate. Actually, there are two valid and distinct directions in which garden design for restored structures can go.

If research into family records, photographs, paintings or drawings of the garden exist, or if parts of garden structures or plantings are still in evidence, an authentic restoration may be possible. Documenting the details of old gardens takes time and effort. Authentically restored sites such as Thomas Jefferson's Monticello have ongoing staffs of archeologists, landscape architects and horticulturists. They work full-time researching the available evidence so that authenticity is given the highest possible priority. Such gardens are important because they can offer insights into lifestyles of important people and times. Authenticating which plants were grown is also important.

Recent years have seen a revival of interest in many of the older cultivars of ornamental and edible plants, not only for reasons of nostalgia, but also because many of these plants possess resistance to insects and disease, or tend to be extremely hardy and long-lived in comparison with modern hybrid cousins. Many plant improvements have occurred over the years, but in the rush to obtain brightness of color, larger flower and fruit size, characteristics such as fragrance, drought resistance, and plant form were sometimes sacrificed. For this reason, horticulturists at Monticello and other important gardens make considerable efforts to obtain and reintroduce plant species and cultivars that are authentic to the garden. Organizations such as the Southern Garden History Society have been formed and are strong advocates of authentic restoration of our garden heritage.

Before attempting a garden restoration, it may be wise to consult a landscape architect who specializes in this type of work. An observation that can be helpful in establishing early garden design on a site is to watch carefully for bulbs to come up at various seasons. Often these plantings will emerge and identify geometric patterns, walks, or other insights into an earlier time for the garden. Carefully observing depressions and mounding of soil can also identify patterns that once were part of the garden design. English archeologists have learned that the use of aerial photographs under low-level light conditions such as sunset or early morning can sometimes reveal ancient marks on the land.

The second type of valid garden design for restored structures is the more common. Most homes or other structures retain little evidence of what was in the garden. Usually, plants are not as long lived as buildings, and gardens are changed even more often than the structures they surround. In a situation of this sort, the owner may wish to study the chronological period and other authentic gardens in the neighborhood to gain insight into how the garden might have been designed and what plants it could have contained. This approach is more practical for most people and allows the development of a design that more nearly fits the needs of the current situation, while authentically reflecting the spirit of the past. With renewed interest in garden restoration, and a greater availability of period garden literature, more resources are now available than ever before for this type of research.

The cottage gardening style is becoming popular again for restored or modern structures and can be appropriate for either. Suggestions, photographs and plant information in this text should be sufficient to provide a

Bottles edging the walks add an interesting touch to this south Louisiana cottage garden.

basis for designing and installing such a garden. Cottage gardens were known to surround a wide variety of 19th century structures from Greek Revival mansions to modest farm cottages. When executed well, cottage gardens provide, in the words of A.J. Downing, a "peculiar beauty." They also offer an authentic style that translates easily to modern settings.

3 Arranging Perennials in the Garden

The aim of the classic English perennial border is the creation of beautiful landscape pictures. The border maker must begin with very definite objectives in mind. Plant material should then be carefully selected by the rules of artistic design to achieve the chosen objective.

COLOR

The most obvious canon of artistic design in border making is color. Like an impressionist painting, clumps or "drifts" of bloom and foliage colors compose border design. The Classical English borders from the turn of the century utilized either "single theme" colors or subtle gradations of pastels. In the plans with which Gertrude Jekyll illustrated her book of 1908, *Colour Schemes for the Flower Garden*, she often began at the far end of her borders with blue grays and grays, passing on to blues, whites, pale yellows, pale pinks, and from there shading into stronger yellows, then to oranges and reds, and then gradually paling again into the light pastels with the addition of lilacs and purples. Almost always, springtime in these herbaceous gardens featured light yellows and pale lilacs, amid whites.

On the other hand, special "color theme" gardens were also popular in classically designed English borders. Perhaps the most common of these was the white garden, a display of white flowers accented with gray foliaged plants. The archetype of all English white gardens was Vita Sackville-West's creation at Sissinghurst Castle in

"Drifts" of blooms illustrate the element of color in border design.

The use of structural material can contribute to perennial garden color.

Kent. The English also favor gold gardens with conifers or shrubs, blue gardens, and red gardens which also include pinks and rose. Of course, the show of color in a herbaceous border depends upon the succession of bloom, and should be planned so that some areas are offering a colorful display while other drifts are only exhibiting their foliage. As Jekyll said, "It is impossible and even undesirable, to have a garden in bloom all over, and groups of flower beauty are all the more enjoyable for being more or less isolated by stretches of intervening greenery" (114).

Remember that color comes to the landscape from several sources. In addition to perennial and annual flowers, structural materials such as walls, fences, pavings and buildings can contribute a colorful note. Trees, shrubs, turf and groundcovers also play their part, and their seasonal changes pose intriguing challenges. Seasonal changes of plant materials provide a challenge in subtle uses of color. Even the brightest flower colors are subdued by the neutral values of green, which are present in abundance with them. In outdoor light, and with patterns of shade and shadow, color is an all-important tool in the hands of the clever designer. For this reason it is important in choosing plant material to see the plant at its maturity, to form an accurate judgment of its color and other artistic considerations. Tours of nurseries and public and private gardens are almost essential in this regard.

LINE

The word "line" has many connotations, but practically all relate to direction. In design disciplines, line is usually a mark made by pencil, ink, brush or other device to form the basis of the design pattern as distinguished from shading, shadows or colors. In garden design all types of lines are employed to create interesting space relationships. As lines serve for definition of space, they must be considered one of the most valuable tools in the hands of a designer.

Lines may be either straight or curved. Since herbaceous borders use line to define their shape, the overall design of the border is greatly enhanced and strengthened when backed with a wall, fence or tall, dark green hedge. In England, yews (*Taxus* sp.) or holly (*Ilex* sp.) furnish the materials for these features. In Texas and the Gulf South there are numerous species suitable for this task, such as yaupon (*Ilex vomitoria*), cherry laurel (*Prunus caroliniana*), southern wax myrtle (*Myrica cerifera*), Texas mountain laurel (*Sophora secundiflora*), or Japanese yew (*Podocarpus macrophylla*).

Whether designing a cottage garden or a herbaceous border, the lines created by these walls, fences, hedges, and the edges of the planting areas themselves should make strong design statements. When a design relies on curved lines, they should be definite and sweeping.

Edges of the border should be neat and easily maintained, and this implies the use of well-constructed brick, concrete, wood, or metal edging. Edging is especially important when herbaceous borders join turf or ground-cover areas and the line itself becomes an important element of the overall design.

By its crispness, the well-defined edge creates very definite effects. It dramatizes the plants that spill or cascade across it, and it furnishes a strong contrast to the pleasantly muddled look of the plant combinations within the border or bed. Well-designed and constructed edges also make maintaining the garden less of a chore.

James M. Sterling

(Left) The herbaceous border at North Carolina State University in Raleigh, North Carolina, features a dark green hedge that exhibits an element of line. (Below) The White Garden at the North Carolina. State Arboretum provides another example of line. (Right) Curved lines are definite and sweeping.

FORM

Architectural forms are an obvious concern of the landscape designer, but so are plant forms since every plant has a distinctive form in its natural condition. Pruning can modify this, and under its influence a plant may lose its natural identity. Even without this artificial modification, plant forms are less positive than the architectural forms of buildings, walls and walks. So plant forms play a somewhat less positive part in landscape compositions.

Individual plant forms vary from mounds to pyramids and cones, or the cascades of weeping specimens, and it behooves the designer to study these carefully before making selections. Combining individual plants into larger compositions involves other decisions as well. As previously noted, Jekyll favored planting in long drifts rather than clumsy, block-shaped patches. In borders, plants arrange themselves most naturally into three categories by height: the tallest plants fall to the back of the border; the midsize ones, to the center; and the shortest, up front. Some irregularity in this order is desirable, however, to prevent an appearance of boring predictability.

Individual flower forms are extremely important in composition with perennials. Spike and ray flowers are the two most basic flower forms although there are numerous variations and other forms. Familiar examples of spike flowers are the salvias, lythrum and gladiolus. These provide dramatic statements in the border, but are best when contrasted liberally with ray flowers such as daisies, coreopsis, and asters. Some flowers like alyssum (*Phlox subulata*) and various sedums contribute large masses of color from numerous tiny flowers. The flower form in these plants is less important or distinctive than the larger and more individual ray and spike flowers. Instead, these mass flowering plants serve an important role in providing unity and linkage among the many species that may constitute a well-designed border.

(Below) Plants can project a variety of forms: mounds, pyramids, cones, and cascades. (Right) The two basic flower forms are spike and ray flowers.

Dissimilar textures heighten the effect.

TEXTURE

As a product of the plants' surface qualities, texture appeals to the senses of sight and touch. More specifically, the texture of a plant is a result of the relationship of various parts of a plant, the size and arrangement of the leaves, the composition of the twigs into limbs and to the overall structure of the plant. Texture is relative, and placing two dissimilar textures in close proximity heightens the effect of both. The garden canna appears even coarser planted next to the fine-textured herb rosemary. The ferny yarrow gives an even softer effect next to the broad, smooth-leaved *aspidistra*. And a carpet of *Sedum acre* seems neater in contrast to the spikes of *Lythrum* 'Morden's Pink'.

Blending these combinations of textures offers a fascinating method of developing the principle of contrast in the landscape. Using plants exclusively of similar texture creates monotony in a composition, where a variety of textures will add interest and distinction. Form is very closely related to interpretation of texture and the difference is often only one of scale as it is viewed in a composition. The majority of plants used in herbaceous borders are of intermediate texture. As in any art composition, too much variety of texture can result in visual confusion.

Pattern is a repetitious arrangement of forms.

PATTERN

Pattern implies the repetition or reappearance of combinations of plants, structures, colors, textures, lines or forms. When used with restraint and forethought it helps to create unity and richness in a composition. When overused it becomes monotonous. Pattern may be defined as an arrangement of forms repeated within a design. *Parterre* is a term that describes ornamental garden areas in which the flower beds and paths form a pattern. Other examples in the design of herbaceous borders and cottage gardens could be repeating arrangements of several varieties of climbing roses on a wall or the reappearance of certain bulb groupings or specimen plants within the border. Pattern may also serve in paving designs, fences and walls to add interest and detail to the garden.

CULTURAL COMPATABILITY AND THEME GARDENS

Another, and important, consideration in the choice of border plants should be cultural compatability of the various species. Extremes of climate, soil, sunlight, and moisture are all factors that will shape the process of selection. Plants from vastly different climates are rarely good companions in the garden. However, if only native or naturalized flora are used, this may not be a problem.

Theme gardens may be created around cultural requirements as well as color of perennials. Specific site characteristics often suggest certain types of gardens. Bog and water gardens, rock gardens, meadow gardens, shady woodland gardens and dryland plantings are all possiblities.

(Left) Here is one type of garden. (Below) Among the factors in the selection process are climate, soil, sunlight, and moisture. (Bottom) Herbs and perennials form a theme garden.

CLARITY OF DESIGN

Perhaps the cardinal canon of design is simplicity or clarity. This implies the elimination of confusion, and portraying the entire composition in a clear, concise and orderly relationship among all the components. Jekyll stressed this by suggesting that one picture at a time be created by dividing the garden into a series of "rooms."

The ideal herbaceous border or cottage garden is the combination of many materials that actually create tapestries of color throughout the seasons. Clarity of design and a feeling of orderliness are achieved by the addition of carefully placed hedges, walls, walks, fences and edges that provide enclosure and line to the composition.

4 Buying, Planting, and Caring for Perennials

Gardeners may choose plants, cuttings or seeds to start their perennial landscapes. There is a great satisfaction in growing one's own plants from seed, but for today's busy families, plants offer easier and faster results. In some instances, however, plants may not be available; with rare and protected plants, it may not be legal to collect more than seed. Our ancestors often grew new plants from seed, then traded or shared plants with friends and relatives. This practice of sharing plants is very much alive today among dedicated gardeners and can add greatly to the joy of growing perennials. Basic information on starting plants from seed, cuttings and division will be discussed later in this section.

Retail garden centers and nurseries have sprung up throughout the U. S. since World War II. Until that time, the only source of plants for most gardeners, besides exchanges with friends and family, had been mail-order nurseries. Today, most communities of a few thousand population or more have a seasonal or year-round retail garden center. Usually these small outlets offer only a minimal variety of plant materials, since they can stock only those items that their wholesale suppliers find

it profitable to deliver in relatively small quantities. But sometimes they grow unusual plants that are favorites in the community. With this thought in mind, good gardeners often enjoy visiting smaller nurseries and may have obtained some of their favorite perennials from them.

Recent years have seen a marked increase in the quantity and selection of bedding plants. Sales of these "color plants," usually offered in 6-packs, 4-packs or individual 4-inch containers, have grown much faster than other parts of the nursery industry. It appears that homeowners have grown weary of large expanses of turf relieved only by a scattering of trees and clipped evergreens. Well-planned commercial and community landscapes are using seasonal color in large quantities and homeowners like what they are seeing. While the bedding plant segment of the nursery business continues to grow, customers are asking why they cannot have more perennial plants that provide seasonal color year after year. Thus, we are seeing retail garden centers and mail-order sources offering many more perennial plants.

CONTAINER-GROWN PLANTS

Another major change within the nursery industry in recent years has been an increased use of container-grown plants. These offer advantages to both nurserymen and customers, since container-grown plants are easier to maintain in the sales yard and suffer almost no shock in transplanting. As a result, the vast majority of plants now sell in the containers in which they are grown. Only a few years ago certain bedding plants such as pansies were offered as bare-root plants and sold in bundles of 25, 50, or more. However, the shelf life of bare-root plants, even when well packaged, is only a few days; those grown in containers keep for several weeks or more.

Bare-root divisions or seedlings of most perennials still enjoy seasonal sales during the cool weather of late fall, winter and early spring when they may be easily and economically transported through the mail and held for a week or more without serious damage. Container-grown plants, however, may be transplanted successfully far later in the season, so they extend the nurseryman's season while providing gardeners with the opportunity to try a new plant as soon as they discover it.

Containerized perennials are usually sold in peat or paper-based containers that can be set directly into the garden without being removed. Plants growing in the small, restricted areas of these pots may need watering once or more per day during dry weather. Usually, sphagnum peat moss is the main ingredient of the medium in which the plants are grown. Since this resists moisture once it has dried, it is essential to water container-grown plants regularly, as often as once or twice a day in hot weather. It may also be necessary to soak the containers in water for a few hours prior to planting to make sure they are thoroughly moistened. For all but a few plants such as *Asclepias* (butterfly weed), it is best to loosen or cut some of the roots in the container so that they will move out into the surrounding soil more easily after transplanting. This practice is recommended primarily for transplanting during the cool seasons since in the stress of extreme heat any disturbance to the root mass may be too much for young plants. Perennials grown and sold in plastic pots as packs must be removed from their containers when planted. Generally the root mass will slip easily from the pot if the plant is held upside down and a few gentle taps are delivered to the container's bottom. It is equally important for the root mass to be loosened or cut when plants are grown in plastic containers.

The cost of plants relates basically to the size of the container. Although a one gallon or 6-inch pot of perennials may create more of an instant effect than a four- or six-pack, the cost is usually much less for the smaller plants. Most perennials grow quickly, and to create "drifts" and other mass color effects in the landscape requires considerable numbers of plants. If the desired plants are available only in large sizes, these may sometimes be divided after a short period of time to quickly increase numbers.

Container-grown perennials can be easily transplanted into the garden.

WHEN TO PLANT

With most plants now being grown in containers, planting may be done at most any time. The amount of care necessary to establish a perennial during August may, however, be several times that of the same plant set out during October. A simple rule to keep in mind is that ideally, perennials should be set out about six months prior to bloom. Perhaps more easily remembered is that spring-flowering perennials should be set out during the fall, and fall-flowering species should be set out during spring. Summer-flowering perennials are usually set out in early spring. With our relatively mild winters, spring-flowering plants may sometimes be set out during late winter or very early spring, although fall planting allows the plant more time to acclimate and grow before flowering. This, in turn, usually results in more flowers and larger plants. When growing perennials from seed, start a season or at least a few weeks earlier for most species. The individual plant descriptions of perennials featured in this book suggest the best times and methods of propagation.

When new plants are set out, the first few days and weeks are critical and are sometimes referred to as "hardening off." This process is especially important for bare-root plants and seedlings since they must establish new roots to take up moisture before they wither and die. To help your newly planted perennials, it is important that they be kept uniformly moist. For especially tender species it may be necessary to provide temporary shading for a few days until the roots can begin to function efficiently. Our ancestors sometimes did this by placing a standing shingle in the ground adjacent to the plant, to shade it through much of the afternoon. To keep wind and sun from the plant, old-time gardeners also sheltered them in cylinders they made by cutting the tops and bottoms from cans. After a few days, when the plants had settled in, they would remove these protective devices. Special care during the establishment period is especially important for plants that are being brought from a greenhouse directly to the garden. It is best for greenhouse-grown plants to spend a few days out of doors in partial shade before they are set into the landscape.

PREPARING THE SOIL

Most of the perennials described in this book are adapted to a fairly wide range of soil and cultural conditions. It is very important, however, to know the preferences and requirements of plants before selecting them. Many soil types, from heavy clays to sands are common to our region. Soil is composed of particles that range in size from relatively large, in the case of sands, to medium in the case of silts, to very small in clays. Heavy clay is a term sometimes used to describe soils high in clay content. Few soils in Texas contain a sufficient amount of organic material and nutrients to support really vigorous growth. Loam-type soils are ideal and are composed of a mixture of sand, silt and clay. If your soil is less than ideal and amending it is not practical, limit your plant choices to the relatively few native and introduced plants that will grow under your existing conditions.

Before preparing the soil, remove weeds and grass by hand, or kill them with a contact herbicide such as glyphosate (Roundup). If nutsedge or other serious weed pests are present it may be necessary to make several applications of herbicide. It is best to begin this process a month or more prior to tilling the soil since glyphosate-type herbicides require one to two weeks to effectively kill growing vegetation.

Drainage

The most common inadequacy of coastal soils is drainage. Heavy clay soils and relatively flat terrain usually result in poorly drained soils. Small air spaces between particles coupled with little or no slope to the land will cause water to linger on the surface and in the soil itself. As water replaces air spaces in the soil, it deprives roots of the oxygen they need, creating an environment conducive to diseases. Poorly drained soil is responsible for more plant failure in our area than any other single cause. The remedy is raised beds, which work well but involve a considerable expenditure of time and materials to construct properly.

To create a raised bed suitable for perennials, annuals and other ornamental and vegetable plants it is generally much better to work with existing soils than to remove them completely. Digging a deep hole in heavy clay soils creates a pond that holds water like a tub and drains too slowly into the surrounding, native soil. Instead, build the soil up by adding large volumes of organic material, perhaps some sandy loam soil, and fertilizer. These amendments should be thoroughly mixed with existing soils to a depth of about one foot. For most planting areas spread 6″–8″ of organic material evenly over the surface of the proposed planting site before tilling. Composted pine bark, sphagnum peat moss, leaf mold or similar materials are all good for this purpose. The end result is a planting area that is 8″–10″ higher than the surrounding grade. Even after rains, natural settling and decomposition of organic materials, the planting area will remain several inches higher than the adjacent ground, and water will tend to drain off sufficiently quickly to prevent prolonged reduction of oxygen levels in the soil.

Soil preparation is likely to be more important for perennials than for annuals since most perennial plantings are left undisturbed for one to two or more years, while annuals are likely to be replanted several times each year. The logical time to rejuvenate perennial beds is during the fall when most species may be easily divided and reset. With our long, warm growing seasons, perennials and other ornamental plants tend to grow more rank, and organic materials decompose more quickly than in cooler climates. This usually translates into a need to rework planting areas and to divide perennials more frequently than in most other parts of the nation.

Soil pH

Whether your soil is acid or alkaline will have an important bearing on what plants will do well. Soil acidity is described by the term pH. The pH range is from 1–14, with the lower numbers being more acid. Neutral soils are in the range of 7.0. A soil test is the best way to determine the pH of your soil. These are usually available at modest cost, through your local County Extension Agent. Although it is generally best to select plants that will grow in, or near, the natural pH of your soil, it is possible to alter the acidity or alkalinity of your planting areas.

Most plants thrive in slightly acidic soils at a pH range of from 5.5 to 6.5, but this is an ideal that occurs only rarely in our region. From West Texas to the east-central parts of the state soils tend to be alkaline. From the Trinity River east in Texas eastward through the Gulf South, soils are usually acid. If a soil is too acidic, the pH too low, it may be necessary to add lime. By raising the pH, lime can release nutrients that would otherwise be unavailable to the plants. Lime also provides calcium and improves the structure of clay soils. Agricultural gypsum, another form of calcium, is better suited for use on alkaline soils since it improves the structure of heavy clay soils without raising the pH. It is most effective when thoroughly tilled into the planting mixture, and like lime, it tends to last for several years. Sulfur is sometimes used to reduce the pH of alkaline soils. It may take several months to take effect. Iron sulfate can provide supplemental iron to deficient plants, but this is only mildly effective in lowering pH. In addition, iron sulfate leaves a rusty stain if spilled on concrete or stone.

Salinity

Salt in water and soils is a common problem in the Gulf South. Sodium is the main culprit and cannot be readily removed from water. For information about the amount of salt in city and community water, contact the municipality. The Soils Testing Laboratory at your land grant university through County Extension Agents can test private water sources. The best treatment for saline soil conditions is to make certain that drainage is good. Rain tends to leach salts from the soil, but can only do this if the soil allows the water to pass through and drain away the salts. Poorly drained, salty soils are probably the most difficult medium in which to grow ornamental plants. Only a few species will tolerate these conditions.

Fertilization

Soil fertility is an important consideration in growing ornamental plants. The three elements most likely to be deficient in soil are nitrogen (N), phosphorous (P), and potassium (K). The three numbers on the fertilizer label refer to these elements in that order. An example is 13-13-13 fertilizer; a fifty-pound bag of triple thirteen contains 13 percent each of nitrogen, phosphorous and potassium. The remaining 61% of the material is an inert "spreader."

Nitrogen is the element most often deficient in our soils. Plants use nitrogen relatively quickly, and it tends to be mobile, moving easily in soils, water and plants. It can also burn plants if too much is applied in one application. Slow-release sources of nitrogen such as Osmocote, Nutricote and sulfur-coated ureas have been developed in recent years to provide longer-lasting sources of nitrogen. These are effective, but also expensive. Similar results may be obtained by adding small amounts of ammonium sulfate or ammonium nitrate every six to eight weeks during the growing season.

Phosphorous is important for good flower and root development of plants. Phosphorous is represented by the middle number on the fertilizer label. Superphosphate is a rich source of this nutrient as is bone meal, an organic fertilizer that provides a slower "feed." Because it isn't as mobile, phosphorous tends to last much longer than nitrogen and may not need to be added nearly as often. Over-application of phosphorous can cause micronutrient deficiency symptoms similar to those found in plants grown in highly alkaline soils.

The role of potassium is not as clearly defined. It is necessary for healthy stems, drought and cold resistance, but it is rarely severely deficient in our soils. The addition of large amounts of composted organic material lessens the need for heavy applications of fertilizer. Mulches, however, and other non-decayed organic materials actually use nitrogen, phosphorus and potassium in the decomposition process, and their application may create a need for additional applications of a balanced fertilizer.

The best guide to fertilization is, once again, the soil tests offered by your County Extension Agent. If a soil test is not practical, however, a general rule is to apply and till-in two to three pounds of an all-purpose fertilizer such as 13-13-13 per 100 square feet of bed area. After plantings have been established, an application of about half that amount, evenly distributed over the surface of the soil several times per year, is usually sufficient.

It is ideal to prepare the soil several months or a season ahead of actual planting. This is especially beneficial in heavy soil where exposure to frost and rains can help break up the tight texture of the soil. Gypsum is also helpful in this process.

Mulches

Mulches are almost a necessity in our climate. They help insulate the soil and plant roots from extremes of heat, cold and drought while also reducing weed problems. Mulches are most beneficial during the long summer season when they can significantly reduce soil temperatures and slow the evaporation of valuable moisture. Applying several inches of pine bark, leaves, pine needles, hay, or similar material in spring will usually suffice for the entire growing season. Cold-sensitive plants benefit greatly from a winter mulch, which can provide protection from freezing temperatures to their root zones. Since imported mulches may be costly, the use of local materials is logical. Gravel and crushed-stone products are sometimes used, and coastal bermuda grass hay is a good, inexpensive mulch available through much of our region. Since coastal bermuda grass does not produce viable seed, its use as a mulch should not add to the weed problem in planting areas, if the source of the hay was a pure stand. Even old coastal hay is fine for this purpose and may be good for little else.

PROPAGATING PERENNIALS

All of the plants described in this text may be propagated by at least one of three methods: cuttings, seed, or division. Cuttings and divisions are known as asexual propagation, which means that they produce an actual clone of the original plant. This is especially important in reproducing plants of historical significance, since it results in a new plant that is actually a living part of the original, the one from which the cutting or division was taken. It is important to maintain true replicas by this method since seedlings of most plants will vary genetically, even if only slightly, from the parent plant.

Starting New Plants From Seed

Reproduction by seed is popular with nurserymen because it generally enables them to raise large numbers of the same plant quickly and economically. Another advantage of this type of reproduction is that it discourages the passing on of diseases from parent to offspring, an all too common result of asexual propagation. In addition, some plants are difficult to root from cuttings and slow to increase by division, making seed propagation in these cases the only fast and reliable method. Also, it is far easier to transport seeds than plants, so that propagation from seed offers the most practical and convenient way to add new species from distant areas to our gardens.

Since growing plants from seed is a sexual means of reproduction, however, the seedlings may not closely resemble the parent. Seedlings of "wild type" specimens tend to be relatively stable in nature, but cultivars (generally defined as varieties that originate or persist under cultivation) or hybrids, (crosses between two species of a genus) are likely to produce widely varying offspring. Few of these offspring are likely to be as desirable as the parent. An example would be *Coreopsis lanceolata* 'Baby Sun', which commonly produces seedlings that are not nearly so compact as the original plants or seed you purchased. Commercial seedsmen overcome this difficulty by carefully controlling the pollination of the flowers so that each generation reproduces the original cross. This, of course, is one reason that the seed of cultivars and hybrids is more expensive. If you want to be certain of obtaining a true cultivar, you need to purchase seed from a reliable source, or to reproduce them through asexual means such as cuttings or division.

Seed should be ordered or purchased as soon as it becomes available since fresh seed usually germinates better. If it cannot be planted immediately, store the seed in the lower part of the refrigerator. Freezing does not harm the seed of hardy perennials, but neither is it necessary, as some gardeners believe. Some seeds do require a period of chilling to germinate, but a few weeks in the lower part of the refrigerator is usually adequate. If you plant the seed outside during the fall or winter, the naturally occurring cold weather will satisfy this requirement.

The best place in which to start seed of perennials is a cold frame or greenhouse. Most species need little, if any, protection from cold. In fact, excessive heat is more likely to injure seed and seedlings than cold. For spring blooming species, it is best to start the seed as soon as the weather begins to cool in the fall. Early spring is a good time to sow seed of perennials out of doors, but if the hot summer weather arrives while the seedlings are still too small to transplant, keeping them alive until fall may be difficult.

Many good gardeners concoct their own mixtures of soil, peat, and compost in which to start their seed, but professional nurserymen and a growing number of amateurs prefer the convenience of premixed, soilless potting media. Damping-off is a fungal disease that can occur under many conditions, but is less likely when commercial potting mixes are used. Application of fungicides such as Captan will also help prevent damping-off. After filling your pots and trays with the growing medium of your choice, press down on it lightly and evenly with a flat object to firm, but not pack, it into place.

If you plant several species of perennial seed in a single tray, be sure to leave enough spaces between rows of seedlings so that you can remove the quick germinating ones without disturbing the slower starters. Sow the seed in rows, as evenly as possible, and label the container immediately with the date and name of the plant. Watering at this point is best done by setting the pots or trays in a large container of water, so that the bottom ¼ or ⅓ of the container is submerged. When water has penetrated to the point that the surface of the media is obviously moistened, take the containers out of the water and allow them to drain. Then place the containers in a cold frame or greenhouse for germination.

After the seedlings have germinated, expose them to an increasing amount of fresh air by propping open the cold frame, or removing from the seedlings any covering within the greenhouse. Applications of a weak solution of a water-soluble fertilizer such as Rapid-Gro or Peters should begin at this time.

If a greenhouse or cold frame is not available, seed may be started inside the home in any shallow wood, metal or plastic container that is at least 3 inches deep. Milk cartons, foam cups, or peat pots work well, but make sure to punch holes in the bottoms of these containers so that water will freely drain from the soil.

Maintaining proper soil temperature is important for success with seeds. About 75° F is ideal with cooler temperatures often retarding germination. If possible, keep air temperatures at 70°–75° F during the day and

Dividing perennials helps keep them neat.

60°–65° F at night. A useful guideline for most plant species is to cover the seeds with only enough media to make them disappear, but check the planting recommendations on the seed packet for specifics. Cover the containers with plastic or place them in plastic bags, especially if you must leave them unsupervised for a couple of days. Remove this covering as soon as most of the seed has germinated, and then be sure that the new seedlings get maximum exposure to light. Most seed do not require light to germinate, but seedlings need maximum light as soon as they emerge from the soil.

Dividing Perennials

There are actually two very good reasons to divide perennials: to keep them vigorous, and to provide more plants. Such division also keeps your "drifts" and "clumps" of plants from overtaking one another and blurring the design composition. Finally, some plants tend to grow outwards from their original center, a tendency that leaves an unattractive dead or vacant space unless the plants are divided and reset.

It is important to divide plants at the proper time. Generally, it is best to avoid the hottest summer months. A rule of thumb is to divide perennials during the season opposite to that of their bloom. Spring flowering plants respond well to fall division while fall flowering types usually prefer division in early spring. This rule is certainly not inflexible; summer flowering perennials, for example, should be divided in fall or early spring rather than wintertime. Most perennials need four to six months after this disturbance to re-establish their root systems and grow sufficiently to provide a good landscape display. For this reason, it is also best to plant spring flowering bulbs in the fall, though in this case also, there are exceptions, and the gardener should be sure to read the information supplied for each species, since some bulbs also demand special treatment.

Another common question concerns how often plants should be divided. This, of course, varies with the individual plant species. Some need dividing every year, while others do best when left alone for two, three or more years. Since our climate has such a long growing season, plants that may need dividing every three or four years in cooler areas may need to be divided every one to two years for us.

To divide an established clump of a perennial, use a sharp spade to dig around the periphery of the plant; then cut the clump into sections. With some plants this is a simple process, but many others, such as shasta daisies, physostegia, phlox and cannas need extra attention. If divisions of these more finicky types are to survive, each must include 1–3 growing points or "eyes." If there is an old and partially dead center to the clump, discard it since divisions from weak plants usually prove inferior. If you wish to replant the same area in the border with plants you have dug up and divided, be sure to spade up the soil and add organic material and fertilizer before replanting.

Starting New Plants from Cuttings

For many perennials, rooting stem cuttings offers another inexpensive means of multiplying stock. The chances of success in this operation depend largely on the type of plant. Most of the perennials recommended for our area are dicotyledons (dicots), which means that when seedlings appear they have two seed leaves or cotyledons. As a class, dicots root readily. Monocot plants, that bear only one seed leaf, generally respond poorly to this type of propagation. Daylilies, irises and ornamental grasses, for example, are monocots, and these are usually propagated by seed or division. Sometimes commercial propagators clone these plants by means of a sophisticated laboratory technique known as "tissue culture." Tissue culture techniques can reproduce an exact replica of the parent plant from a few plant cells obtained from stems, roots, leaves or flowers. Valuable new cultivars of daylilies, irises, hostas and others are sometimes commercially propagated by tissue culture. This process requires expertise and facilities that are beyond most home gardeners, and it isn't practical for the production of only a few plants. It is a fascinating process that is becoming more important as the technology improves.

Anyone who has grown a begonia from a leaf cutting knows the stem is not the only part of a plant that will produce viable cuttings. But for perennials, stem cuttings are the most common and useful type. Known to our ancestors as "slips," stem cuttings are usually about 6"–8" long and include a terminal (tip) bud and several or more axillary (side) buds.

Commercial nurseries root cuttings in plastic-covered beds equipped with an intermittent mist system. This keeps the humidity very high while the cuttings are rooting. With such a system, cuttings root easily even during the summer. Homeowners without such facilities will achieve a better "take" during the cooler spring and fall seasons. Our grandparents created a protected and highly humid environment for rooting cuttings by placing them under a fruit jar in a well-prepared and partially shaded area of the garden.

To create a small, portable rooting environment take a 6"–8" plastic pot, fill it with a mixture of ½ sphagnum peat moss and ½ sharp sand (builder's sand) or perlite. Moisten thoroughly by partially emerging the container and media in water until the surface indicates it is moist. Remove the pot from the water and let it drain. In choosing material for cuttings, look for new growth and avoid old, woody stems. Use pruning shears or a sharp knife to remove cuttings from parent plants. Take 8 to 10 cuttings that are 6"–8" long and remove the leaves on the lower half of the cutting. If a rooting hormone such as Rootone is to be used, take a small amount from the package and place it where you can dip or roll the base of each cutting in the material. Rooting hormones are not necessary, but can increase the rooting percentage of difficult to propagate species. Gently tap each cutting after dipping to remove excess. Using a pencil or similar dibble, make holes in the rooting media so that the cuttings may be inserted without removing the rooting hormone or damaging the cutting. Firm the media around each cutting using your fingers, and water lightly to settle the media.

Using three or four small bamboo stakes or similar supports stuck into the pot around its edges, make a tent with clear plastic from a cleaner's plastic bag or similar material. Place the propagation unit where it will receive bright light but no direct sun, since temperatures inside the plastic tent can very quickly become too hot.

Most species will take three to five weeks to establish enough new roots to be transplanted. Usually, very little, if any, supplemental watering is necessary when the cuttings are kept under the plastic tent since there is so little evaporation. As soon as the rooted cuttings are taken from the unit and placed into individual containers, a mild solution of water-soluble fertilizer may be applied. Like young seedlings, these newly transplanted, rooted cuttings are tender and susceptible to changes in their environment. They need extra care and attention during their first few weeks.

Ann Hathaway's cottage garden in Stratford-upon-Avon, England, illustrates the use of stakes as support for vining plants.

KEEPING PERENNIAL PLANTINGS NEAT, ATTRACTIVE AND HEALTHY

The amount of time and effort necessary to keep perennials at their best varies with the seasons, but keeping a fairly close watch on the plantings can prevent major problems. Tasks likely to need attention include staking, dead-heading and control of insect and disease problems.

Staking

Many newer cultivars of perennials are more compact and may not require the support of stakes. Some, however, will need these structures if they are not to flop over into adjoining plants and spoil the effect of your design. An important fact to remember about staking is that once the plant shows a need for stakes it is actually too late to provide them effectively. By providing support early in the growing season, the structures are less conspicuous and the total effect much more natural in appearance.

Our ancestors often used twiggy brush or stakes cut from nearby woods to support the tall-growing or vining plants they grew in their gardens. This is still a practical way to stake some plants, although most gardeners prefer to use specially constructed wire rings or bamboo stakes. Another option is the steel stake coated with green plastic; this is generally available and blends well into the natural environment. Bamboo stakes arranged in a circle or triangle and encircled with twine or jute string work especially effectively in providing support for large clumps. To fasten plants to any of these supports use plastic covered wire ties.

Dead-Heading and Pinching

Our long growing seasons make pinching and pruning advisable for many species of perennials. Some plants, such as most of the Salvias, are much more attractive if given an occasional clipping during the warm summer months. Light applications of fertilizer and thorough watering after pruning or pinching help plants recover quickly and return to flowering.

Dead-heading involves the removal of spent flowers and stems, both to keep plants in an attractive condition and to prolong their season of bloom. If this maintenance is neglected, many species of perennials stop producing flowers and instead redirect their energy to the production of seed. Often, too, the spent flowers are unsightly. The petals of some species drop away neatly as the flowers fade, but those of many other perennials will hang on as they wither, unless the whole flower is removed. Dead-heading doesn't improve all plants, however. Some perennials produce a dividend of colorful fruit and seeds after they flower. In these cases, removing the spent flowers will cheat the garden of an added season of interest. Developing a familiarity with the habits of your plants as you choose them furnishes the best guide in this matter.

Insects and Diseases

When populations of certain insects grow out of balance, they may cause serious damage to our ornamental plantings. Sometimes natural predators will control

the problem if given an opportunity, but often after major damage has been done. Chemical controls may be the answer, but if they are used, it is essential to read the labels and follow the necessary precautions. Care in this matter is especially important since chemical products and the recommendations for their use change quickly. An objective source of information on insect and disease control is your local County Extension Agent. Many nurserymen can also supply well-informed, current guidance on these problems.

The most common insect problem of ornamental plants is aphids. These are small, soft-bodied creatures that suck on plants' new growth. Malathion, Diazinon, and Orthene are chemical controls that work well on these pests. If a nonchemical choice is desired, soapy water in a strong spray from the hose can be of help.

Spider mites are also a frustrating problem in many gardens. These tiny creatures are almost microscopic in size but can cause major damage to plantings. The first symptom of a spider mite attack on your plants is a mottled, discolored look of the leaves, followed by fine webbing. By the time the webbing appears, severe damage has occurred. Chemical controls are available, but total eradication is difficult. Insecticidal soaps seem to be fairly effective. Since spider mites are nearly immobile,

Dead-heading can prolong the season of bloom.

Tall fencing is a common method of control against deer.

washing them off with a hard stream of water sometimes helps. For this reason, a heavy rain tends to lessen infestations, while a long spell of hot, dry weather will aggravate the problem. Some plants, such as African marigolds and tomatoes, are extremely susceptible to these pests.

Pill bugs, snails and slugs are especially harmful to young seedlings. Special baits are available to control these pests, but they tend to be a recurring problem. Saucers of beer attract snails and slugs, reportedly luring them to a happy death.

Much of Texas and the Gulf South has a large population of native deer that can be a major problem, as they browse ornamental plantings. The only sure control is tall fencing. Some plants are less attractive to deer, but when these four-legged pests are really hungry, they will eat anything.

The most common diseases of perennials are caused by fungi. Powdery mildew looks like flour dusted on the foliage, buds and blossoms of some plants. Fungicides such as Funginex or Benomyl will usually control this problem, which tends to be more prevalent during spring and fall. "Damping off" is a term used to describe another fungal disease that attacks young seedlings. Usually, the use of sterilized media or commercially prepared potting mixes will prevent this problem. Sanitation is an important part of the treatment for any fungal infection. Diseased portions of plants should be removed, if possible, and destroyed to prevent spread to adjoining ones. Diseases that affect the roots of plants are the most serious. They are not nearly so likely to occur in soils that are well drained and kept slightly on the dry side.

The following lists of perennials are provided as a quick reference for use in the garden. Be sure to read the more detailed descriptions in the text to help determine your ultimate decisions.

PERENNIALS FOR SHADY OR PARTIALLY SHADED SITES

Achillea millefolium
Alstroemeria pulchella
Aquilegia
Aspidistra elatior
Bletilla striata
Ceratostigma plumbaginoides
Clerodendrum
Crinum
Dianthus
Equisetum hyemale
Eupatorium
Ferns
Hemerocallis
Hibiscus coccineus
Hosta

Hyacinthus orientalis
Hymenocallis
Ipheion uniflorum
Irises
Leucojum aestivum
Lilium
Liriope Muscari
Lobelia Cardinalis
Lycoris
Narcissus
Ophiopogon
Ornithogalum
Oxalis crassipes
Phlox
Physostegia virginiana

Plumbago auriculata
Ranunculus
Rhodophiala bifida
Ruellia
Saxifraga stolonifera
Saponaria officinalis 'Flore Plena'
Scilla hyacinthoides
Setcresia pallida
Sprekelia formosissima 'Orient Red'
Stokesia laevis
Tulbaghia violacea
Tulipa
Viola odorata
Wedelia trilobata
Zantedeschia

PERENNIALS FOR SUNNY, RELATIVELY DRY SITES

Achillea
Agave
Allium
Anisacanthus Wrightii
Antigonon leptopus
Aristolochia
Artemisia
Asclepias
Aster
Asparagus
Aurinia saxatilis
Bougainvillea spectabilis
Callirhoe
Canna x generalis
Centaurea cineraria
Cheiranthus 'Bowle's Mauve'
Coreopsis
Cuphea micropetala
Datura
Dianthus
Echinacea
Erythrina herbacea
Gaillardia
Gaura Lindheimeri
Graptopetalum paraguayense
Grasses (Native)

Hamelia erecta
Helianthus angustifolius
Hemerocallis
Hesperaloe parviflora
Hibiscus
Hippeastrum x Johnsonii
Ipheion uniflorum
Irises
Ixora coccinea
Justicia
Lantana
Liatris
Lycoris
Lythrum salicaria
Malviviscus
Mirabilis Jalapa
Muscari racemosum
Narcissus
Oenothera
Opuntia
Passiflora
Pavonia lasiopetala
Penstemon
Perovskia atriplicifolia
Plumbago auriculata
Polianthes

Poliomentha longiflora
Ratibida columnaris
Rhodophiala bifida
Rosmarinus officinalis
Rudbeckia
Ruellia
Salvia
Santolina
Sedum
Senecia Cineraria
Setcreasea pallida
Solanum
Solidago altissima
Sprekelia formosissima 'Orient Red'
Stachys byzintina
Sternbergia lutea
Stigmaphyllon ciliatum
Stokesia laevis
Verbena x hybrida
Tagetes lucida
Tulipa
Westringia rosmariniformis
Yucca
Zephyranthes

PERENNIALS TOLERANT OF BOGGY SOIL

Aspidistra elatior

Canna x generalis

Cyperus

Equisetum hyemale

Eupatorium

Kosteletskya virginica

Hymenocallis

Louisiana Irises and *Iris pseudacorus*

Lobelia Cardinalis

Setcreasea pallida

Tradescantia

Typha latifolia

PERENNIALS HAVING GRAY OR GRAY-GREEN FOLIAGE

Agave americana

Centaurea cineraria

Chieranthus 'Bowle's Mauve'

Dianthus (some cultivars)

Graptopetalum paraguayense

Grasses (some species)

Perovskia atriplicifolia

Rosmarinus officinalis

Santolina Chamaecyparissus

Sedum potosinum

Senecia Cineraria

Stachys byzintina

PERENNIALS THAT FLOWER IN LATE SUMMER OR FALL

Achillea

Anisacanthus Wrightii

Antigon leptopus

Aristolochia

Asclepias

Bougainvillea spectabilis

Canna x generalis

Chrysanthemum nipponicum

Clematis dioscorifolia

Crinum

Cuphea micropetala

Datura

Dianthus carophyllus

Echinacea

Eucomis bicolor

Eupatorium

Gaura Lindheimeri

Gerbera Jamesonii

Ginger Lilies

Hamelia erecta

Helianthus

Hemerocallis

Hibiscus

Ixora coccinea

Justicia

Lantana

Lycoris

Malvaviscus

Mirabilis Jalapa

Oxalis crassipes

Pavonia lasiopetala

Physostegia virginiana

Plumbago auriculata

Polianthes

Poliomentha longiflora

Rhodophiala bifida

Rosmarinus officinalis

Ruellia

Salvia

Saponaria officinalis 'Flore Plena'

Solanum Rantonnetii

Sternbergia lutea

Stigmaphyllon ciliatum

Verbena x hybrida

Tagetes lucida

Tulbaghia violacea

Wedelia trilobata

Yucca

Zephyranthes

PART TWO

Perennials for the Garden

5 Perennials Past and Present

Once a mainstay of gardens in our area, perennials are enjoying a renewed popularity that seems sufficient to re-establish them as important sources of color and seasonal interest for today's gardeners. Growing conditions in Texas and the Gulf South are significantly different from other areas of the nation to require different plants and cultural practices. Our ancestors grew many perennials in their gardens and some of these may still be found in old gardens, cemeteries and abandoned homesites in our region. Many of these classic garden subjects are enjoying renewed popularity as today's gardeners seek the best adapted species for their landscapes.

The following dictionary of perennials includes a large number of the oldest and newest species that are useful as garden ornamentals in our area. Perennials may be defined as plants that persist from the same root part from year to year. Many of these plants will also set seed and sometimes propagate themselves in that manner, as well as from divisions and cuttings. While this bonus is welcome, many of these volunteer seedlings will not "come true": they may differ considerably from the par-

ent plant. This is particularly true in the case of modern hybrid plants.

Though the availability of perennials is improving, sadly this does not apply to many of the fine old plants of yesterday. For these standbys, the gardener often searches catalogs and garden centers in vain. As word of the usefulness and beauty of these plants spreads, no doubt they will become more widely available. Fortunately, propagating perennials is easy, and sharing plants with family and friends is a tradition among good gardeners. The source list found at the end of this book should also help you to locate hard-to-find plants. Often, the plant societies included in this list are the best guides in this kind of search.

A list of perennial flowers could easily number in the thousands, for the possibilities are nearly endless. It is the author's objective, however, to limit his selections to a manageable number by including only those dependable plants that will bring success to the home or professional gardener.

HOW THE PLANTS ARE ARRANGED

Within this dictionary, the major plants are listed by scientific genus and arranged alphabetically. Common names and the family name follow. The major reference

used for nomenclature of the plants is *Hortus Third*, published by Macmillan Publishing Company in New York. Under each major listing, the species and cultivars are

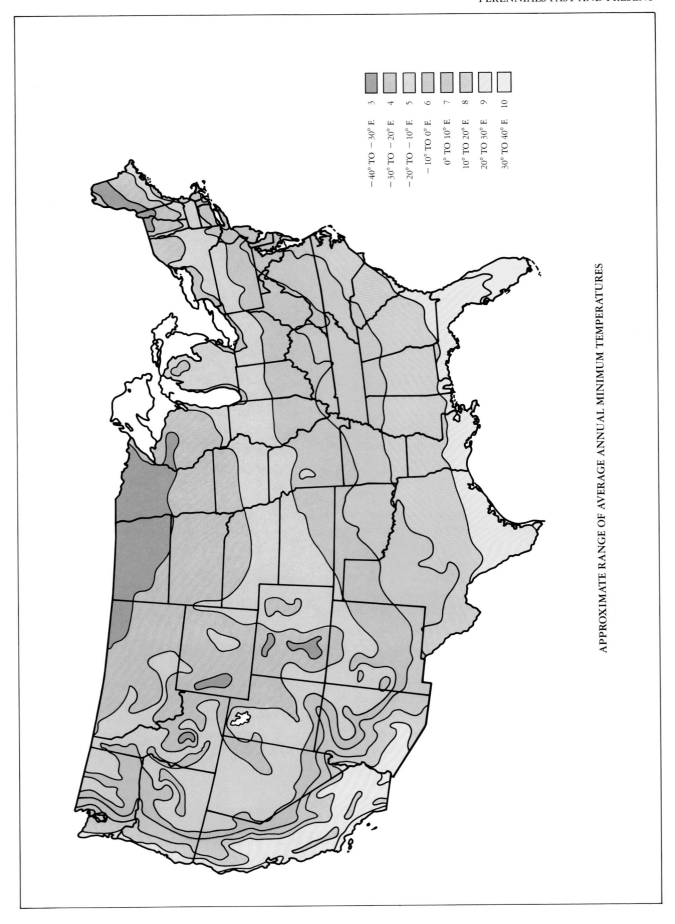

APPROXIMATE RANGE OF AVERAGE ANNUAL MINIMUM TEMPERATURES

described with emphasis on cultural requirements, landscape value, flowering time, and other relevant information. The approximate height of the plant is indicated for the time when the plant is in flower. Recommended sun exposure is abbreviated with the use of symbols indicating full sun, partial shade and full shade. If two symbols are shown, the plant will usually do well in either exposure, but in especially hot climates it is safer to select the location with more shade.

Wherever the author has deemed it necessary, he has appended to the binomials (Latin names) below guides to their pronunciation. Those with a knowledge of the classics will note that botanical Latin often differs markedly from the language of Caesar and Cicero, in which the accent usually falls on the next-to-last syllable. Indeed, pronunciation of botanical Latin can best be characterized as idiosyncratic. Often there is no one accepted way to pronounce a name. This guide doesn't seek to resolve those conflicts. Instead, it offers only an indication of how a contemporary, well-educated nurseryman pronounces the plant names, since the point of this list is to assist the reader in locating plants.

HARDINESS

Cold hardiness is a major factor to consider when selecting perennials, as it is with any kind of plant materials. The U.S.D.A. Hardiness Zone Map is the standard guide to limits of cold tolerance, though it is fraught with caveats when applied to Texas and the Gulf South. Our special conditions of soil and moisture increase plants' vulnerability to cold, and even if our temperatures don't reach extreme lows, still they can drop very quickly. Microclimates, warm or cold pockets within the landscape, also affect plant hardiness. The warm microclimate that lies at the foot of a south-facing wall or evergreen hedge, for example, can provide a safe haven for a plant several zones beyond its usual limit of tolerance.

The hardiness zone number listed is an approximation of the coldest region in which the plant is reliably hardy. Most plants will grow well in the zones south of this region. There are, however, exceptions to this rule with plants that require periods of cold induced dormancy that are insufficient in areas having very mild winters.

The longevity of perennial plants is affected by many factors such as dividing at the proper time, water management, soil type and condition as well as adaptability of the species to the local climate. A major reason for failure with perennials in Texas and the Gulf South is that our growing conditions are sufficiently different from the rest of the country to require a vastly different set of plant materials and cultural requirements. Our long growing seasons, widely varying soils, rainfall, humidity and temperature extremes are a challenge to gardening that can only be successfully overcome with a large dose of specialized information.

PERENNIALS FOR THE SOUTH

Achillea millefolium
(ak ill LEE ah mil ee FOL ee um)
YARROW

Family: Compositae   ○◗
Zone 3   1′–2′   Spring, Early Summer, Fall

A sometimes-used common name for the yarrows is "sunfern." This aptly describes their foliage and preference for at least partial sun. *Achillea millefolium* is native to Europe but naturalized in the Southeast, so that it is often considered a wildflower in Texas. In spite of their delicate appearance, yarrows are relatively drought tolerant and withstand heat well. They prefer a good soil with little competition from trees and other competitive plants, but can exist in less hospitable surroundings.

Yarrows may be propagated from seed or division. They are prolific spreaders, but can easily be kept in

Achillea millefolium—White-Flowering Yarrow

A. millefolium 'Fire King'

A. filipendulina 'Coronation Gold'

bounds by occasional division or the removal of unwanted plants. Fall division is ideal, but other times,
except the hottest summer months, work almost as well.
The yarrow's attractive, ferny foliage is evergreen
through most of Texas and the Gulf South. They bear
their large, flat heads of flowers over a long season, and
the blossoms are excellent for drying. To maintain some
of the original color, cut and dry the flower heads before
pollen forms. If cut later, the flowers are still useful
for dried arrangements, but will usually turn brown.

The white-flowering yarrow found growing most
often in our area is *A. millefolium*. It has all the virtues of
the species, but most selections have flowers of a less than
pure white that can have a somewhat dirty appearance.

A. millefolium 'Fire King' is probably the most
popular and available of the pink-flowered selections of the
naturalized species. Flower color is dark bright pink in
spring but fades to paler tints as the heat intensifies.
Growth and flowering slow down or nearly stop during
the heat of summer to be followed by occasional rebloom
and growth during the fall. *A. millefolium* is well adapted
to nearly all areas of Texas and the Gulf Coast. It is the
yarrow species of choice for the areas near the Gulf Coast
since it seems to withstand the high humidity and hot
night temperatures better than the other forms.

A. filipendulina 'Coronation Gold' is the most popular garden form of yarrow but is not as well adapted to areas
close to the Gulf. For more inland locations, it is fine.
Its gray-green foliage is coarser in texture than that of
A. millefolium, and not so finely cut. 'Coronation Gold' is
a useful plant for locations in Zone 8 and north. Other
A. filipendulina cultivars worthy of note are 'Moonshine',
which is a beautiful combination of pale and bright
yellow flowers, and 'Gold Plate,' which is similar to
'Coronation Gold', but taller and with larger flower
heads. The extra height and flower size of 'Gold Plate'
make staking a necessity.

Agapanthus africanus
(ag ah PAN thus   af ree KAN us)
BLUE LILY OF THE NILE

Family: Amarylidaceae
Zone 8   2'–3'   May–June

Agapanthus can be spectacular in the garden, but
rarely naturalizes in Texas and the Gulf Coast. Its blue or
white flowers appear in funnel-shaped, round, terminal
clusters during May and June. A white form, 'Albus,'
bears its showy flowers on tall stems. 'Peter Pan' is dwarf,

Agapanthus africanus—Blue Lily of the Nile

rarely exceeding 18 inches in height. In areas where they are not winter hardy, Agapanthus is an excellent container plant.

Agapanthus is a fleshy-rooted perennial that should be divided every three to four years. They bloom better when their root systems are slightly restricted, which explains their popularity as container plants. The foliage is evergreen most winters in Zone 9.

A major requirement for Agapanthus is well drained soil since the rhizomes will rot in wet locations. A three- to four-inch mulch of pine straw, coastal bermudagrass hay or similar material is good insurance against winter damage and summer moisture stress. For mass effect space plants about 18–24 inches apart. The dwarf form is most effective planted with 1 foot spacing. Water soluble fertilizers applied several times during the growing season are helpful.

Agapanthus orientalis is a wedgewood-blue type that may bear 40 to 100 individual flowers per spike. The foliage of this species is soft and reflexed, and its overall height is about 2 feet. Agapanthus is very popular in California and Southern Europe. *Agapanthus africanis*

sometimes sells as *A. orientalis* or *A. umbellatus*. With good management they can be useful in parts of Texas and the Gulf South.

Agave americana
(a GAH vee   a MER ee kan a)
CENTURY PLANT

Family: Agavaceae   ◯◐
Zone 9   4′–6′   Evergreen

The common name Century Plant derives from the erroneous belief that the plant must attain an age of 100 years before it flowers. In fact, it usually matures in ten to twenty years. After flowering just once, the plant dies, but small plants almost instantly proliferate around the base of the failing parent. Century Plant is a native of tropical America and popular as an accent in dry, harsh settings. It will rot in wet soils and prefers full sun exposure. Leaves are thick, heavy and gray, with sharp points on the ends and stout prickles along the edges. Flowers are greenish-yellow in heavy clusters on a stalk that may be from 10′–20′ tall.

Agave americana—Century Plant

A. Scott Ogden

A. Scott Ogden

A. victoria-reginae—Queen Victoria Maguey

A. victoria-reginae, Queen Victoria Maguey, is cold hardy as far north as Dallas and an interesting Agave. It is relatively spineless, with white leaf margins that make the plant resemble an artichoke. *A. victoria-reginae* is native to shady canyons of Northern Mexico, but will also grow in the sun. Its formal-looking rosettes grow for about 20 years before blooming and dying.

A. lophantha 'compacta' is a fairly compact Maguey that suckers readily and soon forms large clumps. The attractive spine-edged leaves have a pale green midrib. It is hardy from Central Texas southward.

Agaves make a dramatic impact in the landscape. They are best adapted to sunny, dry sites and are sometimes featured in containers. Spines on the tips of the leaves may be clipped to reduce possibility of injury. Propagation occurs by removal of suckers from mature plants.

Allamanda cathartica
(AL la man dah ka THAR ti ka)
ALLAMANDA, GOLDEN TRUMPET
Family: Apocynaceae   ○◑
Zone 9   10′−20′   Summer

Allamanda is not reliably root hardy except in Zone 10, but established plants frequently return through most of Zone 9. They are native to South America where they are known for their profuse blooming. All through the warm seasons, the reddish-brown buds open to golden-yellow blossoms 3 inches across. This vine has

a tendency to sprawl unless trained on a trellis, stake or similar structure. Cultivar 'Grandiflora' offers a more compact form, one that is sometimes trained as a shrub. Allamandas flower most prolifically after the vigorous vegetative growth of spring has passed, when a slight moisture stress and lower soil fertility triggers a burst of blossoms.

Allamandas prefer rich, well-drained soil and moisture. Best exposure is partial or full sun. Propagation is usually from cuttings.

ALLIUM

Allium
(AL ee um)
ORNAMENTAL ONION
Family: Amaryllidaceae

Ornamental onions are important garden plants in other parts of the world and deserve wider use in the South. The species described here are all easily grown and form clumps that may be divided every two to three years. The onion scent is apparent only when the foliage is crushed. Sources for most of these onions are limited, but several are native and may be easily grown in the garden from seed collected in the wild. Ornamental onions are best set out in fall but may be transplanted at any time with ordinary care.

Allium neapolitanum—Naples Onion

A. *Drummondi*

A. *Coryi*

A. *canadense* v. *cristatum*—Rose Leek

Allium neapolitanum
(AL ee um   nee oh POL ee tan um)
NAPLES ONION
Zone 8   1′ – 1½′   Early Spring   ◯◐

The Naples Onion is one of the few European onions adaptable to the South. Snow white flowers appear on 1–1½ foot scapes and are especially showy. Since the flowers appear very early, it is good to place the plants in locations that offer some protection from late freezes, at the foot of a south-facing wall, rock or shrubbery.

A. *Drummondii*
A. DRUMMONDII
Zone 8   1′   Very Early Spring   ◯◐

A. *Drummondii* is commonly native over most of Central Texas and flowers in shades from chalk-white to deep wine-rose. It is very dwarf and blooms in February and March. A. *Drummondii* is worthy of garden use as an edging plant or in "drifts" near the front of the border, and is very drought tolerant. A lovely orange-flowered hybrid of this species and A. *Coryi*, a yellow species from the deserts of West Texas, was once distributed under the name 'Margaret Kane'; presumably, it is now lost to cultivation.

A. *canadense* v. *cristatum*
ROSE LEEK
Zone 8   1′   Early Spring   ◯◐

The Rose Leek is another of our beautiful native onions. It has attractive rose-colored flowers and bright green foliage, a useful foil for larger spring bulbs. As a native of the Texas Coastal Bend, Rose Leek performs well on heavy hardpan soils. The flowers have a sweet scent similar to that of carnations, a characteristic that the Rose Leek shares with the very similar North Texas A. *canadense* var. *hyacinthoides*.

A. *canadense* v. *Fraseri* has wide grayish foliage with globose white flower clusters.

A. *canadense* v. *Fraseri* is a larger-growing species of wide, grayish foliage that bears globose flower clusters of chalk white. It blooms about April 1 and makes large bulbs up to 2 inches in diameter. It is native from Central Texas through the Great Plains and is, therefore, cold hardy in all areas of Texas and the Gulf South. This species was formerly known as *A. acetabulum*.

A. *stellatum*
PRAIRIE ONION

Zone 5   1'–1½'   Fall   ○◑

The Prairie Onion is a choice, fall-blooming onion native to the Great Plains and the heavy, black soils of North Texas. The attractive, purplish-pink flower clusters are an especially welcome addition to the fall garden. The leaves are flat and shorter than the scape.

A. *tuberosum*
GARLIC CHIVES

Zone 8   18"–20"   Mid to Late Summer   ○◑

Garlic Chives are very well adapted for use in the kitchen garden since the leaves furnish a good, mild source of garlic flavor. The scent is, however, destroyed by cooking. Flowers are chalk-white and occur from mid to late summer when few other perennials are blooming. Because the attractive clumps of foliage increase by rhizomes rather than true bulbs, Garlic Chives may be readily divided at any time. To keep the clumps attractive, dead-head as soon as the blooms fade and before seed forms. Otherwise seedlings may sprout in unwanted areas of the garden.

Alstroemeria pulchella
(al stroh MAY ree uh   pull CHELL uh)
PERUVIAN LILY

Family: Alstroemeriaceae   ◑
Zone 8   2'–3'   Late Spring, Summer

Peruvian lilies are closely related to the Alstroemerias sold in florist shops, but are much more easily grown in Texas and the Gulf South. The flowers are reddish-orange with green edging to the tubular florets. This is an interesting color combination, but not very striking in the garden. To show to best effect, it needs a strong green background. The flowers are long lasting both in the garden and as cut flowers.

Alstroemerias thrive in partially shaded locations and good, moist soil conditions, although they are fairly aggressive and will naturalize in less hospitable locations. They are normally propagated by division of

A. *stellatum*—Prairie Onion

Alstroemeria pulchella—Peruvian Lily

A. Scott Ogden

Amsonia Tabernaemontana—Texas Blue Star

A. Scott Ogden

Anisacanthus Wrightii—Anisacanthus

A. ciliata

rootstock or seeds. Periodic division is not necessary to the continued health of the plant.

Alstroemerias are interesting and unusual plants that are most effective near the center of the border, or interplanted in ground covers such as ajuga, English ivy and similar plants that thrive in partial shade.

Amsonia Tabernaemontana
(am SO nee uh   ta bur nay MON tan uh)
TEXAS BLUE STAR

Family: Apocynaceae   ○◖
Zone 4   2′   Spring, Early Summer

Amsonias are native wildflowers of the Southeast. The pale blue coloring of their flowers, neat growth habit, and ease of culture make them worthy of garden culture. *A. Tabernaemontana* occurs naturally in moist locations in Central Texas, but is very adaptable to a wide range of growing conditions. They form clumps of graceful stems with lanceolate leaves and light blue, star-shaped flowers in terminal clusters. The color is pale blue and is more noticeable in the landscape when combined with white or yellow flowers.

Propagation of Amsonias is normally by division in the fall, although cuttings and seeds are also practical. If grown in rich soil, plants can become rank and loose. Stems should be cut halfway to the crowns after blooming is completed. Amsonias will grow in either acid or alkaline soils and are drought tolerant and long-lived.

A. ciliata is a narrower leaved species often found on dry, sandy, soils. It thrives on sunny, sandhills, but also does well under ordinary garden culture.

Anisacanthus Wrightii
(a neese a KAN thus   RIGHT ee eye)
ANISACANTHUS

Family: Acanthaceae   ○◖
Zone 8   3′–4′   Spring, Summer, Fall

Anisacanthus is native to West Texas, New Mexico, and Mexico. The 2″ long red-orange, tubular flowers it bears throughout the growing season are colorful in the landscape and among the best for attracting hummingbirds. Foliage is thin, small and lance-like. Plants have little form or mass, but with occasional pruning, make an acceptable display in the border. Anisacanthus prefer sunny locations and well-drained soil. They are very drought tolerant and bloom through the most intense heat. Propagation is from cuttings or the seeds that often self-sow in the vicinity of parent plants. Frost damage may occur in severe winters, but roots are usually hardy. Plants should be severely pruned in early spring and whenever necessary to maintain form and flowering during the growing season.

Antigonon leptopus
(an TIG o non   lep TO puss)
CORAL VINE

Family: Polygonaceae   ◑
Zone 8   10' – 15'   Late Summer, Fall

This native of Mexico is widely cultivated in Texas and the Gulf South for its striking, lacy pink flowers. It is a vigorous vine with heart-shaped leaves that needs the support of a trellis, fence or tree. The first hard freeze of autumn kills all the top growth, but established plants return readily the next year from sweet potato-like tubers that some sources describe as edible.

A. leptopus is easily grown, but must have good drainage and at least a partially sunny exposure. It is very drought tolerant and really begins its landscape display after the first good rains of late summer and fall. A white form *A. leptopus* 'Album' is sometimes available. Propagation is by division or seeds. It is best to start the seeds

early in the spring in order that the vines will grow and develop tubers before frost.

A. leptopus is an integral part of many Texas and Gulf South gardens. At its best, it frames a garden like fine lace. The foliage is attractive and sufficiently dense to provide summer shade on trellises and arbors.

AQUILEGIA

Aquilegia
(ak wi LEE ji uh)
COLUMBINE

Family: Ranunculaceae   ◑●
Zone 5   18" – 24"   Spring

Columbines are elegant plants with ferny foliage and abundant flowers in blends and solids of yellow, blue, purple, red, and white. The hybrids so popular in other parts of the nation tend to be cool-season annuals in Texas and the Gulf Coast. There are, however, at least three species that are native to Texas and fairly long-lived when grown in good, well-drained soils. Columbines prefer partially shaded locations, but will grow and flower in fairly dense shade or full sun if the soil contains a high percentage of organic material and drains well.

As a rule, Columbines are not long lived, but they reseed freely. Seeds sown in early fall will sometimes flower the first spring. Established clumps should be divided in the fall after the second flowering, or discarded in favor of new plants. They become nearly dormant during the hottest period of summer and resume growth after the first cooling rains of fall.

Antigonon leptopus—Coral Vine

A. leptopus 'Album'

Aquilegia canadensis—Wild Columbine

Aquilegia canadensis
(ak wi LEE ji uh   kan a DEN sus)
WILD COLUMBINE

Zone 5   1'–2'   Spring   ◐●

A. *canadensis* is native to rocky river banks in the Hill Country of Texas. The foliage recalls that of maidenhair fern, but slightly coarser. Flowers are a soft blend of red and yellow and occur from mid to late spring. They barely ascend above the luxuriant spring foliage. This is one of the best blooming plants for partially or nearly fully shaded locations.

A. Hinckleyana
HINCKLEY'S COLUMBINE

Zone 5   18"–24"   Spring

Bright, solid chartreuse-yellow flowers with long spurs appear elegantly on long stems well above the beautiful foliage of Hinckley's Columbine. Native to a few stream banks in the Big Bend area of Texas, it is a well-adapted subject for Texas and Gulf Coast gardens. Readily grown from seed planted in the fall, or by the division of mature clumps, A. *Hinckleyana*, like other Columbines, cross-pollinates readily with other Aquilegia species; this makes it difficult to keep a pure seed source if more than one species is included in the garden.

A. *longissima* is very similar to Hinckley's Columbine but has an even longer spur, which can exceed 4 inches in length. Both are beautiful and useful plants that are currently very limited in availability.

Aristolochia elegans
(a ris to LO kee a   EL ee ganz)
DUTCHMAN'S PIPE

Family: Aristolochiaceae   ○◑
Zone 9   8'–10'   Vine   Summer

Dutchman's Pipe is a most interesting vine that was once common in cottage gardens of Central and South Texas. It is a slender, woody climber native to Brazil. The leaves are triangular to three inches long and more

Hinckley's Columbine is well adapted for Texas and Gulf Coast gardens.

A. Hinckleyana—Hinckley's Columbine

Aristolochia elegans—Dutchman's Pipe

or less heart shaped. The flowers are among the most unusual in the plant world. Typically, they are about three inches long and one inch wide and shaped like a Dutchman's Pipe. Color is an odd brownish-purple with a yellowish-green tube. Since the color is somber, the flowers, though large and interesting in shape, may go almost unnoticed. Blooms appear during the summer over a long period, a few at a time.

Dutchman's Pipe is easily grown in most any garden soil. Basic requirements are a sunny or partially sunny location and a fence or trellis for support. Propagation is by seed, layering, or cuttings. Self-sown seedlings often occur near the parent plant.

A. durior also goes by the name Dutchman's Pipe and is more commonly available. It does not, however, live long in the warm winter climate of the Gulf Coast. *A. durior* is much hardier than *A. elegans* and will tolerate very cold winters. Easily grown from seed, it is sometimes cultivated as an annual in warm winter areas, where it provides quick foliage cover for trellises.

Artemisia
(ar ti MEZ ee uh)
MUGWORT, TARRAGON, WORMWOOD, SOUTHERNWOOD

Family: Compositae   ○◑
Zone 3 and 4   3′   Summer

Sometimes known as "Dusty Millers" in Texas and the Gulf South, artemisias are grown primarily for their foliage. Artemisias are a bit frustrating; they include some of the best gray-foliaged plants for the border, but the various species tend to be either overly aggressive in the garden, or prone to rotting in areas of high humidity. Cold hardiness is not a problem since most types are hardy into Zones 3 and 4.

Traditionally, artemisias were grown for their aromatic, insect-repellant and medicinal qualities. They thrive even in poor, dry soils, and are usually propagated by division. Sunny locations are preferred.

Artemisia abrotanum, or 'Southernwood,' is pungently aromatic. This cultivar's green, feathery foliage was used historically to scent stored linens and to repel insects. Today, its fresh, long-lasting perfume makes the foliage a preferred material for bouquets, wreaths and dried arrangements. A compact grower, Southernwood prefers good drainage and may prove short-lived in areas of high humidity. The flowers are yellowish-white, nearly round, and occur in loose panicles. Established plantings profit from light fertilization, especially after harvest. Propagation is usually from cuttings. Tangerine, lemon, and camphor scented cultivars are available.

A. absinthum is known as "Common Wormwood" and was formerly well known as the source of the liquer

absinthe. Tolerant of poor soil, this species type grows to about 3 feet and is easiest to establish if planted during the winter in Texas and the Gulf South. Though by nature an expansive herb, Common Wormwood may be contained and shaped through shearing. Foliage is silver-gray in color and attractive in combination with other perennials.

A. annua, or 'Sweet Wormwood,' is a reseeding annual that is well adapted to our area. It is more greenish than gray in color, but is an excellent companion plant for perennials.

A. dracunculus is the true French tarragon. It is a gem for cooking but is not well adapted to Zones 8, 9, and 10. If grown in containers and protected from the heat and humidity of our summers, it will sometimes survive, but is not recommended as a landscape plant for our area.

A. ludoviciana is probably the most common of the artemisias in our area and has naturalized from the Hill Country to the Texas Panhandle where it is an indicator of good, well-drained soils. Although one of our best adapted silver-foliage plants, it can be invasive, especially in sandy soils. The running roots can be controlled with metal or plastic barriers set 8″ – 10″ deep.

Artemisia abrotanum—Southernwood

Artemisia Schmidtiana 'Nana' 'Silver Mound'

Upper leaves are lance-shaped, and the lower ones are lobed. Shoots emerge close together and make a handsome display in spring, followed by a more lax summer growth habit. The foliage withers with the first hard frost, and should be cut back to the ground at that time. 'Silver King' and 'Silver Queen' are closely similar cultivars often confused in the nursery trade. 'Silver Queen' is somewhat smaller in size with more finely cut foliage. Naturalized on many old homesites in Texas, *A. ludoviciana* supplies a traditional material for floral bouquets. It is one of several plants sometimes known as "Dusty Miller," and the best adapted, most useful artemisia for our area.

A. Schmidtiana 'Nana,' commonly known as 'Silver Mound,' is a cultivar of unknown origins, though the species is native to Japan. At its best, this is a wonderful plant whose tight, neat mounds spread to a width of 18″, without exceeding a height of 6″. Like some of the other artemisias, 'Silver Mound' tends to "melt" in the Gulf Coast heat and humidity. It is more dependable in areas away from the immediate coast, where it can be a spectacular addition to the border. If left unstaked, the clumps tend to flop by midsummer. This can be partially prevented by a modest trimming before the plants flower. Propagation is by cuttings and division.

A. vulgaris, the "Mugwort," grows well in a wide variety of soils and exposures. The green variety grows to about 3′ tall and may become a pest, but the silver one, though larger growing, spreads slowly and is not invasive. This latter type finds many uses in the landscape, especially in a gray garden where its tarnished-silver foliage adds a distinctive yet harmonious note. Shaping with pruning or hedge shears encourages a less weedy appearance. This herb is associated with St. John the Baptist, since he wore it around his waist in the wilderness to ward off evil spirits. Its many uses have won this plant a place in many stories and legends.

Other useful artemesias include *A. pontica*, Roman Wormwood, which grows 1½′–3′ tall and has lacy, gray foliage. It responds well to pruning and may be used as a

A. ludoviciana

Asclepias tuberosa—Butterfly Weed

low hedge. *A. lactiflora* is native to China, grows 3′–4′ tall and is good in a semi-wild garden. *A. stelleriana*, Beach Wormwood, has a beautiful, soft white cover on the foliage. As long as it has dry, sandy soil in which to grow, it, too, remains proof against our heat and humidity.

Asclepias tuberosa
(as KLEP ee us   too be ROE suh)
BUTTERFLY WEED

Family: Asclepiadaceae   ○◑
Zone 3   2′–3′   Summer

The flat-topped umbels of the Butterfly Weed are 2″–5″ across and usually bright orange. They are among the most showy of our wildflower perennials and can be useful in the garden. Bloom usually occurs in mid to late summer in their natural environment, but often earlier in the garden. The lance-like leaves are neat and attractive before and after the relatively long blooming season. The flowers are excellent and long-lived when cut. They are also attractive to butterflies, especially the gaudy Monarchs, which add a second burst of color to the plant.

There are two factors that somewhat limit the use of Butterfly Weed in landscape settings. This plant must have good drainage and is best adapted to relatively dry, sandy soils. The major problem, however, lies in transplanting. The long tuber-like roots must not be broken when being moved. Even young plants are sensitive to this problem and are best grown or obtained in containers and, after planting, left undisturbed in the landscape. Once established, they tend to be long-lived and increase in floral display each year. Bright, sunny locations are best.

In her book *A Southern Garden*, Elizabeth Lawrence extolls the virtues of *Asclepias tuberosa* and recommends combining clumps of them with June flowering daylilies (103). Butterfly Weed sometimes repeats it, flowering in August when few other plants brave the heat.

Propagation is usually from seed, although by digging deeply and by taking care not to break the roots, mature clumps may be divided in early spring. For seed propagation, collect mature seed in late July or August, remove the small, downy appendages and store in an airtight container in the lower part of the refrigerator until spring and plant. Several years are required to produce large, bushy clumps. Colors vary from yellow to near-red, but most seedlings will be orange. The only way to be assured of obtaining other colors is by dividing clumps or taking root cuttings. A superficially similar, much more easily propagated native of Northern Mexico, *Asclepias curassivica*, is popular in South Texas gardens. Known there as "Mexican Oleander," its ever-blooming clumps may be readily divided.

Aspidistra elatior
(as pi DIS truh   il ah TEE or)
CAST IRON PLANT ◐●

Family: Liliaceae
Zone 8   2′–3′

The tough, leathery, evergreen leaves of Aspidistra are stemless and sprout from thick roots and rhizomes. Individual leaves usually measure about 4″ in diameter and about 1½′ in length. Common names such as cast iron plant or barroom plant arise due to the ability of the plant to persist under adverse conditions and low light.

In fact, poor soil and drought have little more effect on the Aspidistra than to slow down its already modest growth rate. Direct sun will burn its foliage and extremely windy sites will cause a tattered, unattractive appearance. Cold weather in most of Texas and the Gulf South does little to the handsome, almost artificial-looking foliage. Small, purple-brown flowers appear in spring near ground level but are relatively inconspicuous.

The best use of this native of China is to mass it in shady borders under trees and similar shaded situations. Aspidistra is frequently used in containers and sometimes for indoor or atrium environments. A green and white variegated selection is sometimes available. The intense dark green foliage and ease of culture make Aspidistra one of the best choices for shaded areas. Propagation is by division in early spring. Since growth rate is slow to moderate, the cost of these plants tends to be higher than that of most other ornamentals. Another plus for this plant is its value as a cut green for floral decorations. The leaves last for weeks when properly handled and can be wired into unusual shapes.

Any reasonably good garden soil is adequate for Aspidistras. Occasional deep watering in dry spells and the periodic removal of damaged or dying old leaves are the only major cultural tasks. Annual application of an all-purpose fertilizer will hasten growth.

Aster x
(AS ter)
AUTUMN ASTER ○◐

Family: Compositae
Zone 5   2′–3′   Mid to Late Fall

This plant is the only aster I have found to be truly reliable in Texas and the Gulf South. It thrives in Central, West, North and East Texas and tolerates the coastal humidity. Trying to find the correct name for the plant has, however, been frustrating and unsuccessful. It differs from *A. frikartii*, by offering no spring or summer flowers. It is, however, sometimes sold under that name.

The 2′–3′ mounds and 1½″ lavender flowers occur in October and November and usually last until frost. Leaves are lanceolate, somewhat hairy, grayish green, and larger earlier in the season before the flower stalks begin to develop. They are especially nice in the fall border when combined with the yellow-gold flowering *Tagetes lucida*, Mexican Marigold-Mint.

Culture is among the easiest of garden perennials. A sunny, well-drained site and any reasonable garden soil usually produce excellent results. Propagation is by cuttings or division of older clumps in early spring. For neat garden appearance stems should be cut close to the ground after flowering. Tips may be pruned in mid-summer to shorten height, but staking is usually not required in sunny locations. Mature clumps are usually long-lived even when left undivided for many years.

(left) *Aster x*—Autumn Aster (Above) The Autumn Astor bears lavender flowers.

Autumn Asters are valuable for their opulent display of flowers in mid to late fall and because they are so easily grown. Their drought tolerance is outstanding, making them useful in Xeriscape and other resource-efficient garden situations. They are fairly common in rural Texas gardens and occasionally available from local nurseries.

Asparagus officinalis—Garden Asparagus

A. densiflorus 'Sprengeri'—Asparagus Fern

Asparagus officinalis
(ah SPAR a gus   oh fish i NAL is)
GARDEN ASPARAGUS

Family: Liliaceae   ○◑
Zone 6   4'–5'   Ferny Foliage

Although primarily considered a garden vegetable today, *A. officinalis* was often planted in old-time Texas and Gulf South gardens as an ornamental. The ferny, fine textured, dark-green foliage is excellent when combined in bouquets with flowers. The foliage usually dies back to the ground with the first hard freeze, and should then be cut back, to return early the next spring. New shoots may be cut and enjoyed as vegetables for several weeks in the spring without seriously weakening the plant.

Asparagus thrives in a variety of conditions, but prefers sunny locations and well-drained soil. An application of fertilizer in late winter will promote more and stronger spring and summer growth. Most of the varieties sold as vegetables are suitable for ornamental use. 'Mary Washington' is an old favorite. Asparagus were often part of the cottage gardens of Texas and the Gulf South. They may be propagated by division in late winter or from seed in spring. Their fine texture, drought tolerance, and general ease of culture make asparagus good candidates as perennials. Old clumps increase slowly and do not normally require division to remain healthy.

Asparagus densiflorus 'Sprengeri'
ASPARAGUS FERN

Zone 9   Lime-Green Foliage   ○◑

Although commonly called a fern, *A. densiflorus* 'Sprengeri' is not a true fern since it reproduces by seed instead of spores. It is quite useful in the Gulf Coast area where the long, graceful arching stems of small, lime-green needles are valued for hanging containers and pots, as a ground cover or mass planting. When root bound, older specimens sometimes produce attractive red fruit.

Asparagus Fern is tolerant to salty conditions and may be used in seaside plantings. Fleshy root nodules enable the plant to store moisture and withstand extended dry periods. Frost-damaged foliage should be cut back to the ground. Occasional applications of nitrogen fertilizer help keep the foliage rich and green. Heavily root-bound plants may be cut with a sparp knife into several divisions and repotted almost any time during the growing season. Masses of Asparagus Fern in sunny or partially shaded areas can provide fine texture and lush green to flowering borders. *A. densiflorus* 'Myers' is an even finer textured and darker green variety with very ʼense foliage, shorter and less arching stems. It is most useful as a container plant. *A. retrofractus* has tufts of green threadlike foliage and many slender stems. It is also useful as a container plant in Zones 9 and 10. *A. falcatus* is sometimes known as Sickle Thorn and is an attractive, climbing form with rigid spines. It is useful in areas having mild winters. *A. setaceus (plumosus)* is a tall, climbing asparagus that is much used by florists. It has spines with reflexed tips that help provide support as the plant climbs. It is evergreen in areas having very mild winters.

Aurinia saxatilis (Alyssum saxatile)
(aw REN ee uh   saks a TIL is
BASKET-OF-GOLD

Family: Cruciferae	◐
Zone 3 6″–12″ Spring	

This useful plant can only be recommended for western and northern parts of Texas and the Gulf South. It must have good drainage and tends to rot in areas of high humidity. Flowers are a bright daffodil-yellow and

Aurinia saxatilis—Basket of Gold

Bletilla striata—Chinese Ground Orchid   A. Scott Ogden

occur in early to mid spring. *A. montanum*, Mountain-gold, is smaller and more compact but equally as attractive in the landscape. It is most effectively displayed in a spot where the plants can hang over the edge of a raised bed. The life of *A. saxatilis* may be extended by pruning plants back about one-third after flowering. Propagation is sometimes by division, but usually from cuttings.

Lobularia maritima is the annual referred to as sweet alyssum and should not be confused with the plants described above. Sweet alyssum does reseed in some landscape settings, but is not a perennial.

Bletilla striata
(blay TIL uh   stree AH tah)
CHINESE GROUND ORCHID

Family: Orchidaceae	◑●
Zone 8 2′ Spring	

B. striata is one of the few terrestrial orchids suitable for general cultivation in Texas and the Gulf South. They thrive in the shaded or partially sunny garden with a moist humus-rich soil, but they will also grow satisfactorily in sunnier, drier locations. The spikes of purplish-pink flowers emerge in early spring and may be damaged by late spring freezes unless mulched annually.

A white form, *B. striata* 'Alba,' is also available and has leaves with white-striped margins as well as the white flowers. The foliage is large and handsome. Propagation is usually by division of established clumps in late summer or fall.

Bougainvillea spectabilis
(bo gin VIL ee uh   spek TAB il is)
BOUGAINVILLEA

Family: Nyctaginaceae	◐
Zone 9 20′ Summer and Fall	

Bougainvilleas are extremely showy vines that are useful as container specimens outside their normal range. Even a light frost kills the leaves, while temperatures in the twenties usually freeze the whole vine back to ground level. Colder temperatures can completely kill even established specimens. Though the flowers are inconspicuous, the paperlike bracts that surround them are beautifully and intensely colored in shades of red, orange, pink, purple and blends. The stems are armed with spines that are large and sharp.

When grown in containers, Bougainvilleas can be pruned to become more shrubby than vinelike. They also bloom better when root bound, although their performance is best when fertilizer and water are regularly applied. Sunny, hot locations promote spectacular displays of bracts that can occur from spring till frost,

A closeup of 'Barbara Karst' shows its beautiful blooms.

though the most intense displays usually take place in September, October and November.

Well-established plants often bloom several times during the growing season. If severely damaged by frost, however, outdoor specimens may not bloom at all the following year. Frost-damaged wood should not be removed until late the following spring when the true extent of damage can be determined.

Propagation is from cuttings taken during the growing season. Transplanting Bougainvilleas is complicated by the fact that their root systems are not fibrous and do not hold a ball of soil well. Extra care should be taken during this operation to disrupt the roots as little as possible. Bougainvilleas are very drought tolerant. They are truly hardy only in Zone 10 but are used extensively in Zone 9, and as container plants where winter protection can be provided in Zone 8.

There are many varieties of Bougainvilleas on the market, and the gardener will find plenty of scope for exploration. 'Barbara Karst' produces masses of ruby-red flowers and is one of the best for training into a shrub in a large container. 'Convent' (purple) and 'Sundown' (salmon) are vigorous, free-flowering varieties, as are many of the dwarf types that are especially well suited to container-growing.

Bougainvillea spectabilis 'Barbara Karst'

Callirhoe involucrata—Wine-cups

Callirhoe involucrata
(ka LIR o ee   in vol lu KRA tuh)
WINE-CUPS

Family: Malvaceae   ○◗
Zone 4   1'–2'   Spring and Summer

This is a native Texas wildflower that deserves more widespread use in the garden. The plant forms a trailing mound that can cover a 2'–3' circle with its deeply cut, gray-veined foliage and 2″ red-violet flowers. These flowers are cup-shaped and somewhat tulip-like in appearance. The foliage of the Wine-cup dies back to the

ground in late summer or early fall, to re-emerge in winter or very early spring from the plant's thickened, carrot-like roots.

A good choice for the front of a sunny border, Wine-cups are relatively short-lived, but new seedlings often spring up to surround the mother plants. New plants may be raised from seed planted in late winter and transplanted into the garden in early spring. The trailing stems do not root as they touch the ground, as one might expect, but 4″ cuttings taken below a node may be rooted under mist in early summer. A related species,

C. digitata, the Standing Wine-cup, grows in an upright manner, offering a better perennial alternative where more height is required. Because of its greater stature, the Standing Wine-cup is a better plant for center or rear of the perennial border than *C. involucrata*.

Wine-cups are deep rooted and require little supplemental irrigation. They are useful in containers where they spill over the edges in a handsome manner. With regular watering and dead-heading, the blooms can continue for several months.

Canna x generalis
(KAN nuh   jin er AL is)

CANNA

Zone 7   2'–6'   Early Summer till Fall   ◯◑

Cannas were once an important ornamental in Southern gardens and are currently enjoying a renewal of popularity. They are natives of the tropics and subtropics and have thick, branching rhizomes. Cannas have been in cultivation for some time; the Indian Shot, *C. indica*, was known as early as 1570. The work of breeding and improving this species was begun in the 1840s by a Frenchman, M. Annee. He introduced the first hybrid, "Annei," in 1847 or 1848.

Cannas are among the easiest of perennials to grow and are available in a wide variety of flower colors and plant sizes. The foliage is banana-like and varies in color from green to reddish purple, bronze and variegated. Bloom season can last from May until November in some areas.

Rhizomes purchased in early spring bloom well the first year if planted in sunny locations and good soil. In colder climates, the rhizomes (bulbs) are dug and stored

Canna x 'Iridiflora Rubra'

Canna x generalis—Canna 'Pfitzer Dwarf'

Canna x 'Striped Beauty'

S. J. Derby

after frost and replanted the next spring. Cannas respond to good growing conditions, but few plants can withstand more abuse. Removing spent flowers and seed pods induces repeat flowering as well as guaranteeing a neat appearance. Dividing established clumps every three or four years helps to prevent overcrowding, but is not essential.

Many varieties of cannas are available. Among the most useful are the Pfitzer Dwarfs, which range in size from 2½'–4' tall and produce large heads of brightly colored flowers in yellow, pink, orange, salmon and red. The major pest of cannas is a leaf caterpillar whose depredations cause leaves to abort and become unsightly. Applications of insecticide to the foliage or to the root zone with systemic materials will usually control the problem.

Cannas are usually propagated by division of mature clumps. New varieties are obtained from seed which should be soaked in warm water or have their seed coat knicked with a file before sowing.

A large, vigorous, tall-growing canna with long, tubular flowers and brilliant red coloring is sometimes found in old Southern gardens. This seems to be *C. x* 'Iridiflora Rubra', one of Annee's hybrids and a plant this pioneer introduced sometime around 1858. Distributed under the name of 'Ehemannii,' this is a striking variety that seems to have some resistance to the caterpillars that cause leaf roll. *C. iridiflora* is a tall species canna with attractive ginger-like foliage and pendant flowers in bright crimson. This is a beautiful addition to the back of the border and was once a winner of the Royal Horticulture Society Award of Merit. *C. x* 'Striped Beauty' is a more recent introduction with interesting green and cream, variegated foliage. This hybrid bears yellow flowers marked with creamy patches. It grows quickly and easily, though it remains relatively dwarf, not exceeding a height of 3'–4'.

Centaurea cineraria
(sen TAW ree uh   sin er RAY ree uh)
DUSTY MILLER

Family: Aetheopappus   ◯◑
Zone 8   1'–3'   Gray Foliage

C. cineraria is one of the most handsome of the silver-gray foliage plants. It is easily grown from cuttings in summertime, or from seed in the spring. There are several plants that go by the name "Dusty Miller." This one is very popular in California and grows well in light, well-drained, alkaline soils. It does tend to be short-lived.

Flowers appear singly in summer, are about 1" in diameter and purple in color. Plants should be trimmed back after flowering. The foliage is very silvery in color and furnishes a wonderful contrast to the greens of the border. Leaves are strap-shaped with broad, rounded lobes. This plant is a relative of the Cornflower or Bachelor's Button and is somewhat similar in appearance.

Ceratostigma plumbaginoides
(ser at oh STIG muh   plum bag ee NOY deez)
BLUE PLUMBAGO

Family: Plumbaginaceae   ◯◑
Zone 6   1'   Summer

This plant is confused by many with *Plumbago auriculata*, a flower that belongs to the same botanical family, and is also called Blue Plumbago but which is a more tropical, less hardy species. *C. plumbaginoides* is poorly adapted to areas close to the Gulf Coast, but flourishes in the Texas Hill Country where it is sometimes used as a groundcover. It prefers sandy, fertile soil and although it tolerates partial shade, it does not compete well with tree roots. The diamond-shaped leaves and clusters of bright blue flowers are an attractive combination. *C. plumbaginoides* is a good companion plant for early flowering

Centaurea cineraria—Dusty Miller

Ceratostigma plumbaginoides—Blue Plumbago

Cheiranthus—'Bowle's Mauve' Wallflower

'Bowle's Mauve' Wallflower is good for massing in borders.

spring bulbs since the Plumbago is not an aggressive competitor and its foliage does not emerge until after many bulbs have finished blooming. Propagation is usually by division of established plantings. The brilliant maroon-red fall color of the foliage is one of this perennial's outstanding characteristics.

Cheiranthus
(ki RAN thus)
BOWLE'S MAUVE WALLFLOWER

Family: Cruciferae ◯◗
Zone 6   2′   Spring

Most wallflowers perform very poorly in the heat and humidity of the Gulf South, but 'Bowle's Mauve,' an introduction of the famous English horticulturist E. A. Bowles, performs fairly well. Wallflowers are relatives of stock, a fragrant, cool season annual popular in old gardens of the South. 'Bowle's Mauve' is a handsome mounded plant with lavendar-purple flowers. It may

be grown from seed started in early spring or from tip cuttings.

This is a neat and attractive plant for massing in the border, though it requires a sunny location and very well-drained soil, and individual specimens tend to be short-lived. It is growing well in my Central Texas garden, but I doubt that it will prove well-adapted to areas close to the Gulf. Nevertheless, 'Bowle's Mauve' is definitely a prospect for those interested in experimenting with worthwhile plants.

Chrysanthemum x morifolium
(kris AN the mum   mor ee FOL ee um)
GARDEN CHRYSANTHEMUM

Family: Compositae ◯◗
Zone 6   1′–4′   Fall

Garden mums are probably the showiest of all fall-blooming perennials. They are relatively easy to grow, though hobbyists often devote much time and effort to

Chrysanthemum x morifolium—Garden Chrysanthemum

James M. Sterling

Mum variety 'Grandchild'

'Minn Gopher' is considered a cushion mum.

'Yellow Jacket' mums can be repotted for outside use.

cultivating them to perfection. Colors range from reds, purples, whites, yellows, pinks and lavenders to bronzes; almost every color but blue.

Chrysanthemums are sensitive to day length and produce flowers as the days become shorter in the fall. Spring's short days may also trigger a bloom, but both the quality and quantity of the flowers will be much better in fall's cool weather than at the onset of summer's heat. Since spring flowering also tends to weaken plants, any buds that do appear then should be removed.

Thrifty gardeners often try to recycle potted mums from the florist's shop into their gardens after they have enjoyed the flowers in their homes. While the plants may survive, they really aren't worth the effort or the space in

the garden. The varieties that have been bred for greenhouse forcing and florists' sales are not nearly so well adapted to outdoor use as the garden varieties developed specifically for landscape display.

Garden mums need full sun and well-drained, well-prepared soil. To remain vigorous in Texas and the Gulf South, the plants should be divided or restarted from cuttings each spring, as soon as they begin growing rapidly. To prevent disease problems, it is recommended that new side shoots be separated from the clump and reset. Even better is to take 4″–6″ tip cuttings in March or April, root them in a mixture of peat moss and sand, or a commercially prepared potting mix, then plant them directly into the garden on 16″–18″ spacings.

Mums have a wide range of colors.

Mums are among the easiest of all plants to root and are usually ready to set into a permanent location 3–4 weeks after sticking. It is best to settle them into the bed or border before the arrival of really hot weather. Aphids are the major insect pest, but they may be readily controlled by applying chemicals labeled for that purpose.

Pinching is an important part of the cultivation of all kinds of garden chrysanthemums, except the so-called "cushion mums." Most varieties should have the soft growing tips "pinched out" whenever they reach 4"–6" long. For large plantings this can get to be a big job, but can be speeded up and done almost as well by using hedging shears. In our climate, pinching may be necessary every two or three weeks during May, June, and early July. By mid-July or early August in northern parts of our area and September 1 along the Gulf Coast, pinching should cease so that the plants can put on a final burst of growth as the buds are beginning to set. Application of a balanced fertilizer according to label instructions every 4–6 weeks from early spring until mid-August is helpful since mums tend to be heavy feeders. They also need regular and generous watering during dry spells.

Garden mums are not always readily available from garden centers in the spring. Plants ordered from mail-order sources tend to look pretty pitiful when they arrive, but these rooted cuttings will grow quickly and can produce spectacular effects by fall, if well cared for. Garden centers and nurseries usually stock a good selection

James M. Sterling

Mums are easily rooted from tip cuttings in spring.

of heavily budded plants in 4″, 6″, and 1 gallon containers during August and September. This method of planting mums has grown more popular in recent years. It is, of course, more expensive, since the larger plants cost more, but it saves the homeowner the trouble of nursing the plants through the long hot summer. Plants should be cut to near ground level after hard frost in the fall.

Selecting appropriate varieties is a key to success with chrysanthemums in our area. It is possible to have flowers as early as the end of August and as late as November by a judicious choice of early, mid-season and late flowering varieties. Early flowering types, while they provide the first blooms, do not offer lasting floral displays in our area, since the buds tend to open while our weather is still too hot. For this reason, mid-season and later types should make up the bulk of our plantings. Some of the many good choices and their colors include the following: 'Lipstick' and 'Ruby Mound,' red; 'Jackpot' and 'Yellow Cloud,' yellow; 'Stardom'and 'Liberty,' lavender-pink; 'Grandchild,' two-tone pink; 'Starlet,' honey-bronze; and 'Pancho,' orange to bronze.

Varieties recommended especially for Houston and the Gulf Coast area include the following: 'Megumi'-yellow anemone, 'Seizan'-yellow anemone, 'Daphne'-white single, 'Ginger Ale'-light bronze anemone, 'Haresugata'-red anemone, 'Texas Hombre'-bronze anemone, 'Thisle Hill'-Lavender anemone, 'Adorn'-pink single, 'Baby Tears'-white single, 'Frolic'-white single, 'Grenadine'-pompon bronze, 'Lancer'-lavender single, 'Redcoat'-red single, 'Ruby Mound'-red pompon, 'Target'-yellow single, 'Tinker Bell'-purple single, 'Westpoint'-yellow single, 'Yellow Jacket'-yellow spoon, and 'Zest'-red single.

Garden mums can be very effective when planted in "drifts" within perennial borders. Individual plants should be spaced 18″–24″ apart. They also adapt easily

to container growing. Indeed, through careful, painstaking training, hobbyists are able to grow in various sized containers spectacular chrysanthemum cascades whose blossoms number in the dozens or even hundreds. Individual flower types vary from singles, spoons, quills, doubles, and pompons. Colors are rich, and flowers are long lasting in the landscape or when cut. Growing mums in the field for sale as cut flowers on All Saints Day is still practiced in some Gulf Coast areas, although not nearly so commonly as it once was.

Chrysanthemum x superbum (C. maximum)
SHASTA DAISY

Family: Compositae   ◯◑
Zone 5   1′–3′   Spring

Shastas are perennials that may be easily grown in our area, but satisfaction and success depends on a careful selection of varieties. Cultivars that bloom as early as possible and are compact in growth habit are preferred because Shastas suffer during periods of heat and drought and sprawl in our warm, humid spring weather. A compact Shasta that I collected from an old garden blooms in College Station by April 1, and lasts until early to mid-June. It is fairly similar to 'Little Miss Muffet,' which is commonly available from the seed catalogs. My experiences with the very large and double flowering forms, on the other hand, have not been successful.

Shastas like a deep, rich soil and fairly moist conditions. Even with supplemental irrigation, I sometimes lose plants during the heat and humidity of August and September. The first rains of fall give them new life and

Shastas are among the best perennial cut flowers.

no amount of cold seems to cause them to suffer. It is best to divide Shastas every fall, sometime between the first of September and mid-December. Single divisions placed one foot apart at this time make a solid mass by spring. If planted later in the season, the divisions will take root and grow, but they will not produce the same quantity of flowers. As soon as the blossoms begin to fade, the flower stems should be cut as close to the foliage mounds as possible. Shastas are among the best perennial cut flowers. They produce so many flowers that cutting some for the house detracts little from the garden display.

Chrysanthemum x superbum—Shasta Daisy

C. nipponicum
NIPPON DAISY

Family: Compositae ◯◑

Zone 5   2′   Fall

Nippon Daisies have become very popular in the Southeast, and the limited trials that have been made of them in Central Texas look promising. The plant could best be described as a woody, bush-form of Shasta Daisy. Since they are shrubby, mature plants cannot be divided, although it is reported that sometimes a few rooted branches can be found near the base of the plant. Spring-rooted cuttings are said to make substantial, blooming-size plants by fall. Plants are naturally compact in form and should not be pruned, since such treatment may retard the fall bloom sufficiently that it will fall prey to frosts. Experience is limited with this plant in the Gulf South, but I suspect that it will do better inland than next to the coast.

Sweet Autumn Clematis can have a vanilla-like scent.

Clematis dioscorifolia (C. paniculata)
(KLEM a tiss   DI ass ko ree fol ee ah)
SWEET AUTUMN CLEMATIS

Family: Ranunculaceae ◯◑

Zone 7   20′–30′   Early Fall

The large flowering clematises do not thrive in the heat and humidity of the Gulf Coast area. They can, however, with considerable nurturing, be made to flower for several or more years in more inland parts of our region. Sweet Autumn Clematis, *C. dioscorifolia*, however, is a different matter. The clouds of whitish flowers it bears in late summer or early fall are small but fragrant, while the vine itself is vigorous and easily grown. On good soils, in fact, it often flourishes to the point of becoming invasive. The major merits of the plant are its late summer bloom, which comes when little else is in flower, and the wonderful vanilla-like scent it so freely bestows on the garden. This clematis is visually effective on arbors, trellises, and even growing into trees. It needs several hours of direct sunlight daily to produce flowers.

Sweet Autumn Clematis is a native of New Zealand, although it has naturalized in a few areas of the South. It usually freezes to the ground each winter and may be cut back at that time. Propagation is from cuttings or the root sprouts which can appear some distance from the mother plant. *C. virginiana*, commonly called "Virgin's Bower" or "Woodbine," is native to areas of Texas and the Gulf South. This vine bears a heavy crop of cream-colored flowers in late summer, and as these fade, they are replaced by a silvery haze of plumed fruiting structures. *C. drummondii*, from Central and West Texas, produces a similar effect and is sometimes known as "Old Man's Beard."

Clematis dioscorifolia—Sweet Autumn Clematis

Clematis texensis is a rare native of Texas.

C. texensis is a rather rare native of Texas whose flowers are urn-shaped and red. It is a dainty grower in most gardens, but can make a handsome display in mid- to late summer. *C. texensis* is too tender to be grown well in England but was introduced into cultivation there in 1868. European breeders greeted it with great excitement because it differed so drastically in flower form and color from existing garden clematises. Attempts to cross it with other species and cultivars, however, have met with only limited success. The best forms of *C. texensis* are a bright scarlet in color, but such plants are not common. *C. texensis* 'Duchess of Albany,' with pink bell-shaped flowers, performs well in our area.

C. integrifolia, a shrubby native of the Balkan peninsula, produces its cornflower-blue four-petaled flowers continuously from spring till fall and enjoys alkaline soils. *C. Armandii* is sometimes known as "Evergreen Clematis" and is native to southern China. Its glistening white flowers are about 2½" across, and are borne on branched clusters during March and April. Although a slow starter, *C. Armandii* grows vigorously once established. It is reported to be well-adapted to the New Orleans, Louisiana, and Charleston, South Carolina, areas, where it is sometimes trained up trellises for screening purposes. Its leaves scorch badly when the plant is exposed to sodium in the water or soil.

The best known of the newer clematises were bred by Jackman, a renowned English nurseryman, in 1860. The result of crosses between *C. lanuginosa* and 'hendersonii,' these produce large, spectacular flowers. The 'Jackmanii' hybrids are still among the most popular clematises today.

Clematis vines are frail and thin, requiring support to be effective. Because hybrids such as 'Jackmanii' flower on new wood, they should be lightly pruned immediately after flowering. As the old adage has it, clematises like to have their heads in the sun but their feet in the shade, and these vines do grow best where their roots remain cool during the hot months. A heavy mulch of leaves or pine bark is recommended, and some growers advocate placing a large stone immediately over the root zone of the plant to provide extra protection from the heat.

Clerodendrum x speciosum
(kler oh DEN drum   spee si OH sum)
CLERODENDRUM, JAVA SHRUB

Family: Verbenaceae ◯◗
6–7′   Summer

Clerodendrum are tropical plants, but they return from the roots reliably each year in most of Zones 9 and 10. They have huge, dark glossy-green leaves, and flower

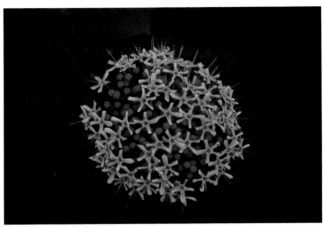

Clerodendrum Bungei—Cashmere Bouquet

over a long season. Flowering is much more prolific following mild winters. *C. speciosissimum* produces spectacular, pyramidal panicles of red flowers followed by green and blue-black berries in showy bracts. They are often found in old gardens of the region and thrive in full sun or partial shade. Though it prefers a rich, moist soil, the Java Shrub will grow almost anywhere. Frost-injured wood should be cut back at the end of winter. Propagation is usually from root sprouts or seed.

C. Thomsoniae, Bleeding Heart, is an evergreen vine in Zone 10 that produces branched clusters of heart-shaped crimson flowers with white calyxes. This species is useful in greenhouses and other protected locations. When used as a container plant, a heavier bloom may be induced by restricting the plant's supply of water and fertilizer.

Sometimes known as Cashmere Bouquet, *C. Bungei* is a semi-woody perennial common in parts of the Deep South. It normally reaches a height of 3′–5′ tall and produces flat corymbs of tightly clustered, fragrant, rose-red flowers in summer. Although well adapted to many locations, *C. Bungei* blooms best in partially sunny areas. Propagation is usually by transplanting the root sprouts that spring up freely around the parent plant—so freely, in fact, that they can become a pest in areas of good soil.

Coreopsis lanceolata
(ko ree OP sis   lan see oh LA tuh)
COREOPSIS

Family: Compositae ◯◗
Zone 6   1′—3′   Late Spring, Summer

Coreopsis are among the most useful native perennials of our region. Very tolerant of both heat and drought, they require little care to produce lavish amounts of color in the garden. *C. lanceolata* tends to be rather tall, about 3′, and sprawls as it reaches its peak flowering. This failing, which is especially obvious in the aftermath of a heavy wind or rain, is aggravated by an abundance of water and fertilizer. Its foliage is long and slender, and the 2″ yellow, daisy-like flowers appear on long, slender stems from mid-spring until really hot weather in July.

The good news about Coreopsis is the introduction of cultivars such as 'Baby Sun' and 'Sunray,' both of which are more compact and less sprawling in character. 'Sunray' is a semi-double golden orange and 'Baby Sun' is more yellow. Both stay in the 18″ height range and have

retained all the good characteristics of the species. 'Gold Fink' is a very compact selection that forms dense tufts of foliage and can be used as a ground cover in small areas. It is not, however, as well adapted to the Gulf Coast as the other two cultivars. There 'Gold Fink' often proves shortlived, melting during the heat of midsummer. Better success can be expected in central, west, and northern parts of the Gulf Coast states.

Coreopsis clumps should be divided every 1–2 years and will usually bloom from seed the first year.

Coreopsis lanceolata—Coreopsis

Close-up of 'Baby Sun'

Coreopsis cultivar 'Baby Sun'

Seedlings will appear in large numbers around established plants, but will not breed true. To maintain the dwarf character of the special cultivars, it is necessary to propagate them through the division of existing clumps or purchase fresh seed. Mature clumps sometimes form plantlets called "proliferations" on the tips of floral stems. These may be removed and set in moist potting soil, where they will quickly root. "Proliferations" will develop the same form and size as the parent plant.

The seed heads that Coreopsis plants produce at the end of their bloom cycle are unsightly and should be removed. In dead-heading these, it is best to make the cuts as close to the foliage as possible to avoid leaving an untidy mass of stubble. Removing spent blossoms and stems often stimulates another cycle of flowering.

The last few years have seen the introduction of *C. verticillata* into the nursery trade. Also known as the "Threadleaf Coreopsis," this is a species with very fine-textured foliage. At least three cultivars are available. 'Golden Shower' forms 2′–3′ mounds of airy foliage that, given favorable conditions and adequate care, bear bright yellow flowers all summer and into the fall. 'Zagreb' is a dwarf form that attains a height of about

Coreopsis verticillata cultivar 'Zagreb'

C. verticillata cultivar 'Moonbeam'

18″ while yielding golden flowers. 'Moonbeam' is just slightly larger, and bears lovely, creamy yellow flowers.

C. verticillata cultivars tend to form running thickets of fine stems that may be divided in fall or early spring. All Coreopsis prefer sunny locations and well-drained soil. They prefer sandy soils and perform well with little or no fertilization. In addition to their use in masses and in border plantings, I have grown *C. verticillata* 'Moonbeam' in a large container. There it made a pleasing combination with a gray-foliaged Dianthus that spilled over the pot's edge.

Crinum bulbispernum
(KRI num   bulb is PER num)
CRINUM, ORANGE RIVER LILY

Family: Amaryllidaceae   ○◗
Zone 7   2′–3′   Spring and Summer

C. bulbispernum is probably the most common Crinum found in Southern gardens, often naturalizing in bar ditches and near old homesites. It is easily recognized by its glaucous fountains of foliage. It is very hardy and the parent of many hybrids. The common pink forms are undistinguished, but the white form 'Alba' and wine red 'Rubra' are choice garden plants. The large lily-like flowers and coarse foliage furnish a handsome contrast to finer textured plants.

Crinum are propagated by seed or by removing natural offsets from older plants. They are of easy culture and thrive under a wide variety of conditions. Flowering is more prolific when clumps are allowed to remain undisturbed for several years.

Crinodonna corsii 'Fred Howard' is known as Amarcrinum and is well adapted to Zones 9 and 10. It is a hybrid of *Amaryllis belladonna* x *Crinum Moorei*. Pink flowers rise in August and September from established clumps. Amarcrinum is especially valuable for the delightful primrose fragrance it inherited from *Amaryllis belladonna*, a beautiful South African bulb that, unlike its offspring, fails to grow in the South.

C. Moorei var. 'Schmidtii' is a white flowering form that comes from Natal, a part of South Africa that experiences more heat and summer rainfall than the rest of the country. This is fortunate for Southern gardeners, for this variety of *C. Moorei* performs much better in the South (Zones 9 and 10) than the usual forms, which grow here only in wintertime. *C.* 'Schmidtii,' does, however, prefer the protection of a partially shaded location. The foliage spreads from the long-necked bulbs to form bright green rosettes of corn-like leaves. Snow-white flowers appear atop tall stems in May and June. *C.* 'Schmidtii' is a parent, along with *C. bulbispernum*, of the outstanding *C.x powelli* 'Alba.'

Crinodonna corsii 'Fred Howard'

C. Moorei var. 'Schmidtii'

Crinum bulbispernum—Crinum, Orange River lily

C. scabrum is a spectacular red and white striped Crinum that is the parent of multitudes of hybrid "Milk and Wine" lilies found across the South. In June it crowns its rosettes of rough-edged leaves with boldly striped blooms reminiscent of Amaryllis. This native of Tropical West Africa is slow to produce offsets, but sets seed abundantly. It is hardy only in Zones 9 and 10. *C. Zeylanicum* is a similar species from tropical East Africa

and India; because of its tender nature it is rarely encountered outside of Florida gardens.

C. erubescens (Zone 8) is a native of Brazil that blooms in late summer with spidery, fragrant white flowers atop reddish stems. The compact rosettes spread by underground rhizomes to create a thicket in the landscape. Like many Crinums, this species may be grown as an aquatic. It is often sold as *C. americanum*. *C. americanum* is very similar to, but in every respect inferior to, *C. erubescens*. *C. americanum* is native to brackish estuaries along the Gulf and demands aquatic treatment. *C. asiaticum* produces similar flowers on huge plants with yucca-like foliage, and is hardy only along the Gulf Coast.

CRINUM HYBRIDS

Crinum were one of the first groups of ornamental flowering plants to be extensively hybridized. Even as early as 1837, well before plant genetics were well understood, William Herbert recorded nearly 30 hybrids. Because Crinum are extremely tough and long-lived, many of these old hybrids still lurk in today's gardens, though most have long since lost their proper identities. Although hundreds of Crinum Hybrids have been

C. amabile

Crinum Zeylanicum

C. asiaticum

created in the past 150 years, many of these older, some-times rather homely, varieties are still cherished as family heirlooms.

By far the commonest Crinum hybrids in the South are the group of plants loosely termed "Milk and Wine lilies." These bear white flowers, each petal of which is marked down the center with a pink or wine-colored stripe. As previously noted, most are hybrids of *C. sca-brum* and *C. bulbispernum*, and have in common trumpet-shaped blooms and rather rank foliage. Collectively, this group of hybrids is known as *C. x herbertii.* A second group of "Milk and Wine lilies" has wide open, star-shaped blossoms, and probably originated through crosses of *C. scabrum* or *C. Zeylanicum* with *C. erubescens.* These are primarily late summer bloomers and are ex-tremely beautiful and fragrant garden flowers. *C. amabile*, with its huge, agave-like foliage and enormous clusters of spidery wine-striped flowers, is a distinctive type of "Milk and Wine lily" popular in gardens along the Gulf Coast. Apparently, it is a natural hybrid of *C. Zeylanicum* and *C. asiaticum* and was cultivated in Southeast Asia prior to European contact; it may be the oldest hybrid of all.

In the late 1880s, shortly after the introduction of *C. Moorei* from South Africa, Sir William Bowman of Jolwynds, Dorking, introduced *C. x Powellii*, combining the beautiful campanulate blooms of *C. Moorei* with the hardiness of *C. bulbispernum*. At least two varieties of this cross, the snow-white 'Alba' and the rosy-pink 'Cecil Howdyshel' are popular in Southern gardens.

'J. C. Harvey,' a shell pink trumpet-shaped hybrid of *C. Zeylanicum* and *C. Moorei*, was first offered for sale in Florida about the turn of the century. Its prolific nature and lush corn-like foliage have made it one of the com-monest garden Crinums around the Gulf Coast. About 1930, Louis Percival Bosanquet, a Floridian of English descent, originated 'Ellen Bosanquet,' a well-known wine-red Crinum which today is one of the South's finest garden plants. Presumably, it is a hybrid of 'J.C. Harvey' and *C. scabrum*, although Mr. Bosanquet left no record of his crosses.

Other old Crinum hybrids worthy of garden use in-clude 'Mrs. James Hendry,' a Henry Nehrling cross from early in this century; 'Peachblow,' a choice T. L. Mead hybrid from the same period; and 'White Queen,' a frilled white trumpet from Luther Burbank. Among

C. erubescens

Crinum hybrid 'Ellen Bosanquet'

Old Crinum hybrid 'Mrs. James Hendry'

'White Queen'

'Peachblow'

Crinum x Worsley

'Carnival'

'Parfait'

more modern hybrids, 'Carnival' is an outstanding red of unusual hardiness; *C. x Worsley*, an exciting bicolor; 'Wm. Herbert' a vivid red stripe; 'Parfait' an outstanding blush; and 'Sangria' an unusual cultivar with handsome red foliage and pink blooms.

Crocosmia Pottsii
(kro KOZ mee uh   POT zee eye)
MONTBRETIA

Family: Iridaceae   ◯◗
Zone 8   3'–4'   Spring, Early Summer

Montbretias are interesting and easily grown plants whose foliage somewhat resembles that of the Gladiolus, but whose flowers are borne in a loose abundance on forking, airy branches. The flowers are funnel form, about 1½" across, and bright red-orange. They grow from small, gladiolus-like corms that send out stolons to form new plants. In good soils Montbretias can be invasive, but the flowers are striking in the garden and excellent as cut flowers.

The best displays of Montbretias are grown in the sun in modestly fertile soil. Heavy fertilizing and an abundance of water can cause weak and sprawling growth. It is best to allow the foliage to mature for several weeks after flowering before cutting the plants back. They may be transplanted successfully at any season, but fall or very early spring is ideal.

Cuphea micropetala
(ku FEE uh   my kro PET ah luh)
CIGAR PLANT

Family: Lythraceae   ◯◗
Zone 9   2'–4'   Fall

The 4"–6" long, shiny, dark green foliage and mounding form make this Cuphea attractive even when not in flower. In areas of little or no frost, the plants are evergreen and bloom in spring as well as fall. The flowers are borne in terminal spikes and are tubular-shaped with red and yellow-green coloring. They are very attractive to hummingbirds and may be worth including in the garden for that reason alone. Flowers usually begin to appear in September and continue until the first hard frost.

Where winters are colder, the above ground portion of the plant freezes and should be cut to the ground. The following spring, the clumps will reappear, larger than

Crocosmia Pottsii—Montbretia

The Cigar Plant has bright red
tubular flowers.

Cuphea micropetala—Cigar Plant

Cuphea hyssopiflora—False Heather

False Heather can be planted in
masses or as clipped hedge.

before. Cupheas are very drought tolerant and prefer sunny locations and well-drained soil. They are propagated by the division of existing clumps in the spring, or from cuttings taken early in the growing season. Natives of Mexico, they are very much at home in Central and Coastal Texas where they deserve more widespread use.

    C. hyssopifolia, False Heather, is native to Mexico and Guatemala and a popular, useful plant for Zones 9 and 10. Tiny flowers of pink, purple or white occur in abundance during the summer months. The foliage is ½″ to ¾″ long, very narrow, and evergreen when not exposed to hard frost. It may or may not return from the roots following a cold winter. False Heather prefers a sunny, well-drained location and is fairly drought tolerant. It is attractive in masses or even as a small clipped hedge, and may be easily kept 6″–24″ tall. *C. hyssopifolia* makes a fine container planting, though in that situation it may need protection from the hottest sun during the summer months. Propagation is from cuttings, which root readily during the warm seasons.

C. *Papyrus*

Cyperus alternifolius—
Umbrella Sedge

Datura inoxia quinquecuspida—
Angel's Trumpet

Cyperus alternifolius
(si PE rus   al ter nih FOL ee us)

UMBRELLA SEDGE

Family: Cyperaceae   ◯◑

Zone 8   3'–5'   Foliage

Umbrella Plant is a tropical of unusual appearance
that has naturalized in moist areas of the United States.
The common name derives from the umbrella-shaped
clusters of whorled foliage that perch atop the long,
green stems. The creamy-white flowers that open in a
ring around the leaf clusters' bases are not very showy.
C. alternifolius thrives in boggy soils, and will grow in
pots submerged in water. It has been cultivated as a water garden plant for more than 200 years. The first hard
freeze of autumn kills the foliage to the base, but the
roots survive to sprout vigorously the next spring. Frost-
damaged leaves should be cut back to ground level
during late fall.

Propagation is by division of established clumps,
and is best done in spring just before new growth begins.
C. haspon 'Viviparus' is a dwarf form that is well adapted
to water or soil culture. *C. Papyrus* is the well-known
papyrus of the ancients. The Egyptians made writing paper from this species by cutting thin strips of pith from
the stems and then pressing these sections together while
still wet. *C. Papyrus's* fine textured foliage reaches a
height of 6'–8' under good conditions. A bit more
tender to cold than *C. alternifolius*, it is best grown in
Zones 9 or 10. The foliage is striking in the garden,
especially when silhouetted against a wall. It is also very
popular as a cut material for use in floral arrangements.

Datura inoxia quinquecuspida
(day TOO ruh   in OX ee uh)

ANGEL'S TRUMPET

Family: Solanaceae   ◯◑

Zone 9   4'–5'   Summer

Although a true perennial only in tropical or semitropical areas, Angel's Trumpets, with their graceful,
drooping flowers, can make a dramatic impact in the
landscape. The plants usually spread to a width at least
equal to their height. In areas outside their range of cold
tolerance, Angel's Trumpet is often planted as an annual.
The leaves and seeds of the species contain a strong
alkaloidal drug with narcotic properties that can be poisonous to humans and animals. *D. Stramonium*, the
Jimson Weed, a close relative which has naturalized
throughout the world, is known for its poisonous
qualities.

Typically, Angel's Trumpet flowers measure ten
inches in length and may be white, pink, lavender or
yellow. White and lavender are the two forms most often
seen. These plants are rapid growers and are started from

seed in the spring to flower during the heat and humidity of summer. With abundant fertilizer and water, plants may reach 6′–8′, especially in sunny locations with well-drained soils. Angel's Trumpets make an interesting backdrop to a wide border, and they are a very dominant plant in the garden, both visually and physically.

Dianthus spp.
(die AN thus)
GARDEN PINKS AND CARNATIONS
Family: Caryophyllaceae   ◯◑
Zone 6   6″–18″   Spring

Dianthus may be annual, biennial or occasionally perennial, depending upon the cultivar and the growing

conditions. It is a complex genus, and my efforts to identify the perennial forms that make a good showing in our region have not been totally successful. Most of the Dianthus sold as perennials tend to be biennial in Texas and the Gulf South. They are primarily evergreen, cool season performers and well worth space in the garden.

Europeans consider Dianthus among their garden favorites. The English in particular use them freely in

Dianthus carophyllus

Dianthus spp.—Garden Pinks and Carnations

Garden Pinks range in color from white to purple to bi-colors.

Mat-forming dianthus provides softening effect to mixed borders.

their herbaceous borders and as rock garden and wall plants. In addition to a long flowering season in the spring, most Dianthus offer a very sweet perfume.

Cultural practices for biennial and perennial Dianthus are specific but not difficult. They must have well-drained soil and at least half a day of direct sunlight. Perpetuating favorite cultivars is an easy task for home gardeners. As soon as the fall rains begin and temperatures cool, take 4″–5″ tip cuttings and remove the leaves on the bottom half. Stick the cuttings at least half their length into a well-prepared garden area. Water thoroughly and regularly if rains are not fairly frequent. Fall stuck cuttings bloom sparsely the first spring but abundantly after that. Dianthus are susceptible to fusarium wilt which frequently causes them to die out after the second year. Good drainage and open, sunny locations help prevent this problem.

The mat forming, spring flowering Dianthus soften the edges of a mixed border by spilling out over paths, walls and containers. The dense foliage may be a dark green or bluish gray and forms an evergreen mat about 6″ deep. Flower color varies from white to pinks, purples, reds, and bicolors, and flower stems usually rise 6″–1′ above the foliage mats. Flowers are abundant, long lasting and excellent for cutting.

The garden carnations are classed as *Dianthus carophyllus*. Both garden and florist carnations are included in this species. Most carnation cultivars are poorly adapted to Texas and the Gulf South, but a double red, ever-blooming type is often found in cottage gardens of rural Texas. It has dark, green foliage and may reach a height 18″ when in flower. The small, double red, fragrant flowers are borne in abundance in spring and fall and intermittently through the the rest of the year. This useful antique can sometimes be found in garden centers specializing in perennials. The propagation of this cultivar is similar to that of the other Dianthus, and its lifespan is usually two to three years.

Many new cultivars of Dianthus have appeared on the market in recent years. Most of these are well-adapted as annuals but only a few seem able to withstand our long, hot summers.

D. barbatus, Sweet William, is one type often seen in Texas garden centers, though it tends to be an annual in most areas of the state. Its solid or multi-colored, fringed flowers do, however, offer striking combinations of hues. For the best results, Sweet Williams should be planted in the fall. They may be grown readily from seed or cuttings.

Dianthus is a diverse and interesting genus of about 300 species with many having great garden value. Our climate limits their use but certainly does not eliminate it. There is an obvious need to identify cultivars adapted to our conditions. Until nurseries produce these Texas-friendly selections, gardeners can profit from sharing cuttings of superior performers among themselves. Propagation is easy, and the garden effect can be distinctive.

Echinacea purpurea
(ek in AY see uh   purr PU ree uh)
PURPLE CONEFLOWER

Family: Compositae   ○◑
Zone 4   2′–3′   Spring, Summer, Fall

Purple Coneflowers are among our best adapted perennials. The 3″–4″ daisy-like flowers occur in abundance in spring and repeat well in early summer and fall. *E. purpurea* is closely related to *E. angustifolia* which is native from Texas northward to Canada. Flowers of the native form are usually less intense in color, have more "clasping" petals, and the plants are less compact in growth habit.

A hardy plant, the Purple Coneflower tolerates drought and thrives in alkaline soils. It prefers well-drained soils and performs best in sunny locations. To propagate, lift and divide mature clumps every 2–3 years, or simply allow the flowers to go to seed, since this is a plant that self-seeds prolifically. Division and transplanting are operations best carried out in fall but, with care, they may be attempted successfully at other seasons as well. Cut spent flowers and their stems back nearly to ground level to maintain a neat appearance and encourage re-bloom. Trying to pull off the bristly cones without benefit of a knife or shears usually results in the uprooting of the entire plant.

Echinacea purpurea

Echinacea 'White Lustre'

Close-up of Purple Coneflower

When used in the border, Purple Coneflowers are best placed in the center or back where their rather coarse foliage and stems will be partially masked by lower, denser-growing material to the front. The flowers are very long lasting both in the garden and when cut. The bright purple-pink color is unusual in the garden and quite striking. A creamy-white form, 'White Lustre,' is also available. 'Bright Star' is a cultivar that is usually available and does well in our area. Self-sown seedlings that appear as "volunteers" in your garden will usually develop into valuable plants but may differ somewhat from their parents.

Equisetum hyemale
(ek wee SEE tum   hi em MA lee)
HORSETAIL
Family: Equisetaceae   ○◑
Zone 7   3'–5'   Unusual Foliage

The jointed, hollow and leafless stems of the Horsetail have a prehistoric look to them, and botanically, this plant is a link to primitive, spore-bearing, rhizomatous herbs. Horsetails thrive in boggy soils and may be grown as an aquatic. Their garden value lies in their vertical, evergreen stems and their distinctive, linear appearance.

Horsetails are also known as "Scouring Rush" because the siliceous stems are sometimes used in polishing. They grow from spores like the ferns to which they are akin. In the landscape they are easily propagated by division at most any time of year. Cuttings will root readily if taken with a joint and placed in good, moist, garden soil. *E. hyemale* can be somewhat invasive and difficult to control, forming dense colonies in wet areas.

Erythrina herbacea
(er ith RYE nuh   her BAY see uh)
CORAL BEAN
Family: Leguminosae   ○◑
Zone 8   3'–5'   Late Spring, Early Summer

Native to most of the Gulf South, *E. herbacea* numbers among the showiest perennials of late spring. The foliage is composed of trifoliate leaflets with spiny midribs. These are borne on arching stems in medium-sized bunches that freeze back to the ground every winter in most of our region. Before they can re-emerge the following season, tall, leafless shoots spring up to bear the tall spikes of brilliant red flowers.

Bean-like pods ripen in fall and open to expose shiny, hard seeds that are bright red, very showy and reported to be poisonous. New plants may be easily started by sowing seeds outside in early spring. Seedlings usually require several years of maturing before they will flower.

Coral Bean is a good plant for massing near the back of the perennial border. It thrives in full sun or partial shade, and will grow in most soils, including those that are alkaline, droughty and salty. In better soils

D. Greg Grant

A. canadensis is grown in shady areas.

flowering is more spectacular. Plants should be cut back to near ground level after they freeze each year.

E. cristi-galli is a native of Brazil and is often grown as a small flowering tree or large shrub in Zone 10 and parts of Zone 9. It has many common names such as "Cry Baby," "Fireman's Cap" and "Coral Tree." It owes the name "Cry Baby" to the tear-shaped drops of nectar that drip from the flowers. Since it blooms on old wood, this plant usually produces no flowers in years following a winter of heavy frost damage. Individual flowers are about 2″ long and a beautiful crimson color. After several freezes, plants develop a ragged look, losing most of their landscape value. In tropical areas untroubled by frost, E. cristi-galli is a showy evergreen. Handsome old specimens may sometimes be found in New Orleans, Galveston and along the Texas Coast from Corpus Christi to Brownsville.

Eucomis bicolor
(yew KO mis BY cuh lor)
PINEAPPLE LILY

Family: Liliaceae   ◑
Zone 9   2′ – 3′   July, August

This is another plant with a most descriptive common name, since its fruiting structure does resemble a medium-size pineapple. Pineapple lilies require lots of water, tolerate heat well, and are hardy wherever the ground does not freeze deeply. A native of the Drakensberg Mountains of Natal, South Africa, these relatives of the Scillas are especially valuable in the garden because of their extended season of display. Even after their bloom passes, the ripening seed capsules continue to be ornamental. Propagation is from seed or by the division of mature plants. Eucomises prefer sun or filtered shade and moist soils rich in organic material.

Eupatorium coelestinum
(yew pa TOR ee um   see les TIN um)
BLUE BONESET, HARDY AGERATUM

Family: Compositae   ◐◑
Zone 6   2′ – 3′   Fall

Hardy Ageratum is valuable not only for its hardiness and adaptability, but also for its misty display of fluffy autumn flowers. This plant possesses another virtue as well: it blooms from early to late fall when few other perennials are at their peak. It is especially nice in combination with *Tagetes lucida*, Mexican Marigold-Mint, which flowers at the same time but in a bright golden-yellow color. Hardy Ageratums also combine well with Chrysanthemums. When used in a mixed border, *E. coelestinum* shows to best advantage near the center or back since they are rather tall and sometimes leggy in habit.

Hardy Ageratum will grow in practically any soil or exposure but does best where it receives at least a half day of direct sunlight. It is a native of Texas and the Gulf South. The rhizomatous roots can become invasive in very good garden soils. Propagation is by division of

E. fistulosum—Joe-Pye weed

Eupatorium coelestinum—Hardy Ageratum

mature clumps in early spring. After blooms have faded and foliage has frozen back in late fall, cut back the entire plant almost to ground level.

E. fistulosum, the hollow Joe-Pye weed, is an even taller and more robust plant. Flowers occur in dome-shaped clusters and are purplish-pink in color. They are well suited to boggy soils and thrive at the edge of ponds and streams. Stems may reach six feet or taller.

FERNS

Ferns compose a large group of perennial plants that are grown primarily for their handsome foliage. They are valuable for their general ease of culture and the fact that they grow best in shade or partial shade. Ferns do not produce flowers but reproduce by the spores that form on the undersides of their fronds (leaves). Ferns are particularly useful in woodland gardens. Some are evergreen while others die back in the winter, but all the species described in this text are perennials. Growing new plants from spores is too much trouble for the average gardener. Most ferns, however, may be propagated easily by division of established plants. An exception is Holly Fern (*Cyrtomium falcatum*) which normally grows from a single crown and is seldom divided. Ferns profit from regular applications of fertilizer during the growing season, but are easily burned by plant foods rich in nitrogen. Fish-oil emulsions and slow-release fertilizers yield better results.

There are many ferns well adapted to Texas and the Gulf South, and a good number of these are natives. Culture is similar for all species: rich, well-drained soil, high in organic content, and plenty of moisture. Most ferns not only need lots of water, but also require that it be of good quality and low in sodium. Rainwater or drip collected from an air conditioner are sources of water that are normally low in sodium. Ferns are useful in shaded perennial borders in combination with such plants as Aspidistra and Aquilegias, Liriope and Clerodendrum. The lush green effect of ferns can transform shaded areas into focal points of the border.

Adiantum Capillus Veneris—Southern Maiden Hair Fern

it is not very aggressive. The foliage dies down after the first hard frost and returns early the next spring. Maidenhair is one of the few ferns that prefers an alkaline soil, and the addition of dolomitic limestone to the potting mix helps guarantee the health of container-grown specimens. In addition, soil mixes should include about one-half peat moss, composted pine bark or leaf mold. A winter mulch of bark, pine needles or leaves is beneficial and protection from hot sun and wind is necessary to produce good quality foliage.

Athyrium Goeringianum (japonicum) 'Pictum'
(a THEER EE UM)
JAPANESE PAINTED FERN
1'   ◐●

Painted Fern is available in the nursery trade and quite beautiful, although somewhat more difficult to grow than some of the others described. It is a hardy, deciduous fern with discreetly multicolored foliage and petioles. A native to Japan, it grows best in filtered light and highly organic soils. Painted Fern grows slowly, but may be divided every 3 or 4 years.

Cyrtomium falcatum
(ser TO me um)
HOLLY FERN
2'   ○◐

Holly Fern is a very popular evergreen fern in Texas and the Gulf South. Though more at home from Central Texas and eastward than in the western part of the state, this handsome foliage plant may be grown almost anywhere in Zones 8 or 9 so long as good soil, moisture and

Adiantum Capillus-Veneris
(ad i AN tum   ka PIL us   ven ER is)
SOUTHERN MAIDENHAIR FERN
12″–18″   ◐●

Maidenhair Fern is native to Texas and the Gulf South, usually growing close to rocky streams in spots where drainage is excellent but moisture abundant. It is found even in desert areas, but always close to water. Maidenhair is an exceptionally elegant plant with its twice-divided, fan-shaped foliage and black stems. It is best grown in containers or in small, isolated areas since protection from hot sun and wind are provided. Large clumps may be occasionally divided, but this plant's growth is slow and division is not necessary to its health and well-being. The fronds are pinnately compound and have conspicuous spore cases on their undersides which are often mistaken for scale insects. Foliage is thick and a shiny, dark green. Holly Fern is readily available in the nursery trade. It is useful as a ground cover in shady areas, or as a specimen in containers.

Dryopteris normalis
(dri OP ter is)
WOOD FERN
2′–3′   ◐●

Wood Ferns are well-adapted to our climate and conditions and, consequently, relatively easily grown. They are more vigorous than most ferns and can become very luxuriant. Since they are deciduous, Wood Ferns die back after the first hard frost, but return early the next spring. They prefer well-prepared, well-watered soils

with a high organic content. Propagation is by division. It is an excellent fern for the middle or back of the shaded border, especially in combination with evergreen material such as Aspidistra.

Cyrtomium falcatum—Holly Fern

Dryopteris normalis—Wood Fern

Dryopteris erythrosora—Autumn Fern

Dryopteris erythrosora
(dri OP ter is)
AUTUMN FERN
18″ ◐●

Autumn Fern is evergreen and hardy, with arching fine-textured fronds. Mature foliage is olive-green, but new fronds unfold to a bright copper-red. Cold weather burns the foliage, and though Autumn Fern remains reliably evergreen through Zone 9, it adopts a deciduous habit further north. Autumn Fern prefers well-drained soils high in organic content and moisture. It is native to China and Japan.

Lygodium japonicum
(lie GODE ee um)
JAPANESE CLIMBING FERN
10′–15′ ◐●

Japanese Climbing Fern has escaped from cultivation to naturalize through the lower South and is commonly found climbing on trees and shrubs. Fast growing, it is less demanding than most ferns and tolerates direct sun and periods of dry weather without serious damage.

Nephrolepis exaltata 'Bostoniensis'
(nef roe LEP is)
BOSTON FERN
2′ ◐●

Despite its name, Boston Fern is native not to New England but to the Southern United States as well as Brazil, Africa, and Asia. It is not cold hardy beyond Zone 8, and freezes to the ground each winter in most of Zone 9. Also known as "Sword Fern," it is easily grown in shade or partial sun if provided with a highly organic soil and sufficient moisture. Boston Fern spreads rapidly from runners, which root to produce new crowns. This plant grows well in pots or hanging containers; among the many cultivars used for these purposes are 'Dallas,' 'Rooseveltii,' 'Compacta,' and 'Whitmanii.' Boston Ferns are also suited to use as a groundcover in shaded areas.

Onoclea sensibilis
(oon oh KLEE uh)
SENSITIVE OR BEAD FERN
2′ ◐●

Sensitive Fern is a hardy, deciduous plant, native from Canada and the northeastern United States to Florida. It is a vigorous grower that tolerates poorly drained soils better than most ferns. The Sensitive Fern's fronds are a pleasant yellow-green in color and contrast nicely with darker evergreen shrubs. They are also excellent for cutting and indoor use. During the fall, the foliage turns a handsome yellow; it should be cut back during winter.

Osmunda regalis
(oz MUN duh)
ROYAL FERN
4′ ◐●

Royal Fern is native throughout the South and grows in partially sunny areas of good, moist soil. It is hardy, deciduous and grows in clumps that may be divided after several years or more. Individual fronds may measure 18″ across and are rich green in summer and bright yellow in fall. This is a very good garden fern that is becoming more widely available in the nursery trade. Growth rate is relatively slow.

Polystichum acrostichoides
(pol LIS tick um)
CHRISTMAS FERN
1′–2′ ◐●

Christmas Fern is native to the Southeast and is somewhat like an evergreen Boston Fern. It is an ideal fern in many ways, but grows rather slowly, prefers shade and highly organic, well-drained soil. Propagation is by division. Christmas Fern is cold hardy and evergreen in Zones 8 and 9.

Polystichum acrostichoides—Christmas Fern

Rumohra adiantiformis—Leatherleaf Fern

Rumohra adiantiformis
(roo MOR uh)
LEATHERLEAF FERN
2'   ◐●

Leatherleaf is the fern that is used extensively in the florist trade for greenery. It is also a good landscape plant, though subject to severe damage by cold north of Zone 9. For best results, provide rich soil, plenty of moisture and a good mulch all year. Leatherleaf Fern is a very dark green and is useful as a ground cover or container plant in shady locations. Propagation is usually by division.

Thelypteris kunthii
(thel ip TER is)
MAIDEN FERN, WOOD FERN
3'   ◐●

Maiden Fern is native to Texas and the Gulf South, and is an excellent landscape plant. It tolerates drier conditions than most ferns and grows well on gentle slopes. The fronds are a delicate, light green in color and contrast very nicely with darker green plants such as Aspidistra. Foliage should be cut back to the ground after it freezes, or anytime it looks untidy. Maiden Fern will tolerate morning sunlight. It is an excellent plant to combine with early spring flowering bulbs since it does not sprout until most of them have finished their bloom cycles.

Thelypteris (Macrothelypteris) torresiana
(the lip TER is)
MARIANA MAIDEN FERN
3'   ◐●

As its common name indicates, the Mariana Maiden Fern is native to the Mariana Islands, but it has

been found naturalized in Florida and Louisiana and appears to be moving westward. It thrives in partial sun, forming clumps of upright arching fronds. Mariana Maiden Fern is cold sensitive, but it recovers quickly from frost damage in Zone 9. It is a vigorous plant that propagates naturally by spores, yet it is not normally invasive. Mature clumps may be divided every three or four years in the early spring.

Gaillardia x grandiflora
(gay LAR dee uh   gran dih FLO ruh)
BLANKET FLOWER
Family: Compositae   ○◐
Zone 3   1'–3'   Summer

G. x grandiflora is a garden hybrid that is sometimes perennial in Texas and the Gulf South. *G. pulchella* is the annual, native form so common along Texas roadsides. Both thrive in relatively poor soils and difficult growing conditions. Too much water and rich soils cause rank growth and result in short-lived plants.

Gaillardias are usually single flowered, but semi-double types do exist. A common cultivar is 'Goblin,' which rarely exceeds one foot in height yet bears 3"–4" flowers of red petals tipped with yellow. 'Burgundy' and 'Yellow Queen' are in the 24"–30" range and have solid colored flowers.

Clumps of mature plants sometimes die out from the center. Division is the best treatment for that condition and should be undertaken in early spring. New plants are easily grown from seed, but most cultivars must be propagated vegetatively by division or cuttings to remain true to type. Dead-heading is an essential part of this plant's maintenance since old flower heads hang on for months if not removed. The stems of these bristly seed heads are tough, and sharp shears will be needed to cut them without pulling the entire plant from the ground by its roots.

Gaillardia x grandiflora—Blanket Flower

Gaura Lindheimeri—Gaura

Gerbera Jamesonii—Transvaal Daisy

Gaura Lindheimeri
(GAR uh lin high MER eye)

GAURA

Family: Onagraceae   ◯◗

Zone 6   3'–5'   Spring, Summer, Fall

Gaura is native to Texas and Louisiana and is becoming a popular cultivated perennial in the Southeast. It is reported to be a long-lived plant in Southwestern gardens, thriving with little care. The effect in the garden is an airy, vase-shaped cluster of many fine stems. Branched flower spikes occur from May until frost, their many pink buds opening a few at a time into 1″ white blossoms. Spent blossoms drop off cleanly, but old bloom stems should be removed periodically to keep a tidy appearance and prevent an overproduction of seed.

Propagation is usually from seed. Gaura self-sow generously and young seedlings may usually be found in the vicinity of the parent plant. Not a spectacular plant, but one that can add nice delicate mass to the border. Gaura prefers sandy, well-drained soils where its carrot-like root can search deep for moisture. Once established, they require watering only in periods of prolonged drought.

Gerbera Jamesonii
(ger BER uh   jay mis SOHN eye)

TRANSVAAL DAISY

Family: Compositae   ◗

Zone 8   18″   Spring, Summer, Fall

Gerberas are large flowering daisies that come in beautiful pastels of pink, coral, orange, red, yellow or cream. Flowers may reach 5″ in diameter and can occur over a very long season. The foliage is composed of clumps of large, dandelion-like leaves that provide a coarse-textured effect. Old leaves may be cut off in late winter to provide a neater appearance. Likewise, old bloom heads should be removed to encourage continued bloom.

Mature clumps may be divided in early spring, or seed may be started in peat-amended soil when temperatures are in the vicinity of 70 degrees F. Gerberas are site-specific plants. They must have well-prepared soil that drains very well. For this reason, raised beds are recommended for most areas. Protection from hot afternoon sun during the summer months is another necessity in most of Texas and the Gulf South. Filtered sun is best. Non-matting mulch like pine needles or coastal Bermuda hay can provide winter protection in Zone 8 where freeze damage frequently occurs. Heavy mulches, however, can cause rot.

Gerberas are spectacular both in the garden and as cut flowers. When just the right exposure is found, they can be very rewarding. They are not competitive plants and do not flourish among ground covers. Gerberas are usually sold in lots of mixed colors, and generally the different hues blend easily. If a single-color display is desired, it may prove most practical to divide and reset plants of a favorite color yourself.

GINGERS

Because they are natives of the tropics, ornamental gingers perform very well in coastal areas of Texas and other Gulf States. As members of the family *Zingibera-ceae*, they are relatives of bananas and cannas and share those plants' large, tropical-looking foliage. The bonus with most gingers is their exotic flowers. Although sensitive to cold, some species will thrive northward through most of Zone 8. Gingers like rich, well-prepared soils high in organic content. Although much preferring a moist location, they will tolerate occasional periods of drought. The plants we call gingers actually include many genera; we will discuss a number of the more useful ones together in this section so that they may be more conveniently compared.

All gingers prefer filtered sunlight, while some are most at home at the edge of a pond or stream. Their blooms vary in size, color and form, but all are borne in large, bracted heads or spikes. In their natural habitat gingers grow as understory plants on highly organic, moist soils. When they find themselves in a favorable environment, they form large clumps that every three or four years should be divided and reset in early spring. If frozen back, old foliage should be removed to just above ground level. Gingers respond well to application of fertilizer during spring and summer.

Alpinia zerumbet
(al PIN ee uh)
SHELL GINGER

Shell Gingers are native from the eastern Himalayas of India to the Malay Peninsula. They are among the more cold sensitive gingers and liable to suffer serious damage in temperatures below about 25 degrees F. The rhizomes are normally hardy to 15 degrees F. They bloom on the previous year's canes, bearing floral racemes that are 12″–18″ long and white or pink in color. Canes that have flowered should be removed at the end of the season. Plants must be established for at least two years and have lots of water before blooms will appear. Even if the Shell Ginger never flowered, however, its large, dark green, lance-shaped leaves would still be handsome enough to warrant growing the plant. When not damaged by frost, Shell Gingers may reach 8′–9′ tall, and

are often considered the grandest of the gingers. A. zerumbet 'variegata' is an exceptionally handsome cultivar with green and white variegated foliage. It is reported to be equally cold hardy as the more common green form.

Costus cuspidatus
FIERY COSTUS

Fiery Costus is native to deeply shaded forests of Brazil. This plant rarely exceeds a height of two feet and bears 4″–6″ eliptical leaves of a dark, shiny green. The flowers appear from summer through fall and are a brilliant golden-orange. It is an excellent choice for color in deep shade, or for container use. Moist soil, high in organic content, and tropical temperatures are required to grow this plant well. It is cold hardy only in Zone 10. Elsewhere it may be grown in containers or other places where it can be protected from the cold.

Costus speciosus
CREPE GINGER

Crepe Ginger, as this plant is commonly called, may reach 10′ in the tropics. Typically, its leaves are 8″ long and about 2″–3″ wide. Flowers are white with yellow centers, and are borne in 5″ spikes adorned with green and red bracts. More enduring than the flowers are the 4″ "cones" that follow, which change from green to dark red, remaining ornamental well into the fall. Crepe Ginger is more sun tolerant than most gingers and usually reaches a height of 6′–7′ tall.

Curcuma petiolata
(kur KOO muh   peh tee oh LAY tuh)
HIDDEN GINGER

Hidden Ginger is among the most cold hardy of the gingers and will survive outdoors through most of

Costus speciosus—Crepe Ginger

Curcuma petiolata—Hidden Ginger

Zone 8. The deciduous foliage is light green and thin-textured, somewhat resembling cannas. Typical mature height is 2'−3'. The foliage normally yellows and begins to die before frost and is late to sprout again in the spring. The flower spikes that appear in midsummer keep so near the bases of the leaves that they may be overlooked unless the plant is examined closely. Color is rosy-pink with purplish margins.

Hidden Ginger may be propagated from division in early spring. It is one of the most useful gingers for landscape purposes since it masses well and provides a handsome, coarse texture in shaded locations.

C. Roscoeana
JEWEL OF BURMA

The bloom of this ginger is a 6"−8" cylinder of pale orange to brick red. The bracts are long-lasting, and though this plant is closely related to the preceding species and is sometimes called the Orange Hidden Lily, its spikes are borne more visibly at the center of the foliage rather than hidden within. Total height of the clumps is about 3'.

Dichorisandra thrysiflora
(die kore ih SAN druh   thri sih FLORE uh)
BLUE "GINGER"

Dichorisandras are not true gingers but belong rather to the family Commelineaceae and are actually more closely related to the spiderworts. Their fleshy canes with their dark green foliage often reach 3'−5' tall. Flowers are borne in terminal panicles of brilliant blue. Plants tend to sprawl in deep shade and thrive best where filtered light is available. They flower from late summer until early fall. Propagation is by seeds, cuttings or division.

Hedychium coronarium
(hay DIH kee um   kor roe NA ree um)
BUTTERFLY GINGER

Hedychium are among the easiest gingers to grow and will thrive in heavy clay soils as long as adequate moisture is available. They are native to India, Southeast Asia, and China, and normally reach a height of about 5'−6'. Flowers are pure white, highly fragrant, and resemble butterflies. Butterfly Ginger should be divided every three or four years to insure continued flowering. As canes finish flowering in the summer, they should be cut off at ground level. Where there is adequate water, Butterfly Ginger may be grown in full sun.

Even if they freeze to the ground, Hedychiums are quite root hardy in Zone 9 and most of Zone 8. Mrs. Margaret Kane, a well-known horticulturist from San Antonio, reports that early or late frosts have no detrimental effect on her Butterfly Gingers. The severe winter of 1983−84, with its low of 9 degrees F. and a 13" snow, didn't prevent her established plants from blooming June through October the next year. Colors vary from white through yellow, apricot, orange and bright red.

H. flavescens
YELLOW BUTTERFLY GINGER

Yellow Butterfly Ginger is very similar to H. coronarium except in flower color. The flower clusters are somewhat larger, and the individual blossoms are yellow with orange patches and cream-colored stamens.

Hedychium coronarium—Butterfly Ginger

Dichorisandra thrysiflora—Blue "Ginger"

H. Gardneranum
KAHILI GINGER

The elongated flower spikes of Kahili Ginger may reach 18″, bearing light yellow flowers with striking red stamens. Fragrance is outstanding, and the bloom season usually spans August and September.

Kaempferia rotunda
(kemp fe REE uh   row TUN duh)
RESURRECTION-LILY

Kaempferias are among the most diverse of the gingers in color, size and foliage pattern. The Resurrection-lily's flowers, short-stemmed but showy, glistening lavender and white, rise from the bare earth before the leaves emerge in spring. The flowers' fragrance is intense and vanilla-like. When they emerge, the leaves are just as decorative, silvery-green and marked with a purple pattern above, purple-hued also on the undersides. The leaves are deciduous and roots are reportedly hardy to 10 degrees F. Total height is from 2′−3′. Resurrection-lily is best grown in filtered sunlight and moist soil.

Zingiber zerumbet
(ZING gih bur)
PINE-CONE GINGER

Naturally deciduous and root hardy in Zones 8 and 9, Pine-cone Ginger is distinctive and attractive. The cone-like inflorescence with creamy-yellow florets is a favorite of flower arrangers, especially after the flowers have passed and the cones turn a rich red. *Z. darceyi* is a very similar species, but it offers in addition an attractive, variegated, white and green foliage. *Z. officinale* is the ginger whose tubers may be found in the produce section of grocery stores, and it is the source of the condiment used for gingerbread and other culinary purposes. The cones of *Z. officinale* are not colorful and the plant is somewhat more tender than the other species mentioned.

Gladiolus x hortulanus
(glad ee OH lus   hort ooh LAN us)
CORN FLAG, SWORD LILY

Family: Iridaceae ◯◐
All Zones   2′−4′   Spring

Gladioli are tender perennials usually grown as annuals in Texas and the Gulf South. Tall, sword-shaped spikes of funnel-shaped flowers are available in many solid colors, as well as some bi-color combinations. Glads must be planted very early in the spring or even late winter so that they will flower before the arrival of summer's intense heat with its onslaught of thrip insects.

High-crowned corms 1½″−2″ in diameter are more productive than older, larger corms. By setting the corms 4″−5″ deep (about 3−4 times their depth), staking may sometimes be avoided, but the flower spikes are very heavy and liable to topple in rain or wind. By planting sets of corms every two weeks through late winter and early spring, it is possible to extend the flowers' bloom over a longer period. Dwarf forms of Gladiolus called

Gladiolus byzantinus—Hardy Gladiolus or Jacob's Ladder

Gladiolus natalensis—Parrot Gladiolus

A. Scott Ogden

miniatures are available and these are generally better for landscape use since their compact growth habit (less than 3') reduces the need for staking.

Gladioli must have a sunny location and well-drained, well-prepared garden soil. Protection from the hot afternoon sun prolongs the life of the flowers. All Gladioli furnish excellent cut flowers and rows of their swordlike foliage are a common sight in the cutting garden. The flower spikes may be cut just as the lowest buds begin to open with reasonable assurance that they will continue opening after cutting.

In Texas and the Gulf South, Gladiolus corms must be dug and stored after they begin to die back each summer. At that time, their tops should be cut off just above the corm. Burn or discard the foliage since it can harbor botrytis infection. Dry the corms for several weeks in a shaded, ventilated area, then pull off and discard the withered roots and the remains of old corms. Dust the new corms with a garden fungicide such as Captan and store in a well-ventilated, frost-free area until planting time next spring. If all of this sounds like a lot of trouble, it probably is, and may be avoided by planting either of the two species-type Gladiolus described below, or by replanting with new corms each spring.

For mixed borders and cottage gardens, there are two species Gladiolus that are excellent perennials requiring little care. *G. byzantinus*, sometimes known as Hardy Gladiolus or Jacob's Ladder, is a delightful plant often found in old cottage gardens in the South. It is a native of Southern Europe where its preference for corn fields has earned it the name "corn lily." It blooms with many of the Bearded Irises, about April 1 in Central Texas. Flower spikes are a beautiful purple and rarely exceed 18″–24″ tall. *G. byzantinus* does best in a sunny, well-drained location, but will grow tolerably well in clay soils. Corms are small in comparison to the modern hybrids, but do not require digging each year and increase nicely even in abandoned gardens. *G. byzantinus* is generally available from spring bulb catalogs, but it responds better to an early fall planting in Texas and the Gulf South. A rare and somewhat less vigorous white form, Cv. 'Albus,' is sometimes found.

G. natalensis (*G.psittacinus*), sometimes known as the Parrot Gladiolus, is an African form from Natal that is easily recognized by its hooded orange and yellow blooms. It was one of the species used to create the modern hybrid glads, and it grows to a height of about 3'. Its foliage appears soon after the last frost, and the flowers open in late April on tall, sturdy stems. The plants grow from large, shallow-grown corms that multiply readily and grow well in heavy soils. Foliage of both *G. natalensis* and *G. byzantinus* may be cut off just above ground level after it yellows in the summer.

Graptopetalum paraguayense
(grap to PET uh lum   par eh gway YEN see)
GHOST PLANT, MOTHER OF PEARL PLANT

Family: Crassulaceae   ◯◐
Zone 9   6″   Early Spring

Ghost Plant is one of several succulents sometimes called "Hen and Chickens" in Texas and the Gulf South. A native of Mexico, it is useful either as a container plant or a ground cover for small spaces. The leaves are loosely arranged in elongated rosettes, very thick and pearl gray

Graptopetalum paraguayense—Ghost Plant, Mother of Pearl Plant

Ghost plant is attractive in containers.

in color. Considerably less striking than the foliage are the grayish flowers that appear in early spring on 4″–6″ stems. Propagation is by stem cuttings of mature rosettes of foliage, or by placing the basal end of individual leaves in garden soil. Leaves and stems are very brittle and easily removed. Ghost Plant prefers a sunny or partially sunny location, well drained soil, and is very easily grown. Graptopetalums are related to Echeverias and grow under similar conditions, although in general, they are less demanding. Their foliage is unique and attractive in container plantings, either alone or as a ground cover for specimen plants.

GRASSES

European and English border makers have long relied upon the graceful character and fine texture of ornamental grasses as integral materials of their designs. Ironically, many of those grasses are North American natives whose potential United States gardeners have only just begun to realize. Appreciation and use of ornamental grasses is increasing in our country, however.

In general, grasses are low maintenance plants that lend themselves well to Xeriscape and other resource efficient landscapes. Most of the ones featured in this text are clump-forming types, although a few are modest "runners" (spread by underground rhizomes). Soil and fertilizer requirements are minimal for most species. Good, deep soils are helpful in establishing the extensive root systems that facilitate drought tolerance, but are not an absolute necessity.

Landscape uses include specimen plantings, containers, and groupings in perennial borders. Foliage color and leaf textures vary, as do the sizes of the plants. Some grasses offer very interesting flower and fruiting structures that add value to the landscape for long periods of time. Even when fall turns to winter and the foliage is dry and dormant, some grasses retain sufficient ornamental value to make them worthwhile landscape subjects. Ornamental grasses are especially useful in landscapes that feature native plants, since their culture and appearance make many of them compatible. Most ornamental grasses may be easily propagated by division of clumps in early spring.

Native Grasses

Andropogon Gerardii
(an druh POE gone   jer ARE dee eye)
BIG BLUESTEM

5′–7′   ○◐

Big Bluestem is native to sandy soils in most of Texas, North Dakota, eastern Montana and Arizona. Its flowering period is primarily from August until November. The inflorescence looks like a turkey's foot; held aloft on a thin stem that rises above the foliage, this "flower" consists of two or several terminal seed heads that emerge from leaf sheaths along the stem. Big Bluestem is a warm season grass with a rhizomatous root system and good drought tolerance. Propagation is by division of mature clumps or seed.

Courtesy of Fort Worth Nature Center and Refuge

Courtesy of Fort Worth Nature Center and Refuge

Big Bluestem's turkey
foot inflorescence

Andropogon Gerardii—Big Bluestem

Bouteloua curtipendula—Sideoats Grama

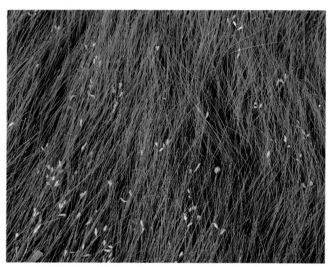

Buchloe dactyloides—Buffalo Grass

Chasmanthium latifolium—Inland Sea Oats

Courtesy of Fort Worth Nature Center and Refuge

Bouteloua curtipendula
(boo teh LOO uh   cur tih PEN doo luh)
SIDEOATS GRAMA
3'–4'

Sideoats Grama is the state grass of Texas. The seed heads resemble oats and hang uniformly on one side of the stems. Sideoats Grama is excellent for mass planting and flowers from June until November. It is native to open grasslands, borders of woods, and roadsides, usually on the better soils and on relatively undisturbed sites. Sideoats Gramma is rhizomatous and propagated by division or seed. It is very drought tolerant.

Bothriochloa saccharoides var. *longipaniculata*
(bo three oh KLOE uh   sa ka ROW ih dees)
LONGSPIKE SILVER BLUESTEM
3'–4'

Longspike Silver Bluestem grows from clumps and is not rhizomatous. It is adapted to clay or sandy soils, tolerates light shade, and is native to southeastern and southern Texas and northeastern Mexico. Flowers appear mostly from May to November and are tufted and feathery. Propagation is by division or seed.

Buchloe dactyloides
(BUH kloh ee   dak til OH ih dees)
BUFFALO GRASS
6"–10"

Buffalo Grass is fast becoming a popular substitute for conventional lawn grasses in Central and West Texas. It is fine textured, blue-green in color, and well-adapted to dry soils and full sun. Buffalo Grass spreads by aboveground runners and self-sown seed. It is a good companion for wildflowers and a suitable low-maintenance ground cover for naturalistic plantings. Seed may be sown at any time during the warm seasons, but is easiest to establish if planted in the spring. Buffalo Grass performs best in dry, sunny areas and turns an even tan during the winter months.

Chasmanthium latifolium (Uniola latifolia)
(kaz MAN thee um   la tee FOE lee um)
INLAND SEA OATS
3'–4'

Inland Sea Oats is a graceful grass that is useful for mass plantings in perennial borders. It tolerates shade well and thrives in a wide variety of soils. The seeds that begin forming in July dry and mature naturally during the fall months. Propagation is by division of the rhizomatous clumps, or from seed which often self-sows in the vicinity of fruiting plants. Inland Sea Oats, like many other native grasses, furnishes attractive cut material for arranging in the home.

Elymus canadensis var. *canadensis*
(EL ih muss   kan ah DEN sis)
CANADA WILDRYE
3′–4′   ◯◐

Canada Wildrye is native to all areas of Texas except the southern portion of the South Texas Plains. It is found mostly in shaded sites, frequently along fence rows, borders of wooded areas and in moist ravines, but tolerates full sun well. It flowers mostly from March until June, but occasionally in summer and early fall. The nodding seed heads closely resemble wheat, and dry to an attractive tan color.

Erianthus giganteus
(air ee AN thus   jeye gan TAY us)
SUGARCANE PLUMEGRASS
5′   ◯◐

Sugarcane Plumegrass is another clumping grass, forming tall, dense tufts of foliage and stems that throw off white, silver, red or purple blooms from early fall through November. The flower heads hold well into winter and are spectacular in the natural or man-made landscape. Propagation is from seed or division of established clumps. Sugarcane Plumegrass is native to wet soils from Florida to eastern Texas and in Cuba, and is especially well-suited to heavy soils and low areas.

Muhlenbergia filipes
PURPLE MUHLY
4′–6′   ◯◐

Purple Muhly is notable for the late fall color it provides in the landscape. The purple panicles can be 4′–5′ tall and they place this plant among the most handsome of the native grasses. It is salt tolerant and flourishes in open coastal woodlands and on sand dunes from the Coastal Plains of North Carolina to Florida, Alabama, Mississippi and eastern Texas. Propagation is by division and from seed.

Muhlenbergia Lindheimeri
(moo len BUR jee uh   lind HIGH mer eye)
LINDHEIMER'S MUHLY
3′–4′   ◯◐

Lindheimer's Muhly Grass is becoming more widely available as a container-grown plant at nurseries than most other native grasses. It is fine textured, bluish-gray-green in color, and attractive at all seasons of the

Courtesy of Fort Worth Nature Center and Refuge

Elymus canadensis—Canada Wildrye

Courtesy of Fort Worth Nature Center and Refuge

Erianthus giganteus—Sugarcane Plume-grass

Muhlenbergia Lindheimeri—Lindheimer's Muhly

year. The bloom stems are graceful and appear primarily during the fall. Propagation is by seed or division of mature clumps in the spring. Lindheimer's Muhly is drought tolerant and will grow in a wide variety of conditions. It has potential as a mass or group plant in perennial borders.

Muhlenbergia reverchoni
SEEP MUHLY
2′　　　　　　　　　　　　　　　　　　　　○◑

　　Seep Muhly is a compact-growing bunch grass with narrow, twisted leaves and light, airy, purplish seed heads. It is well-adapted to dry sites, will grow in poor, gravelly soils, and is sometimes used as a container specimen.

Poa arachnifera
(PO uh　ah rak NIH fer uh)
TEXAS BLUEGRASS
2′–3′　　　　　　　　　　　　　　　　　　○◑

　　Texas Bluegrass is a tufted perennial with long, slender rhizomes. It is a shade-tolerant, cool-season grass with curiously attractive seed heads. Borne on the female plants in early spring, these fruiting structures appear tangled in cobwebs. Propagation is by seed and division of mature clumps.

Schizachyrium scoparium (Andropogon scoparius)
(skih ZA kree um　scoh PAH ree um)
LITTLE BLUESTEM
3′–6′　　　　　　　　　　　　　　　　　　○◑

　　Little Bluestem is a personal favorite because of the striking blue-gray hue its stems turn in late summer. The unusual coloring lasts for about two months, and it provides a beautiful contrast to the greens and tans of other plants at that time of year. Come fall, and through the winter, this grass adopts a striking reddish-brown coloration which is especially apparent in mature clumps. Little Bluestem's roots sometimes penetrate 6′–8′ deep in sandy soils. The plant is strongly vertical in form during the late summer. Seed heads are also attractive, and dry naturally during the fall. Propagation is by division of mature clumps, or from seed.

Introduced Grasses

Cortaderia Selloana
(kor tah DEI ree uh　sell oh AH nuh)
PAMPAS GRASS
8′–10′　　　　　　　　　　　　　　　　　○◑

　　Pampas Grass is a native of Argentina and very popular as an ornamental in Texas and the Gulf South. It prefers well-drained soil and full sun but will grow almost anywhere. The large mounds of graceful, thin leaves arch to produce a fountain effect. The flowers are prominent in late summer and early fall, resembling giant plumes of tannish-white. The margins of its leaves are razor-sharp, and Pampas Grass can be dangerous to small children. The cultivar 'Rubra' yields reddish-pink plumes. The female flowers of both species are more showy than the males. Propagation is usually by division of clumps. Pampas Grass continues to grow larger each year and is difficult to control in the landscape. It is best used on very large sites where its size and sharp leaf margins are not likely to come into close contact with people.

Cymbopogon citratus
(kim boh POE gone　sih TRAY tus)
LEMONGRASS
3′–5′　　　　　　　　　　　　　　　　　　○◑

　　Lemongrass is a true perennial only in Zone 10 and sometimes 9. It looks somewhat like Johnson grass, but

Schizachyrium scoparium—Little Bluestem

Cymbopogon citratus—Lemongrass

Miscanthus sinensis 'Gracillimus'—Maiden Grass

Miscanthus sinensis 'variegatus'—Variegated Japanese Silver Grass

Fountain Grass cultivar 'Atrosanguineum'

Pennisetum setaceum—Fountain Grass

the foliage has a wonderful lemon scent. It is the commercial source for lemon oil and the leaves are sometimes used to flavor poultry and other foods. Propagation is usually by division. Lemongrass is easily grown in a wide variety of situations, but prefers well-drained soil and at least a half day of direct sun.

Miscanthus sinensis 'Gracillimus'
(mis KAN thus   sih NEN sis)
MAIDEN GRASS
4'–5'   ◯◐

The leaves of Maiden Grass are approximately one-half inch wide and marked by a narrow white stripe down the mid-vein. The plant resembles a dwarf pampas grass but is much more mannerly in growth. Both the foliage and the flower heads are curled and its tan-beige winter color is quite attractive. Maiden Grass is useful as a specimen or in masses. It is drought tolerant and easily grown. Propagation is usually from division of mature clumps.

Miscanthus sinensis 'Variegatus'
VARIEGATED JAPANESE SILVER GRASS
5'   ◯◐

Its handsome fountains of silvery-white or yellowish and green striped foliage make Variegated Japanese Silver Grass a very useful garden perennial. *M. sinensis* 'Zebrinus' is similar, but slightly larger growing and with leaf blades marked by horizontal bands of white or yellow. 'Yaku Yima' is a dwarf form, with foliage only about 18" tall and blooms that reach 3'–4'.

Pennisetum setaceum
(pen ih SAY tum   say TAH kee um)
FOUNTAIN GRASS
3'–4'   ◯◐

As Fountain Grass becomes more widely available, it is being planted in our area in masses and as specimens. The leaf blades are narrow and it blooms from August through October. There are several popular cultivars of *P. setaceum* available, such as 'Atrosanguineum,' the Purple Fountain Grass whose foliage and spikes both are purple. Propagation is usually by division. Fountain Grass is visually effective when used as a focal point with low ground covers or perennials.

Hamelia patens—Firebush

Dr. Jerry Parsons

Helianthus Maximiliani—Maximilian Sunflower

Hamelia patens (H. erecta)
(HA may lee uh   ee REK tuh)

FIREBUSH

Family: Rubiaceae ◯◑

Zone 9   4'–5'   Summer, Fall

Few plants do more than survive the heat that comes to Texas and the Gulf South from July through September, but *Hamelia patens* seems to thrive on it. Actually a large shrub or small tree native to Mexico, Firebush is a dependable and useful perennial for the southern half of Texas and other Gulf South states. It freezes to the ground and resprouts each spring, typically offering a 4'–5' mound of reddish orange flowers from early summer until late fall.

In addition to its long blooming season, there are several other significant attributes of the plant. Firebush is very drought tolerant and thrives in almost any soil, as long as it is well-drained. Full sun or partially shaded locations are preferable to shady ones, since those result in rank growth and little bloom. The foliage often turns bright red before freezing back and the small, dark fruit is reported to be edible. In Mexico, a fermented drink is made from the fruit. The leaves and stems have been used for tanning and a concoction from the leaves reportedly is used for various medicinal purposes.

The flower buds of the Firebush appear in great numbers and last longer than the flowers themselves. After maturing, the flowers drop off quickly and the plant requires only occasional shearing to keep it in a nearly perpetual state of bloom. Another common name for *H. patens*, the "Hummingbird Bush," suggests one of the plant's special charms. Its tubular red flowers attract these brightly colored little birds, adding an entirely different kind of display to the garden.

San Antonio area nurserymen are beginning to stock the plant as a result of recent publicity by Extension Horticulturists. Yet *H. patens* is certainly not a "new" plant for our area. Mrs. Margaret Kane, a well-known grower of perennials in San Antonio, has a large specimen that has been in her garden for many years, and the Mercer Arboretum in Houston has a large plant located in a raised bed near its entrance. Firebush is said to be fairly common in Florida.

Propagation is by seed or half-ripe cuttings rooted under glass. Firebush is effective as a container plant, and when planted in masses or at the back of a wide border. Its many fine qualities make it worth growing as an annual in northern parts of our region where severe winters may kill the plant's root system.

Helianthus angustifolius
(he lee AN thus   an gus tih FOH lee us)

SWAMP SUNFLOWER

Family: Compositae ◯◑

Zone 7   3'–6'   Fall

This East Texas native is a good source of late summer and fall color in the border. Like most sunflowers, it is fairly aggressive and requires considerable space. Flowers are 2½" yellow daisies that usually begin to open in September. In good soils, where they reach their greatest height, Swamp Sunflowers may require staking.

H. Maximiliani, the Maximilian Sunflower, is also native to Texas but over a broader range. It is also a larger plant, sometimes reaching 10 feet in height. Maximilian Sunflowers are easily grown and will tolerate considerable abuse. They are best used at the back of the border since they become quite large and reproduce quickly. A sunny location is about the only requirement. Staking may be necessary, especially in good soils. Clumps may be divided in early spring. The yellow daisy-like flowers are about 3" in diameter and produced in great numbers.

H. x multiflorus cultivars such as 'Flore Pleno' and 'Loddon Gold' are spectacular in the late summer garden. Each plant becomes quite bushy and can fill an area approximately two feet square. The flowers are large and double, somewhat resembling chrysanthemums.

A fourth species of sunflower, *H. tuberosus*, the Jerusalem Artichoke, grows about 6'–7' tall, bearing yellow flowers. The potato-like tubers are edible and often sold in grocery stores. Because *H. tuberosus* is very prolific, it is best to harvest all but a very few of the tubers each year to prevent a complete takeover of the garden.

Heliopsis helianthoides scabra
(he lee OP sis   he lee an THOY dees)
HELIOPSIS

This sunflower relative is useful in the border for summer and early fall flowers. The golden-yellow flowers are useful for cutting as well as landscaping. Cultivars are propagated by division or cuttings, while the species itself may be grown from seed. After several years, the size and quantity of a plant's flowers may begin to diminish, and this is a sign that the clump should be divided. Early spring is a good season for that operation. Heliopsis are easily grown, drought-resistant perennials that tolerate shade and poor, dry soil more successfully than most plants.

HEMEROCALLIS—DAYLILIES

Although most people may think of the daylily as a modern flower, according to Chinese literature its ancestors have been in cultivation for thousands of years. Indeed, there is evidence that daylilies were in use among the Chinese even before the development of written language. The earliest references report the plant's use as a food crop. The flower buds, which may still be found on the shelves of oriental markets, are palatable, digestible and nutritious. The root and crown were widely employed as a medicine to relieve pain and, later, juice extracted from fresh roots by pounding was administered to patients suffering from cirrhosis and jaundice.

As early as 70 A.D. a Greek herbalist, Dioscorides, referred to a form of this plant that we now know as the Lemon or Custard Daylily (*Hemerocallis flava*). This had been brought from China to Asia Minor, and is found today in many areas of Texas and the Gulf South. Wherever it has traveled, this plant has been prized for the fragrant, long-lasting, pale yellow blooms it bears in early spring.

The Tawny Daylily, *H. fulva*, is even more at home than the Lemon form in the southern United States. Its tenacious roots make it an excellent soil-stabilizer for steep slopes, and it occurs in such abundance through much of the southland that it is often considered a native wildflower. It is almost beyond belief that such a lovely

Hemerocallis fulva—Tawny Daylily

and aggressive plant reproduces only by root spread, yet this particular species of daylily actually is sterile and sets no viable seed. A double form of the Tawny Daylily (*H. fulva* 'Kwanso') is almost as durable and well-adapted as the single form and marks many homesites and cemeteries throughout the South. For meadow gardens and naturalistic plantings, these species-type daylilies still make valuable additions to the designer's palette. Since the early 1930s, however, the activities of British and American hybridizers have revolutionized this ancient flower.

Dr. A. B. Stout pioneered this new era of research on the genus *Hemerocallis*. Since his initial work, many scientists and amateurs have become involved in hybridizing daylilies, and literally thousands of new varieties have resulted. Whereas daylilies formerly offered the gardener only a yellow, an orange, and a red, this flower is now available in countless shades of near-whites, yellows, oranges, pinks, vivid reds, crimsons, purples, pastels, and handsome blends.

Breeding of daylilies may be as simple or complex as the abilities and facilities of the breeder. The transfer of pollen from one flower to another may be left to foraging bees, or the breeder may choose to take a camel's hair brush in hand and perform this task himself. If the cross is successful, a new hybrid will result. At a more professional level, breeders know which hybrids and species will cross successfully to achieve specific objectives. These may include not only innovations in flower color but also flower form, height, texture, size and season of bloom.

Despite the remarkable progress of the last half-century, two colors, blue, and a pure white, still elude daylily hybridizers. Blue is actually more elusive than white. Next to an Easter lily, perhaps, the "near white" daylilies may look less than pure, but through most of the garden such hybrids as Yancey's 'Gentle Shepherd' really do appear white. The hybridizers have not come even close to a true blue, although there are bluish lavenders and bluish purples.

Classification of Daylilies

Though daylilies are members of the lily family, they are not true garden lilies. Within this family, the daylily counts among its relatives such familiar plants as onions, tulips, and hyacinths. The scientific name of the daylilies' genus is *Hemerocallis*, which derives from two Greek words meaning "beauty" and "day." As this name suggests, an individual daylily flower opens for only a day, but since each scape (flower stalk) bears many buds, and these open in series, a single plant maintains its beauty over a number of days.

Daylilies are fibrous-rooted, hardy, herbaceous perennials. Their roots are finger-like in appearance, and vary in size from tiny and thread-like to large, round and fleshy. There is a crown at the place where the roots and leaves join. The foliage is narrow and long, and assumes the shape of a fan. Basically, all daylilies fall into one of three types, according to their foliage. There are daylilies of the dormant type, which lose their foliage completely during the winter; evergreen, which retain their green

Closeup of seed pod

Nell Crandall

Tawny Daylily is found in many homesites of the South.

Nell Crandall

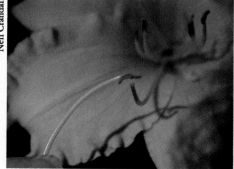

A breeder may choose to pollenate a pistil with a camel's hair brush.

Nell Crandall — 'Betty Woods'

Nell Crandall — Yancey's 'Gentle Shepherd'

Nell Crandall — 'Green Flutter'

Nell Crandall — 'Little Business'

Nell Crandall — 'Janet Gayles'

Nell Crandall — 'Frank Gladney'

Nell Crandall — 'Kindly Lights'

Nell Crandall — 'Becky Lynn'

Nell Crandall — 'Wind Frills'

foliage all year unless there is an unusually severe winter; and semi-evergreen which lose part or most of their leaves during the winter. As a rule, the evergreen day-lilies perform best in hot climates, while the deciduous types prefer cooler locations, although there are exceptions.

A fairly recent innovation in daylilies is the introduction of tetraploids, plants that have twice the ordinary diploid number of chromosomes (22). This doubling to 44 chromosomes is usually brought about by applying colchicine, a powerful alkaloid derived from the autumn crocus *(Colchicum autumnale)*, to the daylily plant. After selecting the diploid variety he wishes to convert, the breeder injects colchicine into its crown with a hypodermic needle. Colchicine is sometimes also applied to daylily seed, but this technique is far less likely to produce useful plants.

There is some controversy among daylily experts concerning the value of this practice, but the tetraploid flowers tend to be larger; the color more intense; the scape sturdier; the substance of both flower and foliage increased; and vegetative vigor greater in leaf, stem and flower. Another advantage lies in the possibilities of future breeding with an increased number of chromosomes. Many tetraploid varieties are now available, some at moderate prices. In fact, there are so many tetraploids

'Double Splendor'

'Little Greenie'

'Velvet Gem'

'Best of Friends'

'Double Whammy'

'Fairy Tale Pink'

today, there is little reason to continue artificially converting more diploids. Originally, if a hybridizer had developed a particularly desirable "tet" and wished to breed it, he first had to create a mate by converting another diploid. With the large gene pool of tetraploid daylilies now existing, however, this is no longer the case.

Daylily Culture

Since daylilies require a minimum of six hours' direct sunlight daily, it is usually best to locate them in areas of full sun. A partial exception to this rule are the red- and purple-flowered varieties, many of which appreciate some protection from the afternoon sun in our hot climate. Lighter-colored flowers reflect more light and can, therefore, tolerate more heat.

Daylilies are not fussy about soil and general culture, but significantly better results are obtained from good, well-drained soils that have been amended with large amounts of organic material such as peat moss, pinebark or compost. Sandy soils need the water and nutrient holding capacity that organic materials contribute, and heavy clays need the aeration and increased drainage they

Nell Crandall

'Inkspot'

Nell Crandall

'Sweetheart Supreme'

Nell Crandall

'Baby Betsy'

Nell Crandall

'Divine Guidance'

Nell Crandall

'Ono'

Nell Crandall

'Double Paprika'

provide. Raising beds 3″–6″ above the surrounding area is an effective way to provide adequate drainage.

Daylilies tend to grow poorly under broadleafed trees such as oaks and pecans. The roots of these trees rob the soil of moisture and nutrients, while the heavy leaf canopies screen too much of the sun. Pine trees, on the other hand, provide a dappled shade that is ideal, and their roots tend to be deep and less competitive.

In Texas and the Gulf South, early spring and very late fall are the best times to plant daylilies, although freshly dug plants may be safely set out at any time during the growing season. If newly dug plants must be

held for a few days before planting, heel them into a prepared bed of soil or compost until they can be placed in their permanent location. Planting during July, August, or September, when temperatures are likely to be in the 90 degrees F. range, is risky and causes the root-stock to rot.

Before setting out new plants, be sure to remove any decayed or damaged roots. Wash and trim the foliage back and prune the roots back to 8″–12″. Work the soil well, loosening it to a depth of at least a foot. Make a mound in the center of the planting-hole and spread the roots out around it. The crown should be placed so that

Nell Crandall

'Siloam BoPeep'

Nell Crandall

'Harry Barras'

Nell Crandall

'Divine Guidance'

it will sit even with the surface of the surrounding soil. Take care not to plant too deeply because daylily roots pull the crown downward anyway, and buried plants tend to rot. If the crown is planted high (even with the surface of the soil), it may be left undisturbed and allowed to clump for a longer period of time. Soil should be firmed and watered well to prevent air pockets. Spacing between plants should be 18″–24″, depending upon the growth rate and vigor of the variety.

Grooming the plants is important to their appearance, especially during the bloom period. Old flowers or "dead heads" should be removed frequently, and the entire scape should be cut out after the last buds open. Unless growing a crop of seed for propagation, it is best to remove the scapes soon after flowering is complete, since the maturing seed robs the plant of moisture and nutrients that could be devoted to the production of the next crop of flowers.

Most modern varieties should be divided about every third year, though some daylilies need this treatment more frequently. The experience and advice of other growers in your area is the best source of information on this matter. To divide rapidly growing clumps, simply slice them into sections with a sharp spade or knife. Prized hybrids, however, should be carefully lifted with a spading fork, the soil gently shaken or washed from the roots, and tubers separated gently so that not a single division is wasted.

Although there are no stems from which to root cuttings of daylilies, small plantlets sometimes appear along the stems. These "plantlets" are called proliferations or "prolifs". When prolifs appear on expensive varieties, they are avidly collected because they offer an additional way to multiply that costly stock. Proliferations will generally bloom in the year following planting. They can be removed and treated like cuttings until they are rooted and set into a permanent location.

Daylilies prefer slightly acid soils in the range of 6.5 and are relatively heavy users of nutrients. Spring is the most important time to fertilize. It is important to keep the fertilizer off the foliage and water it into the soil

thoroughly, immediately after application. Many growers deliver another, lighter feeding in the fall. This application, following the summer dormancy, helps to build food-reserves in the plant, increasing its size and preparing a better bloom for the next season. A low nitrogen fertilizer with a ratio of 3-12-12 or 4-8-12 is best for fall, while a 5-10-10 or 5-10-5 is recommended for spring. In choosing a fertilizer for daylilies, pay close attention to the first number in the formula (e.g., 3-12-12, 5-10-5) since this indicates the percentage of nitrogen, and too much nitrogen causes blooms to slick and wilt in the hot sun.

Older clumps of daylilies should be fertilized more heavily than newly planted ones since the soil becomes more depleted with time. Mulching helps to conserve moisture, reduce heat stress in summer, and keep weeds under control. When daylilies are mulched it may be necessary to add additional fertilizer to compensate for the nitrogen used in the decomposition of the mulch.

Insects and Diseases

Daylilies are not without their problems, primarily those of insect infestation. A few daylilies in the landscape are not likely to attract the problems of extensive collections, but mites, thrips and aphids can cause damage and are especially troublesome when daylilies are grown in proximity to other susceptible plant species. Aphids, small greenish insects that suck juices from the plant and that in the process may transmit diseases, are serious pests. Since these pests like cool weather, they may be present in fall and early spring just as growth begins. A close inspection will reveal the aphids' presence, and they can be controlled with a wide variety of insecticides. As hot weather approaches, aphid problems usually subside.

Spider mites pose another serious threat to daylilies, since they can cause severe damage. A fine webbing appears on the plant as the infestation increases, and may eventually cover the plant completely if the mites go unchecked. Heavy infestations stunt plants, causing a decline of the foliage.

There is a two-spotted spider mite that thrives in cool weather and a red spider mite that comes along when the weather gets hot. The two-spotted spider mite is a little larger but both are so tiny they are hard to see without a magnifying lens. Insecticidal soaps, Pentac and Morestan are miticides safe to use on daylilies when applied according to label instructions. Kelthane is a chemical sometimes used to control spider mites on other ornamentals, but can cause severe burning on daylilies. Good air circulation and exposure to rain and washing can also help control mites.

Thrips are almost invisible to the eye, but can seriously damage blooms of daylilies. By attacking the buds, these insects may prevent them from opening at all, while the flowers that do survive will be discolored and malformed. Thrips are most active in late spring or early summer.

Nematodes are plant parasites that sometimes attack daylilies. Microscopic in size, they are found in the soil almost everywhere. There are many kinds of nematodes, but all attack the plant in the same way: entering the roots in large numbers, these miniature eelworms feed on the plant's root hairs, interfering with its ability to absorb water and nutrients. The typical symptom is a general loss of vigor. Should nematode damage be suspected, contact your Agricultural Extension Agent for instructions about submitting a specimen for positive identification. Infected plants cannot be saved, but the soil can be treated with chemicals or steam sterilization to reduce populations of these harmful parasites.

Diseases of daylilies are few but can be troublesome. Bacterial soft rot can cause the complete loss of a fine daylily in just a few days. Healthy tissue turns to smelly mush when infected with this disease which is prevalent in wet periods, especially on plants in poorly drained soils. Raising the beds and increasing air circulation around the crowns of the plants usually will prevent recurrence of the problem.

Owen Shores Garden, Atlanta, Georgia

'Lady Neva'

'Mountain Violet'

'Jerome Spalding'

Nell Crandall

Landscape at Crandalls, Houston, Texas

'Pojo'

'Country Honey'

Kingwood Garden, Mansfield, Ohio—'Kindly Light' daylilies

Selecting Varieties of Daylilies

The major problem with selecting daylily varieties is the bewildering array from which to choose. The American Hemerocallis Society publishes annual popularity polls and awards medals to outstanding varieties, but daylilies are definitely regional performers. Even within the Texas and Gulf Coast areas, the same variety may vary drastically from region to region in its performance. Another problem is a difference in goals among the growers. Eager collectors of daylilies may be willing to devote significant amounts of nurturing to produce desired results, while less avid homeowners and gardeners prefer dependability and good landscape effect to the latest color blend or flower form.

Still another consideration is the cost of the plants. Some of the newest and most sought-after varieties command very high prices that prohibit their use in landscape displays requiring large numbers of plants.

With all these considerations in mind I have included a few recommendations that may provide some help in selecting daylilies for landscape use. First, I have consulted the most recent popularity polls of the American Hemerocallis Society for the regions that include Texas, New Mexico, Louisiana, Mississippi, Alabama, Florida, and Georgia. In addition, I have included recommendations of knowledgable horticulturists in the Dallas-Fort Worth and Houston areas of Texas for their favorite landscape daylilies. Among the criteria for inclusion in this list are good bud count per scape, attractive foliage, vigor to increase in clump size, relatively low cost, and good availability.

Creating Landscape Effects with Daylilies

Daylilies are becoming increasingly popular as landscape plants. There are many ways to use them effectively. Masses of a single variety is a popular method, especially in commercial and public areas, but also on a smaller scale in the home landscape.

When used in perennial borders and cottage gardens a different look is, in my opinion, more appropriate. The beauty of daylilies is the variety they provide. There are new flowers opening every day, so that if you have a number of clumps of daylilies, your garden changes every day; sometimes the daylilies lend more pink to it, sometimes more yellow, red, etc., etc. . Through a careful combination of the many sizes, colors, flower forms and seasons of bloom, gardens featuring daylilies can be like a kaleidoscope, offering a different pattern each time the position of the viewer is changed.

RESULTS OF RECENT POPULARITY POLLS OF DAYLILY VARIETIES

CULTIVAR	HEIGHT	SEASON OF BLOOM*	BLOOM SIZE	COLOR	FOLIAGE**
REGION 5 (Georgia)					
'Fairy Tale Pink'	24"	MRe	5½"	Pink	SEv
'Becky Lynn'	20"	EMRe	6¾"	Rose	SEv
'Betty Woods'	26"	E	5½"	Chinese Yel	Ev
'When I Dream'	28"	EMRe	6½"	Blood Red	SEv
'Lullaby Baby'	19"	EM	3½"	Lt Pink	SEv
REGION 12 (Florida)					
'Betty Woods'	26"	E	5½"	Chinese Yel	Ev
'Becky Lynn'	20"	EMRe	6¾"	Rose	SEv
'Midnight Magic'	28"	EM	5½"	Black Red	Ev
'Sebastian'	20"	EM	5½"	Purple	Ev
'Little Zinger'	27"	EM	2⅔"	Red	SEv
REGION 14 (Mississippi and Alabama)					
'Fairy Tale Pink'	24"	EMRe	5½"	Flesh Pink	SEv
'Becky Lynn'	20"	EMRe	6¾"	Rose	SEv
'Joan Senior'	25"	EMRe	6"	Near White	SEv
'Janet Gayle'	26"	E	6½"	Pink Cream	Ev
'Ruffled Apricot'	28"	EM	7"	Apricot	Dor
REGION 13 (Louisiana and Arkansas)					
'Joan Senior'	25"	EMRe	6"	Near White	SEv
'Becky Lynn'	20"	EMRe	6¾"	Rose	SEv
'Fairy Tale Pink'	24"	EMRe	5½"	Pink	SEv
'My Belle'	26"	ERe	6½"	Flesh Pink	Ev
'Frank Gladney'	26"	EMRe	6½"	Coral	Ev
REGION 6 (Texas and New Mexico)					
1 'Ono'	18"	EM	4⅜"	Lt Yellow	Ev
2 'Fairy Tale Pink'	24"	MRe	5½"	Pink	Ev
3 'Jerome'	22"	EM	6¾"	Orange	Ev
4 'Little Deeke'	20"	EMRe	4½"	Orange, Gold	Ev
5 'Ruffled Apricot'	28"	EM	7"	Apricot	Dor

* E—Early; M—Midseason; Re—Repeat Flowering; L—Late
** Ev—Evergreen; SEv—Semi-Evergreen; Dor—Dormant; SDor—Semi-Dormant

LANDSCAPE FAVORITES FOR THE DALLAS-FORT WORTH AREA

CULTIVAR	HEIGHT	SEASON OF BLOOM*	BLOOM SIZE	COLOR	FOLIAGE**
'Green Flutter'	20"	L Re	3"	Gr Yellow	SEv
'Mary Todd'	26"	E	6"	Buff Yellow	Dor
'Texas Ranger'	22"	EM	5"	Red	Dor
'Prairie Blue Eyes'	28"	M	5¼"	Lavender	SEv
'Betty Davis'	24"	M	5"	Dk Lavender	Dor
'Melanie Dawn'	26"	M	4½"	Pink & Lavender	Dor
'Persian Peach'	32"	M	5½"	Peach	SEv
'Judy Koltz'	32"	M	5½"	Pink & Peach	SEv
'Sweet Patootie'	24"	M Tetraploid	5½"	Lemon Yellow	SEv
'Stella de Oro'	11"	EMRe	2¾"	Gold	Dor
'Louise Manellis'	14"	EMRe	2½"	Peach	Dor
'Little Business'	22"	EM	3½"	Rose, Red, Green	SEv
'Notorious Fling'	26"	EM	5½"	Dk Purple, Green	Ev
'Broadway Bonanza'	24"	L Tetraploid	5½"	Dark Red	SEv
'Frilly Miss'	20"	M	4½"	Lemon Yellow	Dor
'Double Attraction'	20"	EM	5"	Dbl Gold, Red	Dor
'Double Dream'	26"	M	5"	Dbl Sal-Pink	SEv
'Tetrad'	18"	Re 4 petals, 4 sepaks	4½"	Yellow	Dor
'Wind Frills'	26"	M Spider Form	7½"	Pink	Ev
'Kindly Light'	26"	M Spider Form	7½"	Yellow	SEv
'Lime Painted Lady'	26"	M Spider Form	7"	Gr Yellow	SEv
'Juanita Hammond'	32"	M	4"	Red	Dor
'Bitsy'	18"	EE	1½"	Lemon Yellow	SEv
'Stella De Oro'	11"	E	2¾"	Gold	Dor
'Pixie Parasol'	14"	M	2¼"	Apricot	Dor
'Texas Sunlight'	26"	M	3½"	Gold	Dor
'Double Decker'	26"	M	4½"	Dbl Lt Gold	Dor
'Double Cutie'	13"	E	4"	Chartreuse	Ev
'Sea Warrior'	32"	M	5½"	Orange Yellow	SEv
'Touched By Midas'	30"	M	6"	Gold	Ev
'Shady Lady'	32"	M	5"	Yellow & Red	Dor
'Apple Annie'	28"	E	4½"	Red	Ev
'Best of Friends'	19"	E	6½"	Deep Pink	Ev
'Loving Memories'	17"	E	5½"	Near White	SEv
'Brutus'	24"	ML	7"	Yellow Pink	SEv
'Ed Murray'	30"	M	4½"	Black Red	Dor
'Mary Deans'	26"	M	5½"	Rose Pink	Dor
'Mary Lanham Thomas'	24"	E	5"	Baby Pink	Dor

* E—Early; M—Midseason; Re—Repeat Flowering; L—Late
** Ev—Evergreen; SEv—Semi-Evergreen; Dor—Dormant; SDor—Semi-Dormant

J. D. Oglesby

Garden of Mr. & Mrs. J. D. Oglesby, Houston, Texas—featuring Spider Daylilies

LANDSCAPE FAVORITES FOR THE HOUSTON AREA

CULTIVAR	HEIGHT	SEASON OF BLOOM*	BLOOM SIZE	COLOR	FOLIAGE**
'Abbeville Sunset'	20"	E	6"	Pink, Green	Ev
'Kings Cloak'	25"	EMRe Tetraploid	6"	Wine, Rose	Ev
'Velvet Gem'	28"	EM	7"	Red	Ev
'Mac the Knife'	30"	ML	5"	Apple Red	Ev
'Marie Babin'	24"	MRe	6"	Yellow, Purple	Ev
'Tovarich'	28"	EM	6"	Dark Red	Ev
'Sunny Girl'	21"	ERe	6"	Pink	Ev
'Orange Tex'	24"	EMRe	5"	Orange	Ev
'Leebea Orange Crush'	18"	EMRe Tetraploid	6"	Creamy Orange	SEv
'Clarence Simon'	28"	MRe	6"	Pink Melon	Ev
'Double Talk'	36"	MlaRe	5"	Dbl Orange	SEv
'Double Decker'	26"	EM	4½"	Dbl Lt Gold	Ev
'Double Splendor'	22"	ERe	4½"	Dbl Coral	Ev
'Double Whammy'	24"	ERe	7"	Dbl Orange	Ev
'Mattie Mae Berry'	18"	ERe	1¾"	Lt Yellow	Dor
'Baby Betsy'	18"	EMRe	2½"	Red	SDor
'Little Business'	15"	EMRe	3¼"	Lavender	SEv
'Sweetheart Supreme'	38"	M Spider Form	7"	Lemon Gold	Ev
'Picolata'	40"	MRe Spider Form	7"	Pale Yellow	Ev
'Wind Frills'	34"	EMRe Spider Form	7"	Pink	Ev

* E—Early; M—Midseason; Re—Repeat Flowering; L—Late
** Ev—Evergreen; SEv—Semi-Evergreen; Dor—Dormant; SDor—Semi-Dormant

A list of sources for daylilies, as well as membership and additional information, may be obtained by contacting Elly Launius, Executive Secretary, American Hemerocallis Society, 1454 Rebel Drive, Jackson, Mississippi 39211.

Hesperaloe parviflora

(hes per AL oh   par vih FLOR uh)

RED YUCCA

Family: Liliaceae   ◯◑
Zone 5   4'–6'   Spring, Summer

The common name of this plant is a bit deceiving, since it is not really a yucca and, despite the warning conveyed by "Red," it is not dangerously sharp. It is, however, one of the most useful garden plants available in Texas and the Gulf South. Stiff and gray-green, the long, slender leaves form stemless clumps; like a slightly ravelled cuff, the leaves sprout fine white threads from their margins. Gracefully leaning stalks, 5'–7' tall, bear coral-pink flowers from May through early fall. Individual flowers are about 1½" long and continue opening for many weeks.

H. parviflora seems to grow equally well with little water or a lot. It can be very drought and heat resistant, thriving even in locations with full sun and reflected heat. Partially shaded locations are also suitable, although sunny exposures produce the best clumps. Propagation is from seed or division of mature clumps. Landscape uses include accent specimens, masses in borders, or container-displays. The only routine maintenance this plant requires is the removal of old flower stalks at the end of the bloom season.

HIBISCUS

Hibiscus coccineus

(hi BIS kus   kok SIN ay us)

ROSE MALLOW, TEXAS STAR HIBISCUS

Family: Malvaceae   ◯◑
Zone 9   5'–6'   Summer, Fall

Texas Star Hibiscus is native to the Southern United States but rarely seen in gardens there. The single, red flowers are about three inches in diameter, and they appear atop branches of palmately lobed leaves with three to seven segments. The foliage and flowers are sufficiently attractive to qualify the plant for use at the back of deep borders. Culture is very easy, with well-drained soil, an annual application of fertilizer in spring or early summer, and a sunny location being most important. Propagation is from seed or cuttings. Mulching the plants in wintertime prevents root injury during very cold weather. Old stems, if they freeze, should be pruned back to the ground in early spring. Even if frost damage has not occurred, it is still a good idea to prune back and shape the plants before growth begins.

Hibiscus moscheutos

GIANT ROSE MALLOW

Zone 5   3'–6'   Summer   ◯◑

The Giant Rose Mallow has the largest flowers of any hardy perennial. In some of the hybrids, they may be a foot across. Rich, moist soil and full sun brings the most vigorous growth, but Mallows are very accommodating and will tolerate light shade and less desirable soils. Giant Rose Mallows will flower from seed the first year, if started very early in the spring. Favorite cultivars may be rooted from cuttings during the growing season. Colors range from crimson to white, pink, rose, and colors in between.

Giant Rose Mallows are relatives of the native hibiscus found growing in the ditches of Louisiana and other Gulf South states. They are among the most spectacular and easily grown plants for use in the border. Following the spring and summer growing seasons, the plants freeze back to the ground each fall. Old stems should be cut back to a height of several inches above the ground. New shoots emerge by mid-spring and the plants quickly develop handsome mounds of foliage and flowers by early summer. Individual flowers last only a day, but each plant may flaunt several or more flowers at once.

Close-up of Texas Star

Hibiscus coccineus—Texas Star Hibiscus

D. Greg Grant

Hibiscus moscheutos—Giant Rose Mallow

Pink Rose Mallow

Kosteletzkya virginica—Salt Marsh Mallow

Hibiscus mutabilis—Confederate Rose

Red Rose Mallow

Numerous seedling selections such as 'Southern Belle' and 'Frisbee' are offered in good seed catalogs. Few garden plants provide so much enjoyment for so little care.

H. *mutabilis* is an old-fashioned perennial or shrub better known as the Confederate Rose. It tends to be shrubby or tree-like in Zones 9 and 10, though it behaves more like a perennial farther north. Flowers are 4″–6″ in diameter, double, and they open white or pink, to change to deep red by evening. The variety 'Rubra' has red flowers. Bloom season usually lasts from summer through fall. Propagation is by cuttings which root easiest in early spring, but can be taken at almost any time.

When it does not freeze, the Confederate Rose can reach a height of 12′–15′ with a woody trunk. More typical is a multi-trunk bush 6′–8′ tall. Once a very common plant throughout the South, the Confederate Rose is an interesting and attractive plant that grows in full sun or partial shade and prefers rich, well-drained soil.

Kosteletzkya virginica (kos tel ETZ kee uh), Salt Marsh Mallow, is related to the Hibiscus and a native of fresh or salty marshes near the coast. The flowers are an attractive pink and occur in great profusion in midsummer. Plants may reach 6′–7′ in height and an equal width when grown in good soil well-supplied with water. Propagation is from seed started in early spring or cuttings taken during the growing season. Plants should be cut nearly to ground level after the first killing frost and mulched for winter protection in Zones 8 and 9.

Hibiscus rosa-sinensis, the Chinese Hibiscus, is an elegant flowering shrub that is increasing in popularity throughout the Gulf South. Despite an inherent problem with winter injury, this species of Hibiscus is used more all the time, both as a landscape planting and in containers.

The glossy, green foliage of the Chinese Hibiscus varies considerably in size and texture from variety to variety. Flowers range from 4″ to 9″ in diameter, and may be double or single. Ranging from white through pink, to red, yellow, apricot, buff and orange, the Chinese Hibiscus' flowers resemble in form and general appearance those of its relatives: okra, cotton, mallows, althea, and hollyhocks. The single-flowering cultivars are most often planted for the more dramatic show of their massed blossoms, while the double types offer the collector an exquisite display of individual blossoms.

The flowers of the Chinese Hibiscus are particularly popular as decorations inside the home since they need no water to stay fresh after cutting. Most varieties last only a day, especially during the heat of summer. To save for an evening party, pick the blooms just as they open in the morning, pack them in a sealed plastic bag, and store in the refrigerator. Set the flowers out an hour or two before the party, and they will stay fresh all evening.

History

A brief history of the Chinese Hibiscus helps us understand how this plant came to the West and how we may better manage it in our area.

First classified by Linnaeus in *Species Plantarum* (1753), the hibiscus he cited seems to have been a double red that is widely distributed throughout China, India, Southeast Asia, and the Pacific islands. In each of these locations, evidence of this flower reaches back to the 1600s. In a later description, Linnaeus also included a single red form. Curiously, double forms were more common in China than the single ones in those early times, and the single red came to the West (England) from the South Indian Ocean.

By the opening decades of the nineteenth century, the Chinese Hibiscus had become a popular greenhouse plant in Europe, as plantsmen vied for newly-discovered varieties. Most of these novelties continued to come from Asia, increasingly from the islands of the South Indian Ocean. On the island of Mauritius, Charles Telfair succeeded in crossing the native *H. liliflorus* with older forms of *H. rosa-sinensis* as early as 1820, and by 1900

hybridizing was being carried out on Hawaii, Ceylon, and Fiji, as well as on the mainland of India and Florida.

Culture

Chinese Hibiscus prefer sunny locations and well-drained soils. Keep them well watered during the hottest summer months, and fertilize regularly with a low-phosphorus plant food to stimulate blooming. The fertilizer recommended by the American Hibiscus Society is a 7-2-7 or a 10-2-4, but a 6-6-6 or, indeed, any balanced fertilizer brings good results. Protection from strong winds will help to prevent damage to the flowers.

As a rule, these hibiscuses are not cold hardy. If your region is prone to frost, you must either treat your hibiscuses as annuals or protect them from the weather in the coldest months. During mild winters, plants may freeze to the ground to sprout anew from the base in spring. An application of a loose mulch, pine straw or oak leaves before the onset of cold weather prevents severe winter-injury. Hibiscuses may also be transferred to containers for over wintering in a greenhouse, and then replanted in the landscape the next spring.

Pests

Hibiscus have their full share of problems. They are susceptible to root knot nematodes and cotton root rot. The only effective control for either of these diseases is to choose disease-resistant varieties and to sterilize the soil in which the plants are grown.

Nor is the Hibiscus immune to insect attack. Aphids love the tender new growth that emerges in the spring; corn ear worms and other worms love the flower buds; red spider mites feed on the leaves; scale insects feed on the stems. All of these can cause serious damage but can be controlled by the use of insecticides listed for that application. Never spray your Hibiscus with Malathion.

Bud Dropping

Many factors will cause Hibiscus blooms to drop from the plant before they open. Drought, temperature fluctuations, improperly balanced fertilizers or mineral deficiencies, wind, insects, even the application of unsuitable pesticides can contribute to this problem. In addition, some cultivars are especially prone to bud drop.

Varieties

There are hundreds of cultivars of hibiscus grown, and each year more appear on the market. For help in making your selections, contact the American Hibiscus Society. Texas boasts three local chapters and more members than any other state except Florida, so the exchange of information and varieties increases with each new season. The Chinese Hibiscus' range of colors seems to know no limits: purple, brown, green, grey, and maroon flowered types are available, together with many multi-colored combinations. Flower types include 2″–3″ miniatures, windmill types, cup-and-saucer forms, full- and semi-doubles, even single and double flowers borne together on the same plant.

Propagation

Most Chinese Hibiscus must be propagated by cutting since they will not come true from seed. Varieties that will not root readily are propagated by air layering, or by grafting.

Summer and early fall are the seasons to root cuttings. Take 5″–6″ cuttings of semi-mature growth in the early morning hours, treat with rooting hormones and stick into sand, vermiculite, a or half-and-half mixture of the two. A misting system is advantageous, but if none is available, just keep the cuttings out of direct sunlight.

Hard-to-root cultivars may be air-layered by selecting a stem one-half inch in diameter and girdling it 12″–14″ from its tip. To girdle, remove an inch-wide strip of bark from around the stem; then dust the wood with rooting hormone, pack it in damp sphagnum moss and wrap with polyethylene plastic. When roots become visible around the plastic, cut off the branch below the roots, remove the plastic, and plant.

Hard-to-root varieties may also be grafted onto vigorous rootstocks by means of side grafts, tip grafts and veneer grafts.

A SAMPLER OF TOP-PERFORMING VARIETIES BY COLOR

COLOR	BLOOM	VARIETIES
Red	Single	'Brilliantissima,' 'Gypsy Queen,' 'Rite 118'
	Double	'Lambertii,' 'Dr. Jack Borge,' 'Anderson Red'
Yellow	Single	'Hula Girl,' 'Kinchen's Yellow'
	Double	'Hilo Island,' 'Mrs. James Hendry'
Pink	Single	'Pink Lady,' 'Seminole Pink,' 'Texas Star'
	Double	'Esther Malley,' 'Cile Tinney,' 'Fanny Peck'
Orange	Single	'Cherie,' 'Mrs. Jimmie Spangler,' 'Red Sheen'
	Double	'Jigora,' 'Uma Med'
White	Single	'Madonna,' 'Bride,' 'The Pearl,' 'White Wings'
	Double	'Elephant Ear'
Brown	Single	'Evening Sunset'
	Double	'Brown Derby'
Purple	Single	'Sweet Violet'
	Double	'Marguerite'
Exotic	Single	'Edna Tyler,' 'The Path'
	Double	'Mary Lee Smith,' 'El Capitolio'

Exotic Hibiscus Varieties and Characteristics

'KINCHEN'S YELLOW'—Large 7–8 inch single bloom of medium texture with ruffled edge, clear white eye, bright lemon-yellow body; vigorus upright grower; has performed beautifully in the Houston landscape.

'CALYPSO'—Loose, semi-double of mandarin red heavily veined with chrome yellow, ruffled petaloids growing from style.

'CHERIE'—Single to 5–6 inches, bright yellow-orange body with maroon zone and white eye; very vigorous upright grower that has bloomed very well in the summer landscape.

Steve Moore

'Kinchen's Yellow'

'Seminole Pink'

'Calypso'

'Mrs. Jimmy Spangler'

'Senorita'

'Crimson Ray'

'Cherie'

'Norma'

'Esther Malley'

'SEÑORITA'—Double orange-yellow to about 5–6 inches, can be trained as a single trunk tree.

'SEMINOLE PINK'—Very vigorus and prolific single to about 6–7 inches, clear bright pink.

'MRS. JIMMY SPANGLER'—Bright currant-red single, yellow edges that fade to darker orange-red, flower size at about 4–5 inches but very profuse bloomer, will perform in the landscape extremely well.

'RITE 118'—A beautiful, big 7–8 inch red-orange bloom with yellow streaks and blotches throughout the petals, coral-pink eye, big round leaves on an upright grower.

'ESTHER MALLEY'—An unusual bloomer that will have single and semi-double blooms at the same time, rose-pink to purple depending on weather, white throat often streaked through the petals, crepey texture, very vigorous upright grower.

'LADY BIRD'—A true Texas giant to about 8–9 inches, dark red with paler edges, very dark glossy eye, edges somewhat ruffled, upright grower that will perform beautifully.

'BABY BLUE'—Double 3½ inch bloom; holds color, blooms all year; dark lavender with rosy red tinges to edge and body.

'Summer Sun'

'Miss Piggy'

'Joyce A'

'Rite 118'

'Black Beauty'

'5th Dimension'

'Baby Blue'

'Tylene'

'MISS PIGGY'—Crepey single to 8–9 inches; bright orange edges to rose body, streaked with pink; large dark red eye.

'NORMA'—Tufted single of crepey texture, 7½–8 inches; bright yellow with carmine center; upright habit and well branched.

'CRIMSON RAY'—8–9 inches single yellow with white veins leading into a large red eye.

'SUMMER SUN'—6–7 inches, single with bright yellow edges blending into an apricot body; pink center radiating into body; very overlapping and tufted petals.

'JOYCE A'—Shown in winter color, a tufted single of 7–8 inches; dark red eye will double in size in summer and edges will lighten to yellow.

'BLACK BEAUTY'—Single from New Zealand, 6–6½ inches; red-purple of fine texture; rapid grower of upright habit.

'5TH DIMENSION'—Single, 5–6 inch bloom; vivid gunmetal grey on brilliant orange which fades to yellow; dark red eye; very prolific upright grower.

'TYLENE'—Single, 5–6 inch bloom; lavender blue with touch of pink at edges and in center eye; upright and vigorous.

'Jerry Holst'   'Geisha Girl'

'Ali Uii'   'Pink Rays'

'Lavender Lauren'   'Sleeping Single'

'ALI UII'—Single, 4 inch bloom; very funnel-shaped throat, red with yellow streaks on overlapped side of petals.

'GEISHA GIRL'—Introduced in 1973, 7–8 inches overlapped single; shown is a fresh bloom and a faded, one-day bloom of lighter color; border orange, blotched smokey body to turkey-red satiny eye.

'PINK RAYS'—Single shell-pink to about 6–7 inches; body maroon-red with white veins from center to edges; eye white.

'JERRY HOLST'—Cup-and-saucer double, pale pink of about 7 inches; twisted petaloids; bush tends to be rather sprawling.

'LAVENDER LAUREN'—Single to 6 inches; tufted petals of neyron-rose with carmine areas on overlapped side of petal; carmine eye; tends to grow tall.

'SLEEPING SINGLE'—Single to 7–8 inches; edges of yellow to turkey-red body; lighter veins from red throat, heavy texture and ruffled.

Hippeastrum x Johnsonii
(hip ee AS trum   jon SOHN ee eye)
HARDY RED AMARYLLIS

Family: Amaryllidaceae ○◑
Zone 8   2′   Spring

Hardy Red Amaryllis are among the most spectacular spring-flowering bulbs. Their foliage is strap-shaped and long, sometimes to 24″. Often it does not appear until after flowering and fades away in early autumn. Old clumps can produce dozens of thick flower stems, each topped with six or more funnel-shaped, red flowers. *H. x Johnsonii* is the first hybrid Amaryllis ever recorded; reportedly, it was produced by an English watchmaker named Johnson about 1812. A hybrid between *H. reginae* and *H. vittatum*, *H. Johnsonii* is more tolerant of heavy clay soils and cold than other Amaryllis. Although the individual flowers may not be quite so large as those of the modern Dutch hybrids, *H. Johnsonii* produces many more flowers per stem and is a much longer-lived garden plant than the modern hybrids, which are bred primarily for pot culture. Clumps may be divided and reset in the fall with the necks of the large bulbs left slightly above ground level.

Hosta spp.
(HA stah)
PLANTAIN LILY

Family: Liliaceae ◑●
Zone 5   12″–18″   Summer, Fall

Hostas are becoming increasingly popular in areas where they thrive. They generally do very poorly close to the Gulf, but in the northern halves of the Gulf Coast states, usually starting in Zone 8, they are fairly well-adapted. Though the hyacinth-like flowers are attractive, Hostas are grown primarily for their foliage. Leaves are lance-shaped, rounded or intermediate in shape. Foliage color may be bluish-green, variegated green, yellow or white, or solid shades of light to dark green.

Hosta foliage dies back to the ground during the winter and emerges rather late in spring, making them good companion plants for spring flowering bulbs. They do best in shady or partially shady locations with rich, moist soil that contains large amounts of organic material. Although Hostas need moisture, poorly drained sites should be avoided. Clumps may be easily divided during

Hippeastrum x Johnsonii—Hardy Red Amaryllis

Hosta spp.—Plantain Lily

early spring. Snails and slugs sometimes damage foliage but can usually be controlled with baits or foliar sprays labeled for that use.

Hostas are useful in shady borders and individual clumps can make handsome specimens. They compete reasonably well with the roots of other plants and often live for many years. In our region they are fairly well-adapted from Northeast Texas eastward. When grown in areas that are too sunny, hostas scorch.

New Hostas appear on the market on a regular basis. Some of these are being reproduced by tissue culture and are quite expensive. The following list includes some old favorites and the more popular recent introductions. *H. albomarginata*, (*H. sieboldii*) has spear-shaped leaves with a narrow edging of white and flowers of violet-blue. *H. decorata* makes dense, low clumps with rounded leaves having a showy white edge. *H. fortunei* is a larger growing type with oval leaves. Cultivar 'Aureo-marginata' has leaves edged in yellow that lighten to a cream-color in summer. 'Albo-picta' has pale-yellow leaves edged in green. *H. sieboldiana* has an unusual seersucker

Hyacinthus orientalis 'White Roman'—
White Roman Hyacinth

texture to the bluish-green foliage. *H. ventricosa* has flowers of near-blue and dull, ribbed leaves. It may be easily grown from seed. *H. venusta* has lance-shaped foliage and 6″ spikes of mauve flowers. It is a true dwarf and useful as a border or mass plant.

Hyacinthus orientalis 'White Roman'
(high ah SIN thus   or ee en TA lis)
WHITE ROMAN HYACINTH

Family: Lilaceae   ◯◖
Zone 5   6″   Spring

This is the white French Roman Hyacinth that naturalizes in much of Texas and the South. Blue forms also will naturalize, but bloom later. White forms bloom about February 1, and are extremely fragrant. In North Texas, plant in sheltered areas where early flowers will not be spoiled by frosts. Divide and reset bulbs after the foliage yellows and begins to fade away in late spring. Roman Hyacinths prefer at least half a day of direct sun and well-drained soils. They are particularly nice in naturalized landscapes.

Hymenocallis liriosme
(high men oh KAH lis   leer ee OZ me)
SPIDER LILY

Family: Amaryllidaceae   ◯◖
Zone 7   3′   Spring

This attractive native is found in low places in Louisiana, coastal Texas, sporadically north to Arkansas, and east to Mobile Bay. Except for the distinctive trumpets of

the Peruvian Daffodils, the flowers of all Spider Lilies are similar. For garden purposes, the major differences lie in hardiness, blooming season, the size of the plant, and foliage. *H. liriosme,* the "Lily-Scented Spider Lily" grows best as an aquatic or semi-aquatic and blooms in March and April with large yellow-centered white flowers. Although not as easy a garden subject as other Hymenocallis, it has superior cold-hardiness.

Spider Lilies are propagated by division of mature clumps in fall or early spring. Although their preference is for a wet site, they can withstand considerable summer drought, though in those conditions they will shed their attractive glossy foliage. They respond favorably to well-prepared garden soils, but will grow in sand or heavy clay. Where the ground seldom freezes, Hymenocallis may be planted just below the surface of the soil. From the mid-South northward, however, bulbs should be planted deeply and mulched to protect from winter freezes.

H. sp. "Tropical Giant" is a Spider Lily that is popular throughout the Gulf Coast states. It bears large umbels of flowers in late June and early July and is one of the finest of all foliage plants available for Southern gardens, growing readily wherever abundant moisture is available. The large, dark green foliage and fragrant, white flowers make an excellent accent in the garden. The nickname for the plant was first coined by Wyndham Hayward of Lakemont Gardens, Winter Park, Florida, in the mid 1940s. Although one of the most common Hymenocallis in Southern gardens, this species has apparently never been properly described botanically. Its flowers are easily recognized by the white petals arranged in two alternating planes, one spreading and the other drooping. "Tropical Giant" is especially attractive when used as a specimen where its coarse texture contrasts with finer textured plants. Some dealers have marketed this plant as *H. x* 'Ty Ty.'

H. pedalis, the long-tubed Spider Lily, is a very tropical type with stiff, upright, bright green foliage and long-tubed flowers with drooping petals and a vanilla fragrance. It is popular along the Gulf Coast and especially valuable in sandy, seaside gardens. Flowers appear in midsummer. *H. latifolia* is a very similar type, native to South Florida, with larger, duller green foliage and somewhat shorter floral tubes.

H. acutifolia, the Mexican River Hymenocallis, has deep green, strap-shaped leaves and large, glistening white flowers with frilled cups and gracefully spreading or recurved petals. A late-bloomer (September-November), this species extends the Hymenocallis season into the fall.

H. narcissiflora, the Peruvian Daffodil, is certainly the Hymenocallis species most readily available from

D. Greg Grant

Hymenocallis sp. 'Tropical Giant'

A. Scott Ogden

H. narcissiflora—Peruvian Daffodil

D. Greg Grant

Hymenocallis liriosme—Spider Lily

Marie Caillet

'Sulfur Queen'—*H. narcissiflora* hybrid

A. Scott Ogden

Hymenocallis latifolia

commercial sources. This native of the Andes of South America also outdoes the rest of the genus in the size of its flowers, producing huge trumpet-shaped, frilled cups with incurved stamens. This last character sets it apart from Caribbean, Central and North American Hymenocallises, whose flowers have widely spreading stamens. Since this plant is a native of high elevations it often sulks in Southern heat and humidity. Bulbs should be planted deeply (12″ or more) and mulched heavily. This practice helps keep roots cool while also discouraging this bulb's inclination to prolific offsetting, a habit that encourages the growth of large clumps of foliage, but at the expense of flower production. 'Sulfur Queen,' a pale yellow hybrid with huge bulbs, performs better in the South than other popular types such as 'Advance' and 'Festalis'. *H. narcissiflora* is susceptible to iron chlorosis in alkaline soils and performs best in sandy soils. It responds well to "Gladiolus Culture" and often blooms two or three weeks after planting, if dug and stored each

A. Scott Ogden

H. acutifolia—Mexican River Hymenocallis

season. Left in the ground, it is winter-hardy only in the lower South.

H. x 'Excelsior' is a novel hybrid with small foliage topped by enormous white flowers. A cross of the Florida miniature *H. traubii* with the beautiful *H. narcissiflora* of South America, it combines the best attributes of both parents, making a choice plant for a moist spot in the border.

Ipheion uniflorum
(if ee AHN   yu nee FLOR um)
SPRING STAR, BLUE STAR

Family: Amaryllidaceae   ○◑
Zone 5   6″–8″   Early Spring

This native of Argentina is one of the more dependable small bulbs for early spring. *I. uniflorum* is an allium relative and has an onion scent to the flat, bluish-green leaves. Flowers are broadly star-shaped, about 1½″ across and may be white or colored in varying shades of blue. A long season of flowering adds to the value of this plant. It will grow in a wide variety of climates and exposures, but prefers sandy soils for naturalizing. In alkaline clay soils, plant where bulbs will receive no summer water, or dig and store the bulbs during summer. Flowering begins in February in Central Texas and lasts for 4–6 weeks. The bulbs increase rapidly by stolons and are best divided and reset in the fall. Sunny or partially shaded exposures both seem to provide good displays. This is a useful plant for edging or ground cover in naturalistic areas.

IRISES

Irises are among the most beautiful and diverse perennials. Some groups prefer relatively dry, well-drained locations while others thrive in moist or poorly drained soils. There are good, practical choices among the irises for every area of Texas and the Gulf South. Irises are generally classified as either bearded or non-bearded. Within these broad classifications are numerous subclasses, a few of which are particularly useful as landscape plants when combined with other perennials. This section will concentrate on the selection and culture of these beautiful and well-adapted plants.

Bearded Irises

The best-known of all garden irises, the bearded irises receive their name from the tuft of hair, the "beard" that sprouts from the three lower petals. This class does not thrive in areas adjacent to the Gulf, with their excessive humidity and poorly drained soils. The Texas Hill Country and much of Central, West, North and East Texas are good locations for these aristocrats of

the garden. The northern half of the other Gulf Coast states, and all of Oklahoma and New Mexico, are also well suited to the cultivation of bearded irises.

The bearded irises are subdivided by flower size and height. Tall bearded irises are those with flower stalks over 27″; medians are all those under 27″ and are further divided into miniature dwarfs, standard dwarfs, intermediate, border, and miniature tall. A few are classified as re-bloomers because they bloom again in the fall after having bloomed with their fellows in the spring.

Culture of Bearded Irises

Good cultural practices are the best insurance against disease and disappointment with bearded irises. The rhizomes are tough and can withstand considerable heat and drought, but too much water and poorly drained soils invite disaster. Of good substance, too, are the flowers of the modern hybrid types. A single blossom can last for 3–4 days, and because each of a plant's many buds opens separately, a single plant may remain in bloom over a long season.

Recommended planting time is July through October, although if necessary, irises can be transplanted successfully even while in bloom. Rhizomes dug in midsummer may be stored in a cool, dry place for many weeks before being placed in their permanent location.

Since irises perform best if left undisturbed for two or three years at a stretch, it is logical to prepare the soil well before planting. Bearded irises tolerate a soil pH range of 6 to 9, with a preference for slightly alkaline media (7.0 to 8.0). The bed should be well-tilled and the soil improved by the addition of about one-third organic matter such as composted pine bark, or compost mixed with a low nitrogen fertilizer such as 6-10-6 (high nitrogen fertilizers can cause the rhizomes to rot). Full sun and good drainage are recommended, although locations shaded from the hot afternoon sun may encourage longer-lasting flowers.

When planting, place the rhizomes with their tops barely covered with soil. Spread the roots out as far as possible by forming a mound of soil in the center of the hole and placing the rhizome on top. Place some of the prepared soil over the roots, firm by hand and water slowly until the soil settles and no air pockets are likely to remain. If the transplanting is the result of division, cut each plant's leaves back to about 6″–8″; do not prune undivided transplants, however.

Though sensitive to fertilizer, irises are heavy feeders and do require regular feeding. Apply fertilizer with a ratio of 6-10-6 after bloom in the spring or in early fall. Side-dressing with superphosphate in late February or early March improves growth and bloom. Keep iris plantings free of dead foliage, weeds and leaves. Water

Marie Caillet

Tall bearded irises

Marie Caillet

Shirley's TB's

should be applied on the ground and not from sprinklers.

The spacing at which irises should be planted depends upon both the ultimate size of the variety and the desired effect in the garden. Placing the rhizomes 24"–30" apart allows plenty room for growth. Grouping several or more rhizomes of the same variety together provides a greater concentration of color. By placing the cut ends of the rhizomes close enough to almost touch one another, with the leaves to the outside, a quick and effective display may be achieved. When dividing clumps that have been growing for two, three, or more years it is best to dispose of the old center rhizomes and replant only the best of the outer ones. This is a good way to reduce disease and ensure healthier and better blooms for the next season.

Iris borers are common in other parts of the country, but are not normally found in Texas and the Gulf South. Bacterial soft rot, which results in the decay of the rhizome, can be a problem and is best controlled by cutting away affected parts of rhizomes and exposing the remainder to the sun, or by digging and dusting rhizomes with sulfur.

Suggested Varieties

There are possibly 10,000 to 20,000 bearded varieties. These suggestions illustrate most of the color range, but obviously represent only a few of the possible choices.

TALL BEARDED—These are the largest of the bearded irises and have bloomstalks 27" tall, or more. Recommended varieties and their approximate colors are:

  White—'Laced Cotton,' 'Leda's Lover,' 'Song of
    Norway' (blue-white), 'White Lightning'
  Yellow—'Catalyst,' 'Gold Galore,' 'Lemon Mist,'
    'Temple Gold'
  Yellow-White—'Joyce Terry,' 'New Moon'
  Purple—'Dusky Dancer,' 'Maumelle,'
    'Superstition'
  Violet—'Entourage,' 'Mary Frances,' 'Mulled
    Wine'
  Blue—'Blue Luster,' 'Portrait of Larrie,' 'Sapphire
    Hills,' 'St. Louis Blues,' 'Victoria Falls'
  Red—'Ida Red,' 'Spartan,' 'Lady Friend' (reddish-
    purple)

Iris x albicans—Naturalized bearded irises

Marie Caillet

Spuria irises

Pink—'Beverly Sills,' 'Lovely Kay,' 'Pink Taffeta,'
  'Vanity'
Orange—'Copper Classic,' 'Coral Beauty,' 'Son of
  Star,' 'Sunrise Sunset'
Bicolor—'Camelot Rose,' 'Gay Parasol,' 'Betty
  Simon,' 'Mystique,' 'Edith Wolford'
Plicata—'Going My Way,' 'Graphic Arts,' 'Kilt
  Lilt,' 'Rancho Rose,' 'Stepping Out'

MEDIANS—Although the bud count per stem is
somewhat less on medians than on the tall bearded irises,
the overall number of stalks tends to be more. Some of
the dwarf types start blooming as early as March. The
medians are rewarding in the garden and possibly the
easiest of all bearded irises to grow. Recommended varieties and their approximate colors are:

White—'Avanelle'
Blue—'Blue Pools,' 'Silent Strings'
Gold and Violet—'Brown Lasso'
Apricot Orange—'Marmalade Skies'
Pink—'Pink Kitten,' 'Pink Bubbles,' 'Raspberry
  Blush'
Plicata—'Rare Edition'

REBLOOMING IRISES—Reblooming irises
must complete two cycles of growth and bloom in a year,
which implies that they must continue to develop and
increase considerably after the spring bloom. This longer
season of growth leaves these plants particularly vulnerable to early fall cold spells, which sometimes freeze the
rebloomers' buds. Rebloomers also require more fertilizer than other beardeds, and respond best to a 1-4-4
ratio. Recommended varieties and their approximate
colors are:

Blue-White—'Desiderata'
Pure White—'White Reprise'

Light Yellow—'Dime Spot'
Orchid-White Plicata—'Earl of Essex'
Violet—'Feedback'
Yellow-Brown Plicata—'Grandville'
Peach Pink—'Peach Reprise'

Naturalized Bearded Irises in Texas and the Gulf South

The irises most commonly found growing wild in
Texas and the Gulf South are sometimes referred to as
"cemetery whites." Actually, they are a separate species,

Iris x albicans, and a natural sterile hybrid. Although their individual blooms may last but a day or two, they are extremely hardy and often mark abandoned homesites and old cemeteries, where for several weeks each spring they command the attention of all passers-by. Originally from Yemen, these irises have naturalized so extensively and become such a part of our rural landscape that many people consider them native. "Early Purple" irises are also found in abundance on old homesites and cemeteries in Texas and the Gulf South. These are thought to be a different color form of *Iris x* albicans.

Beardless Irises

SPURIA IRISES—Most of the species that were bred to form the modern spuria hybrids came from Southern Europe, Asia, and Northern Africa, areas that have climates not too different from that of Texas and the Gulf South. Spurias prefer neutral to slightly alkaline soils, full sun, good drainage, and little or no moisture during their late summer dormant period. In most locations, they go completely dormant during late summer, at which time their old foliage may be cut off and completely removed, if desired.

The narrow, tall foliage of spurias resembles that of the Louisiana irises. The sword-like leaves push up in the fall to remain green and attractive all winter. Spurias are among the very best irises for Texas and the Gulf South. They thrive even in neglect and produce strong, tall stems of spring flowers that range from 3′–6′ tall.

Iris ochruleuca was one of the species used to breed the modern spuria hybrids, and flourishing colonies of the parent may still be found in old cemeteries and abandoned gardens. The flowers are white with a large yellow spot on the falls (the three bottom petals again, the same ones that carry the beard in the bearded irises). Like many irises, the spurias are heavy feeders, and even abandoned and neglected specimens can be immediately improved by an application of fertilizer in the fall.

Division is best undertaken in the fall. After lifting the old clumps from the soil, it is important to keep the exposed rhizomes and roots moist until they are replanted, and to resettle them with a thorough watering. Spacing the rhizomes several feet apart gives them room to grow and spread and will delay for several years the need for a redivision. Though the foliage of the spurias differs markedly from that of the bearded irises, the two types prefer the same cultural conditions, and they make good companion plants in the perennial border. Spurias bloom a bit later than the beardeds in the spring, and therefore extend the flowering season several weeks. When cut, the buds continue to open, making them popular for indoor decoration.

Although spurias are successful in areas where bearded irises grow well, they are also adapted to locations nearer the coast where beardeds often fail. Yet spurias also flourish in the dry areas of West Texas and the Panhandle. Spurias are among, if not the most, useful irises for landscape use, yet they are less common than most other types. They deserve much more widespread use and popularity.

Suggested Spuria Varieties

Dark Red-Violet—'Ada Perry'
Yellow—'Archie Owen,' 'Imperial Gold'
Blue—'Betty Cooper'
Lavender—'Highline Lavender,' 'Marilyn Holloway'
White—'Ila Crawford'
White-Yellow—'Feminine Mystique,' 'Ruffled Canary'
Maroon—'Imperial Ruby'
Gold—'Janice Chesnik'
Dark Blue-Purple—'Proverb'

LOUISIANA IRISES—This group of irises can be grown successfully in every area of Texas and the Gulf Texas and the Houston-Beaumont areas. The source of

Iris ochruleuca

this hardiness no doubt lies in their parentage, for the Louisiana irises were bred from species found native in Arkansas, Louisiana, and Texas. Stalk heights vary considerably, from 1′–6′ feet, and flowers from 3″–7″ across. Because all the primary colors are inherent in the various species that contributed to this group, there is no limit to the color range. The Louisianas, for example, include the purest form of red of any iris.

Culture of Louisiana Irises

Louisiana irises prefer an acid soil in the range 6.5 or lower. They like large quantities of both fertilizer and water but their greatest need for both of these comes during the naturally cool and moist fall and winter seasons. They are among the few irises that will thrive in poorly drained soils. Louisiana irises can be effectively used along streams and lakes where they may be inundated periodically by changing water levels. Their foliage is lush and requires heavy fertilization to remain

Marie Caillet

'Swamp Flame'—Louisiana Iris

'Feminine Mystique'—
a Spuria iris

Marie Caillet

'Ila Crawford'—a Spuria iris

healthy and productive. Some varieties go dormant during the heat of summer, leaving dead foliage that should be cut back or removed. New foliage will appear again in the fall.

Fall is the best season for transplanting. Beds should be well tilled and amended with large amounts of compost, peat or pine bark. Rhizomes should be planted just below ground level and kept moist until well established. Clumps spread quickly, and individual rhizomes should be spaced several feel apart to avoid need for annual division. Mulching in the summer protects rhizomes against sun-scald. Winter protection is not necessary but could help prevent the evaporation of essential moisture in northern and dry areas of the region. Azalea-Camellia fertilizers are recommended, along with water-soluble fertilizers designed to lower the soil pH.

After bloom is completed in the spring, the stalks should be cut back to the rhizome. Old rhizomes do not bloom again, but increase to produce the following year's

'Kristig'

'Marie Caillet'

'Charles Arny III'

'G. W. Holleyman'

'Papa Bear'

'Kay Nelson'

'Ila Nunn' & 'Dixie Deb'—Louisiana Irises

'Prof. Claude'—Tetraploid

crop. These flamboyant flowers are attractive to bees, and the visits of these insects often result in pollination and the production of fertile seed in the irises' large seed pods. Ripening seeds sap the plant's strength, so they should be removed unless, of course, the grower has decided to raise new plants from seed. If so, leave the pods in place until they turn yellow-green in July or August, shell out the seeds before they dry and plant at once into pots of well-prepared soil. After providing adequate protection during the winter, the young seedlings may be planted into permanent locations the next March.

Suggested Varieties of Louisiana Irises

There are currently over 1,000 varietes of Louisiana irises being grown and these are but a few of the excellent choices.

White—'Acadian Miss,' 'Blanchette,' 'Clara Goula,' 'Monument'

Yellow—'Dixie Deb,' 'Fading Beauty,' 'President Hedley,' 'Sun Fury'

Red—'Ann Chowning,' 'Freddie Boy,' 'Mighty Rich,' 'Bold Pretender,' 'Rhett'

Purple—'Marie Caillet,' 'Mary's Charlie,' 'Pegaletta,' 'Professor Ike,' 'Professor Claude'

Lavender—'Bryce Leigh,' 'Colorific,' 'Lavender Ruffles,' 'Mrs. Ira Nelson'

Rose—'Charlie's Michele,' 'Charlie's Tress,' 'Faenelia Hicks,' 'Rose Cartwheel,' 'May Roy'

Pink—'Caroline LaPoint,' 'Deneb,' 'Medora Wilson,' 'Professor Paul,' 'This I Love'

Iris japonica—Not to be confused with *Iris ensata*, the better known Japanese iris. *I. japonica* is a choice shade-loving perennial for the Gulf Coast area. It freezes north of a line roughly marked by Interstate 10. This iris spreads its glossy green fans by underground runners. It prefers a moist, organic soil and blooms in April to bear delicate crested blooms of white flecked with lavender. A handsome variegated variety is also sometimes available.

Iris japonica x wattii 'Nada' is a hybrid of *I. japonica* with a subtropical heritage. The glossy green leaf-fans

Marie Caillet

'Fantastic'

Marie Caillet

'Valera'

Iris pseudacorus bears a yellow flower.

Iris pseudacorus

A. Scott Ogden

Iris japonica x wattii 'Nada'

and graceful wand-like sprays of delicate, white, crested blooms are a beautiful addition to Gulf Coast gardens. Propagation is by division of runners and culture is similar to that of *I. japonica*.

Iris kochii—Italian iris. This purple iris is better adapted to Southern plantings than the North European *Iris germanica*. It also has the important trait of remontancy. *I. kochii* is a parent of many of the intermediate hybrid bearded irises such as 'Golden Cataract', a reliable fall and spring bloomer.

Iris pseudacorus—This European native iris has escaped cultivation and may be found growing in wet ditches and along streams and lakes. It is bright yellow in color and considered by some to be a native plant. The foliage is much like the Louisianas and Spurias, being

tall and almost reed-like. The plant is very hardy, healthy and aggressive with clumps becoming very large in time. Although similar to the Louisiana irises, *I. pseudacorus* is not botanically part of that group nor will it cross-pollinate with them. If allowed to set seed, it can colonize large areas.

Although they prefer a wet location, *I. pseudacorus* will grow almost as well on a dry site. They are among the easiest irises to cultivate, thriving even when totally neglected. I have found them to bloom sparingly until well established, which may require several years. The foliage reaches a height of $4'-6'$, and is among the best of any irises. It may be cut back in late summer or early fall, if it has become untidy. There appear to be no major insect or disease problems with this highly vigorous species.

SIBERIAN IRISES—Besides the preceding, there are two more water-loving, beardless irises that can be grown in most areas of Texas and the Gulf South, though they require more attention. These are the Siberians and the Japanese. Siberian irises are natives of cool climates of Europe and Asia and therefore prefer the cooler parts of Texas and the Gulf South. They somewhat resemble Louisianas but the plants and flowers are smaller and more delicate in appearance. Mature foliage and flower stems measure in the range of $2'$ tall. The narrow foliage forms a compact clump that stays green all summer and through the fall. When they finally die back in wintertime, the leaves should be cut back to the ground.

Although they can tolerate some summer dryness, Siberians like to be kept moist and prefer a well-drained soil, high in organic content and with an acidic pH (in the range of 5 to 6.5). Siberian Irises are sometimes grown as companions to the Louisiana irises but do not require the heavy fertilization as the Lousianas, nor do they attain nearly the same size.

The best time to plant Siberian irises is in mid to late fall when cool, moist weather is the rule. Rhizomes should be set about 2″ below ground level with the roots spreading deeper. It is important to avoid air pockets; therefore, thorough watering and firming of the soil after planting are important. Bloom dates vary with the location and season but tend to start at the same time as the tall beardeds in March or April and extend until May. The flower colors are primarily white, ranging to deep blue-purple, but in recent years breeders have introduced new selections with pink, rose, red-purple, and near-yellow blossoms.

Sunny locations are generally recommended, but in the intense heat of Texas and the Gulf South, shade from mid-day through the afternoon results in longer lasting flowers. Cut worms sometimes attack the leaves and flower buds, requiring an application of insecticide such as Sevin.

Suggested Varieties of Siberians

White and Cream—'Anniversary,' 'Butter and Sugar,' 'Star Cluster,' 'White Swirl'

Blue to Purple—'Caesar's Brother,' 'Grand Junction,' 'Lavender Light,' 'Orville Fay,' 'Ruffled Velvet,' 'Sparkle,' 'Steve,' 'Super Ego,' 'ViLuihn'

Pink to Wine—'Augury,' 'Chilled Wine,' 'Pink Haze,' 'Rose Quest,' 'Sparking Rose'

JAPANESE IRISES—Although a bit harder to handle in the average garden, Japanese irises may be grown alongside the Louisianas and Siberian irises. They require an acid soil, plenty of fertilizer and water, but do not need to stand in water during the fall and winter. The flowers of Japanese irises are the largest of any iris and their forms and color patterns are the most unusual; though they offer less range of color than the Louisianas, the Japanese irises offer more variety of markings. One big advantage is their bloom date, which is late enough

'Sparkle'—Siberian iris variety

Deep purple flower of 'Sparkle'

Dutch irises

to extend the iris season in your garden another month. Some growers plant Japanese in with the Louisianas in regular beds and water both on the same schedule. One may also grow them in pots in order to more easily control the amount of water allotted in the different seasons.

DUTCH IRISES—These irises are bulbous and quite different from the rhizomatous types described in this section. Dutch irises prefer rich, well-drained soils, and in those conditions will sometimes naturalize. They also prefer sunny locations but can be grown under deciduous trees where they usually complete their growth and bloom cycles before foliage canopies leaf out to provide deep shade. Although their blooms are quite beautiful, Dutch irises are in foliage and flower for a relatively short time and do not offer the long season of attractive foliage and more permanent characteristics of the other irises discussed. They are spring flowering and are best used in the landscape, like Narcissus and similar plants.

Ixora coccinea
(icks OH rah   kok SIN ay uh)
IXORA
Family: Rubiaceae ◐◑
Zone 10   2′–3′   Spring, Summer, Fall

Ixora is a valuable garden plant where it is not subject to severe winter damage. Plants are mounded in form and bloom spring through fall, yielding dense flat-topped to globular clusters of flowers in red, yellow, yellow-orange, buff, and white. Ixoras are used for hedges and as container specimens in tropical areas, and are tolerant of salt spray. Glossy, oblong green foliage adds to the beauty of the plant and provides a handsome background for the showy flowers. Ixoras thrive in rich, well-drained soils that are slightly acid. For maximum bloom, plant in full sun. Frequent applications of fertilizer throughout the growing season are beneficial. Propagation is from cuttings.

Justicia Brandegeana
(jus TISS ee uh   bran dee JEE ah nuh)
SHRIMP PLANT
Family: Acanthaceae ◐◑
Zone 9   4′–5′   Summer and Fall

Shrimp Plant is a native of Mexico and very popular in the lower South where it is used extensively as a garden perennial and often cut for indoor ornament. The dense 3′–4′ floral spikes resemble shrimp in both form and color, with tubular, purple-spotted, white flowers extending beyond the showy, reddish-brown bracts. Luxuriant in its effect, the Shrimp Plant produces many long-lasting bracts through the summer and fall. A

chartreuse selection 'Yellow Queen' is available and attractive. Leaves are egg-shaped and 2″–3″ long.

Shrimp Plant prefers well-drained soil and some protection from the hottest afternoon sun and winter winds. The plants are drought tolerant, once established, and propagated by division of mature clumps or from cuttings. Winter damaged top growth should be removed in very early spring. Mulching in the fall can be helpful in providing protection against frost damage. Landscape

Justicia variety 'Yellow Queen'

Justicia Brandegeana—Shrimp Plant

Justicia spicigera—Firebush or Mexican Honeysuckle

use includes masses in the center or rear of large borders, and as specimens. Large, old specimens may sometimes be found in New Orleans, Galveston, and along the Texas coast from Corpus Christi to Brownsville.

J. spicigera is commonly known as Firebush or Mexican Honeysuckle. Frequently found in Central and South Texas gardens, it is especially abundant in San Antonio. It is native from Mexico south to Columbia where, reportedly, the leaves are steeped in hot water to produce a bluing used for whitening clothes. Medicinal uses have also been reported. Orange or red tubular flowers occur all during the warm seasons. Plants tend to wilt when very dry, but are quite drought tolerant. Large, spreading clumps may reach 4'–5' tall and as wide. Propagation is by cuttings or division.

Kniphofia uvaria
(nip HOE fee uh   you VAR ee uh)
RED-HOT-POKER, TORCH-LILY

Family: Liliaceae
Zone 6   2'–4'   Summer

Kniphofias are very popular in herbaceous borders of England and Europe. They are not as dependable in the Gulf South, but are sometimes worth the effort in areas a hundred or more miles away from the Gulf. A rich, moist soil is ideal, good drainage and a sunny location essential. Garden hybrids range widely in size, color, and time of bloom. Foliage is grass-like and should be cut off at the base in fall. The flowers of some varieties are bi-colored yellow and orange, others are solid in ivory, yellows, coral, orange, and scarlet. Kniphofia flowers furnish a good contrast in form to daylilies, especially since the two plants often bloom simultaneously. It is best to leave clumps undisturbed. Interplant with shallow-rooted perennials such as Coreopsis. Propagation is by seed or division of mature clumps in the fall.

Lantana camara
(lan TAN uh   KA ma rah)
LANTANA

Family: Verbenaceae
Zone 9   2'–4'   Spring, Summer, Fall

L. camara is native to South Texas and tropical America. It grows well in dry, sunny locations to provide landscape color over a long period. Lantanas will grow in sandy soils near the coast where most other plants are severly damaged by the salt. In northern parts of our region, lantanas should be treated as annuals. In Zones 9 and 10 and part of 8, frost-damaged wood is removed and plants are cut back and shaped each spring.

Flowers of *L. camara* come in bi-color mixtures of yellow, red, pink, white, and orange. They resemble

Kniphofia uvaria—Red-Hot-Poker, Torch-Lily

Lantana camara—Lantana

small verbenas in size and form. Native types seem to be more cold-hardy and reliably perennial than most of the hybrids for sale in our garden centers and nurseries.

L. horrida is sometimes known as Texas Lantana or Orange Lantana and has naturalized over much of Texas. Flowers are yellow-orange and appear from spring till frost. *L. horrida* grows well in dry soils and is effective in mass plantings, and as a ground cover in sunny areas. *L. macropoda* is similar, but flowers are pink and cream.

Lantana horrida—Texas Lantana or Orange Lantana

Lantanas are grown from cuttings or seed and do best in sunny areas having well-drained soils. Frequent tip-pruning during the growing seasons promotes more flowers. Fertilizer should be used sparingly, with one light application each spring usually being adequate.

L. montevidensis is a lavender, trailing form that is also native to South and Central Texas. As with all the lantanas, the foliage is aromatic. Trailing Lantana is useful as a ground cover in dry, sunny areas. It is also attractive in hanging containers and spilling over edges of retaining walls and flower boxes. The berries of all lantanas are reported to be poisonous. Lantanas are excellent plants for attracting butterflies to the garden. This species is listed as *L. sellowiana* in some references. All lantanas are especially useful along the Gulf Coast. Occasional pruning helps to keep them neat and in flower for many months.

Lantana montevidensis—Trailing Lantana

Lawsonia inermis
(la SO ni a   in ER mis)
HENNA, RESEDA, MIGNONETTE
Family: Lythraceae   ○◗
Zone 9   3′ – 10′   Spring, Summer, Fall

Reseda is commonly grown in Mexico and the tropics, primarily for its unusually sweet-scented flowers. These are not very showy but bloom periodically throughout the growing season. The plant is quite tropical and actually hardy without protection only in Zone 10. In some parts of the world, Reseda is used for hedges, its small, simple leaves somewhat resembling privet. Propagation is primarily from cuttings which root easily during the growing season. Fragrance is one of the most distinctive and appealing. In areas where

L. inermis produces a small white flower.

Lawsonia inermis—Reseda, Henna

D. Greg Grant

Leucojum aestivum—Summer Snowflake

The bell-shaped blossoms and dark green foliage of Summer Snowflake make this perennial one of the most attractive spring bulbs.

winter temperatures limit its use out of doors, it is sometimes grown in containers so that winter protection may be provided. Heavy mulching in most of Zone 9 may be sufficient to winter the root system. Even when cut back to the ground by cold, plants recover quickly from the roots, and the bloom is little affected since the flowers occur on new wood. Cultural requirements are simple, with well-drained soil and at least a half-day of full sun being preferred. Drought tolerance is good.

Much of the tropical world knows and grows *L. inermis* as Henna. The leaves of Henna are much used in the Orient for staining the nails, hands, and feet yellow. When applied to the hair and beard, a paste made from Henna leaves quickly produces a bright red color that is considered attractive among some classes of Mohammedans. If an indigo paste is applied next, the hair turns jet black. Sometimes tails and manes of horses are dyed red by the same process. The flowers also are important to the cultures of many peoples. They yield a perfume which is an ingredient of certain oils and ointments used by Egyptians for embalming, and by Jews for baths and religious occasions (Henna is the "camphire" of Solomon in the Bible). The plant also yields a dull red dye sometimes used for cloth, and both the fruit and leaves are reported to be used medicinally in some cultures.

Leucojum aestivum
(lou KOE jum   ES tih vum)
SUMMER SNOWFLAKE

Family: Amaryllidaceae   ◐
Zone 6   1'   Spring

This beautiful spring-flowering bulb has naturalized on many sites in East and Central Texas. It is native to

the stream banks of southern France and prefers moist locations and heavy clay soil. The small (¾"), bell-shaped blossoms appear in March or April and bear a distinctive green spot on the margins of the petals. "Gravetye Giant," a cultivar that is sometimes available, yields somewhat larger flowers than the more common species-type. *L. aestivum* is often sold as *L. vernum*.

The dark green foliage of the Snowflake is among the most attractive of all spring-flowering bulbs. Best landscape effects are achieved with large clumps of bulbs. They also combine well with other spring-flowering bulbs and thrive in sun or the shade of deciduous trees. The foliage is outstanding for several months and clumps may be left undivided for many years without sacrificing flowers. Mature clumps may be divided in late spring after the foliage has yellowed.

Liatris elegans
(lie AT tris   EL ee ganz)
GAY-FEATHER, BLAZING STAR

Family: Compositae   ◐
Zone 6   2'–3'   Late Summer

This is the native form of liatris often found growing along roadsides and hillsides of Texas, Louisiana, Arkansas, Oklahoma, and eastward. Many spikes of frilly, rosy-purple, or white flowers emerge from clumps in late summer. Liatris grow from curious round, woody corms that can be divided, but seldom become sufficiently thick. New plants are usually started from seed. A problem I have found with the native liatris is that it will not remain erect without staking when transplanted to the improved growing conditions of the garden. Staking can help solve the problem, but I have found *L. spicata* to be a better garden subject than its native cousin.

Dr. Jerry Parsons

Liatris elegans—Gay-Feather, Blazing Star

L. spicata is considered the most adaptable of the liatrises. It grows naturally in deep soils, and is fairly drought resistant. Staking is not normally necessary and nursery availability is better than that of the native species. Liatris are handsome in combination with *Rudbeckia fulgida* 'Goldsturm,' which usually blooms at about the same time. The rosy-purple color of the common form is beautiful, but not easy to combine with other perennials. Foliage is narrow and thin, producing an overall fine texture.

Lilium candidum
(LIL ee um   KAN dee dum)
MADONNA LILY

Family: Liliaceae   ◖
Zone 7   3'–4'   Mid-Spring

The oldest garden flower in cultivation, the Madonna Lily is depicted in ruins of Egypt and Crete. It is a native of Asia Minor that bears large white flowers in mid-spring. Madonna Lilies do well in North Texas and the Hill Country where limestone soils are common. Their shallow-growing bulbs produce attractive rosettes of foliage much like a Hosta through the winter, before

A. Scott Ogden

Lilium candidum—Madonna Lily

bolting in spring to produce their sweet-scented flowers. The foliage dies down soon after flowering, and remains dormant until early fall when the growth cycle begins anew. Transplanting and dividing should be done in late summer or early fall. Bulbs should be set in a sunny location, only 1"–2" below the soil surface.

Few of the hundreds of garden lilies available to the gardener return as perennials in Texas and the Gulf South. Many cultivars are late blooming and last only a few days in our intense late spring and summer heat. In addition to *L. candidum*, *L. tigrinum*, *L. regale*, and *L. formosanum*, some of the Aurelian Hybrids such as 'Golden Splendor' and 'Thunderbolt' are worthwhile in our area.

L. tigrinum grows to four feet or more to bear many pendulous flowers of orange spotted with black. The Tiger Lily is believed to be a natural hybrid and it reproduces by bulbils formed in the axils of the leaves, as it is a sterile triploid. It is a very vigorous garden lily, thriving in acid soil areas of the South. In the Far East, Tiger Lilies have been cultivated for many centuries.

Tiger Lilies grow particularly well in East Texas, Northern Louisiana, Mississippi, and Alabama, where they are old favorites with experienced gardeners. Garden lilies require well-drained soil, and their flowers last longer if they receive protection from the hot afternoon

Lilium tigrinum—Tiger Lily

sun. Remove faded flowers, but wait until stems and leaves have turned yellow before cutting them back nearly to the ground.

With care, lilies can be transplanted at any time, even when in flower, but spring and fall are ideal. They need constant moisture while growing and blooming, but withstand dry periods after they have flowered.

Mulch is advised, to keep moisture even, reduce weed growth, and keep the soil cool. Roots are near the surface and may be damaged by hoeing or other cultivation in their immediate vicinity. Flooding is better than sprinkler-irrigation, especially once the plants start flowering, since it does not damage the flower or spread spores of diseases.

L. 'Thunderbolt'

L. 'Heart's Desire'

Lilium 'Golden Splendor'

The Aurelian hybrids are results of crosses of *L. henryi* with various trumpet-shaped lilies such as *L. regale*. 'Golden Splendor' is a lovely yellow, and 'Thunderbolt' a warm orange Aurelian that are grown with some success in our area.

    L. formosanum is known to most of us as the Easter Lily, though it blooms in late spring when grown in the garden. Bulbs should be set 5″–6″ deep to allow for development of the extensive stem rooting system. *L. formosanum* is a native of coral sands along the coast of Asia and is one of the few lilies suitable for the Gulf Coast. It suffers from freezing winter weather and is recommended for Zones 9 and 10. Modern hybrid Easter Lilies should not be confused with *L. formosanum*; they differ in having dark green instead of lime green foliage and will not often succeed as garden plants.

    L. regale is probably the most famous of all lilies. It was discovered by Ernest Wilson growing on limestone soil in Western China. The white trumpets on tall stems resemble Easter Lilies but are much more cold-hardy. They are parents of the Olympic and Aurelian hybrids, and are well-adapted to Central Texas; this is a versatile, adaptable garden lily. Garden lilies are an elegant addition to the perennial border, but well-adapted varieties are few for our area.

Liriope Muscari
(luh RIE oh pee   mus KAY ree)
LIRIOPE, LILY TURF
Family: Liliaceae   ◑●
Zone 7   12″–18″   Summer

    The generic name *Liriope* is often used as a common name for this native of Japan, China, and Vietnam. It is classed as an evergreen perennial herb and blooms in early to midsummer in Texas and the Gulf South. Flowers are almost hyacinth-like but more slender, and may be white or lilac-blue. The foliage is broader than *Ophiopogon japonicus* (monkey grass) and generally taller. The most common forms of liriope typically reach a height of 1′–1½′ and form large clumps that may be divided to obtain new plants.

    There are at least a dozen cultivars of *L. Muscari* current in the nursery trade, but only a few are common in garden centers. All are excellent as ground covers and in borders, while some are useful in containers. The form known as "common liriope" has pale lilac-purple flowers and rich green foliage. This is the liriope most often found in garden centers and is usually considerably less expensive than the improved cultivars. 'Variegata' has creamy-white variegated foliage and must have 4–5 hours of sunlight daily to maintain its coloration. 'Silvery Sunproof' is another popular cultivar, one with

Liriope 'Silvery Sunproof'

Liriope 'Majestic'

more white in its leaves than most variegated types. 'Silver Dragon' is a relatively new cultivar that holds its bright white variegation extremely well in the shade. It spreads by rhizomes that sometimes emerge a foot or more from the original plant and is, therefore, better as a ground cover than a border plant.

    'Majestic' has dark green foliage that can reach two feet in height with rich violet-colored, crested flower stalks. It is probably the most widely available of the improved cultivars. 'Big Blue' is not quite so tall, and has dark blue-green foliage and tapering spikes of flowers that are generally conceded to be the largest of any improved cultivar. 'Munro #1' is the only white-flowering cultivar, and is quite impressive in foliage as well as bloom. It prefers partially shaded locations and may leaf-scorch in full sun.

    L. spicata is a different species entirely, one that has longer leaves (up to 2′) and spreads by rhizomes. The foliage is narrower and looks almost like monkey grass, except in its length. *L. spicata* is not well-suited to borders since it spreads quickly and is generally too aggressive. It does perform well as a ground cover, especially in the shade where its leaves are less likely to scorch during periods of intense heat. The flowers are violet-colored and less prominent than those of *L. Muscari* and its improved cultivars.

Liriope is easily propagated by division. When grown as an edging plant along the front of a border, liriopes should be thinned from the rear to prevent this robust plant from encroaching backward into the planting area, and to make the removal of the plants less noticeable. This is best done every three or four years in late summer, fall, or winter, but may take place whenever convenient or necessary. Dividing mature clumps requires considerable strength and endurance, since the individual plants knit closely together. After division, the individual plants should be cut back one-half to two-thirds of their original height, and should be reset as soon as possible. For ground cover or border plantings, single divisions may be set 8″–10″ apart. Larger divisions and closer spacing provide a quicker effect, but with reasonable care the recommended spacings usually begin to run together within a year.

Liriopes are tough plants, but they respond favorably to good cultural conditions. Their preference is for partial shade and a well-prepared, well-drained soil that is also slightly acidic. The incorporation of several inches of pine bark, peat moss, or compost, and approximately two pounds of a balanced fertilizer or special Azalea-Camellia fertilizer per 100 square feet of bed area is sufficient to establish and promote good growth and flowering. An annual application of a similar amount of fertilizer to the surface of the planting, watered in well, keeps the liriope in good condition. Once established, liriope will tolerate considerable dryness, but occasional deep watering during prolonged dry spells and during the first year of planting are well worth the effort. Old foliage tends to brown at the tips and to lie nearly flat on the ground by January or February. For a tidier appearance, some gardeners cut back their liriope almost to the ground in late winter, just before new spring growth begins. For larger plantings, this task can be done with a lawn mower adjusted to its highest setting.

Lobelia Cardinalis
(lo BEE lee uh   kar din AL is)
CARDINAL FLOWER
Family: Lobeliaceae ◑
Zone 7   2′–4′   August-October

Cardinal Flower is native to the Eastern and Southern U. S. and is one of the most beautiful red-flowering perennials. It grows only on moist soils, and is becoming increasingly rare in its natural habitats. Lobelia is best grown in shade or partially shaded areas, and makes a good companion plant for ferns in the shady

Lobelia Cardinalis—Cardinal Flower

border. Cardinal Flower tends to be short-lived, but its lifespan will be prolonged if the basal rosettes are divided and reset each year in late fall, after flowering. Seedlings often "volunteer" in the vicinity of the parent plant, and are easily transplanted. New plants may also be produced by bending over stems of old plants, and placing soil along the stem in several places. New plants will sprout from the buried leaf nodes or joints.

Soil must be uniformly moist and protection from afternoon sun is essential for success with *L. Cardinalis* in Texas and the Gulf South. Cardinal Flower should not be removed from its natural environment since it is becoming rare, and wild specimens don't often survive transpalnting. The flowers of *L. Cardinalis* offer possibly the most brilliant scarlet of any garden flower. They are about 1½″ long and occur on erect, 12″–20″ stalks. Leaves are oblong and 3″–6″ long with serated edges. It is a beautiful plant, but one that will not withstand heat and moisture stress and is, therefore, recommended only for the special situations where it will thrive.

Lycoris radiata "Guernsey"
(lie KORE is   ray dee AH tuh)
SPIDER LILY, GUERNSEY LILY, HURRICANE LILY
Family: Amaryllidaceae ○◑
Zone 7   12″–18″   Fall

The form of this plant found naturalized in old Southern gardens has been researched at the U.S. National Arboretum at Beltsville, Maryland, and found to be a triploid. This is the reason that it is more vigorous than the type currently being imported from Japan. Foliage appears in fall and dies down in spring. Following the first good rains in September, the bloom spikes quickly come forth with their beautiful red, spidery blossoms on 1″–1½″ stems.

Guernsey Lily can be utilized with ground cover.

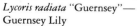

Lycoris radiata "Guernsey"— Guernsey Lily

Lycorus africana—St. Augustine Lily

Lycoris squamigera (Amaryllis hallii)

Guernsey Lilies are good to mix with non-aggressive ground covers such as English Ivy, and for naturalizing in partially shaded or sunny sites. They grow well in heavy clay soils with abundant winter moisture, and are especially fine for planting under deciduous trees. Flowering is usually delayed a year after transplanting. Guernsey Lilies are hardy throughout the South. They should be divided every fourth or fifth year, soon after the foliage dies in spring. If left undivided, the bulbs become so thick they push themselves out of the ground. The strap-shaped foliage is somewhat similar to liriope but has a silver stripe down the center. It remains lush and green all fall and winter, at a time when few garden plants are in good foliage.

L. x albiflora, the White Fall Spider Lily, is similar to *L. radiata*, except for the white or cream color of the flowers. It is believed to be a natural hybrid of *L. radiata* and *L. aurea*. Commercial stocks often include more than one clone under this name. *L. x albiflora* is less hardy than *L. radiata*, but an excellent performer in Central and South-Central Texas, growing well even in the deep shade of live oaks.

L. africana (*L. aurea*), St. Augustine Lily, is a yellow form of lycoris that was reportedly brought to

Florida by the early Spanish settlers. It blooms at a similar time to the other fall spider lilies but with a somewhat larger flower. It is also broader, and larger of leaf. *L. africana* does not bloom dependably west of East Texas but is well-adapted to Louisiana and the eastern Gulf Coast.

L. traubii is similar, and is commonly imported from Japan and sold commercially as *L. aurea*. In fact, this species is more cold hardy than *L. aurea*, though less vigorous in the garden. Foliage of both species appears in the fall and, if frozen in a severe winter, is likely to bloom little if at all the following autumn.

L. squamigera (*Amaryllis hallii*) is the hardiest of all lycorises, blooming in July or August with large, fragrant, lavender-pink flowers. It does not thrive close to the Gulf, but for gardens in Central East Texas, the eastern Gulf Coast, and northward it is a good garden plant that blooms at a time when few perennials are at their peak. Mature clumps are best divided in late spring when the winter foliage has yellowed.

Lythrum salicaria
(LITH rum   sal i KAY ree uh)
PURPLE LOOSESTRIFE

Family: Lythraceae   ◐
Zone 5   2′–5′   Summer, Fall

Although sometimes labeled a weed in England and Europe where it is very common, lythrum is becoming a staple among Southern gardeners. Dense mounds of narrow foliage develop showy spikes of pinkish-purple

Lythrum salicaria 'Morden's Pink'

flowers at the end of each stem, to remain in bloom for a long period each summer and early fall. Light pruning can spark rebloom. Lythrum is reported to grow in either boggy or dry soils, although I have had plants die from apparent overwatering in the heat of our summer. Light shade or full sun are best exposures. 'Morden's Pink,' which matures to a compact 3′ mound each summer, seems to be the cultivar most widely available and cultivated in our area. 'Rose Queen' is reported to be slightly shorter and is increasing in popularity, along with 'Happy,' which is a very compact 18″. Improved cultivars should be propagated from soft stem cuttings taken in summer, or by division in early spring. Lythrum colors are bright and may be toned down by interplanting among gray- or white-flowering plants. They are also effective when combined with the annual dark purple and white forms of Globe Amaranth (*Gomphrena globosa*). Lythrum should be cut back nearly to the ground each fall after freezing.

Malvaviscus arboreus
(mal vah VIS cus   ar BORE ee us)
GIANT TURK'S CAP

Family: Malvaceae   ◐
Zone 8   5′–6′   Summer, Fall

A native of Mexico and Texas, Giant Turk's Cap is an attractive and useful plant. The fuschia-like flowers never entirely open, the swirls of vivid red petals unfolding only partway, but a protruding column of stamens and pistils serves as a magnet for hummingbirds, while many other bird species come later in search of the plant's attractive red fruit. The fruit is reported to be edible either raw or cooked.

Although a semitropical plant, *M. arboreus* often proves root hardy well into Zone 8, if the plant has the chance to establish itself before the arrival of cold weather. Mulching also helps to bring valued specimens through the winter. Frost damaged stems should be removed, and plants pruned and shaped each year in early spring. Giant Turk's Cap is easily grown in sun or partial shade and is exceptionally drought tolerant. Well-drained, fertile soils are preferred, but this plant performs well in a wide variety of soils, moistures and exposures. Propagation is from seed, or cuttings taken during the growing season.

M. arboreus var. *Drummondii* (Turk's Cap, Texas Wax Mallow) is an especially fine variety of the species common in old Texas gardens. Indeed, the frequency with which it is found all along the Gulf Coast from Mexico to Florida is testimony to its popularity as a garden flower, since this variety seems to have spread largely by escape from cultivation. Although this Turk's Cap is

Malvaviscus arboreus—Giant Turk's Cap

Malvaviscus arboreus var. *Drummondii*—Turk's Cap, Texas
Wax Mallow

naturally more compact in its growth than the species, and bears smaller flowers and foliage, it can, on occasion, approach the same impressive size. *M. Drummondii* thrives in alkaline or acid soils and is well-adapted to sunny or fairly shaded exposures. Both forms of Malvaviscus are easily grown and useful in the perennial border, where they often persist for many years with little attention.

Mandevilla x amabilis 'Alice du Pont'
(man deh VILL ah   a MAH bill is)
MANDEVILLA

Family: Apocynaceae   ○◑
Zone 9   20'–30'   Spring, Summer

Although not reliably cold-hardy in most of the Gulf South, this vine is becoming more popular each

year. This is due in part to the plant's precocious flowering. Rooted cuttings begin to bloom when only a few inches tall, and mature specimens flaunt clusters of rich, pink, 2"–4" flowers amid their dark green, shiny leaves from April until November. Since this plant will not tolerate cold, pot or tub culture is the popular method of cultivation. Propagation is from cuttings which are easily rooted under mist with bottom heat.

M. x amabilis 'Alice du Pont' prefers rich, well-drained soil and a plentiful supply of water during the growing seasons. It will grow in full sun, but its blossoms maintain a richer color in the shade. Trellises, stakes, or similar structures are necessary for support. Occasional pruning during the growing season helps to keep plants more compact.

Melampodium cinereum
(me lam POH dee um   sin er RAY um)
MOUNTAIN DAISY, BLACKFOOT DAISY

Family: Compositae   ○◑
Zone 7   4"–12"   Spring, Summer, Fall

Mountain Daisy is a useful perennial for sunny, well-drained locations with alkaline soils. Plants form compact mounds and bloom intermittently over an extended season, bearing small, white, daisy-like flowers with bright yellow centers. The Mountain Daisy is native to the limestone soils of Arkansas, Colorado, and Texas. Like many plants native to arid, stony sites, the Mountain Daisy will not tolerate wet feet; in soggy soils, its root system becomes susceptible to fungal diseases and the plant quickly rots. Irrigate sparingly, and amend heavy soils with sand. Propagation is primarily from fall-sown seed. The plants die down in fall and reappear early in spring, usually in time to bloom with bluebonnets and other wildflowers of the season. A useful perennial when grown with other culturally compatible plants.

Mirabilis Jalapa
(mi RA bi lis   jah LA pa)
FOUR-O'CLOCK

Family: Nyctaginaceae   ○◑
Zone 7   2'–4'   Summer, Fall

Four-o'clocks are among the toughest perennials for our area, and often mark abandoned homesites and cemeteries where they have survived unattended for many years. Often, they even increase in such conditions of neglect, for this species reseeds prolifically; in the garden, if allowed to propagate unchecked, Four-o'clocks can develop into a weedy pest. Flowers are tubular, 1"–2" long, sometimes striped or mottled but more often solidly-colored in shades of red, magenta, lavender, yellow, or white. As their name implies, the flowers open

A. Scott Ogden

Mirabilis Jalapa—Four-o'clock

Monarda didyma 'Croftway Pink'

in late afternoon and stay open well into the evening. The leaves are oval-shaped and about 2″ long. Tops die down with the first hard frost but the roots are hardy over most of the South.

Four-o'clocks thrive in sun or part shade and are quite drought resistant. They prefer moist, loamy soils, but have been known to persist in much less desirable situations. They seem to enjoy the intense heat of mid-summer, even along the humid Gulf Coast, where they have been popular for many years. To prevent Four-o'clocks from taking over a mixed border, remove all but a few of the many seedlings that emerge each spring soon after they sprout. In colder climates the tuberous roots may be dug and stored in a cool, but not freezing, location and replanted the next spring. Propagation is by seed. Division is not a practical means of increasing this perennial, since mature plants develop a deep taproot and resent any disturbance.

Monarda didyma
(mo NAR da   di DEE muh)
BEE BALM, OSWEGO TEA, WILD BERGAMOT

Family: Labiatae   ◯◑
Zone 4   2′–3′   Spring, Early Summer

M. didyma is not very well adapted to Gulf Coast gardens, but does perform well in central and more northern parts of the region. Individual flowers surround a rounded head that is attractive even after the flowers have faded. Bee Balm most often blooms early in our region and withstands summer heat and drought only with difficulty. They are among the most popular perennials in other parts of the world but are marginal in our area. Many colors are available, but two of the most popular are the soft pink 'Croftway Pink' and bright red 'Cambridge Scarlet.' Bee Balm grows best where it

enjoys protection from the hottest afternoon sun and is easily propagated by division of the spreading clumps.

M. fistulosa, Wild Bergamot, is a common wild-flower of Texas and the Gulf South. When moved into the garden it often outgrows the typical 2′ stature it adheres to in the wild. If cut to the ground after it flowers, Wild Bergamot will produce an attractive mound of new foliage that persists through the remainder of the growing season. The lavender flowers are prominent in May and early June.

Muscari racemosum
(mus KA ri   ra se MO sum)
STARCH HYACINTH

Family: Liliaceae   ◯◑
Zone 5   6″–8″   Spring

This is the purple-flowering, musk-scented plant that has naturalized over much of Central, North and occasionally East Texas. It is sometimes known as "Grape Hyacinth," but naturalizes much better for us than *M. armeniacum*, the commonly sold grape hyacinth which

Muscari racemosum—Starch Hyacinth

does poorly in our area. Starch Hyacinth blooms during March and resembles small bluebonnets from a distance. Foliage is grassy and comes up each fall and lives all winter. It thrives in clay or sandy soils and is propagated by seed and division.

Although fairly common in our area, availability is restricted to market bulletins, sellers of specialty bulbs, and collecting from naturalized populations. Bulbs should be planted in the fall about 2″ deep in sun or light shade. Divide established clumps after several years or when they become crowded.

NARCISSUS—DAFFODILS

Daffodils are among the first flowers of spring and can create memorable displays in southern gardens. Some types will naturalize in Texas and the Gulf South, though very few do so near the coast. Fragrance is another asset of these plants. Daffodils can begin blooming as early as December and January, while some flower as late as April and May. The flowers of the later-blooming types do not last as long, since they are exposed to the hotter weather of late spring.

From a scientific viewpoint, all daffodils belong to the genus *Narcissus*. This can be confusing since the name "narcissus" also functions as a common name when it isn't underlined or italicized, and the first letter isn't capitalized. So, *Narcissus* is the genus or generic name for all daffodils, while "narcissus" is a common name for only certain types. In common usage, the large, trumpet-shaped types are often referred to as daffodils and the small, cluster-flowering sorts as narcissus, though even this varies in different parts of the country.

Daffodil Culture

Daffodils prefer a sunny location. They will, however, bloom fairly well in open shade under deciduous trees that allow the sun to reach the plants during late fall, winter and early spring. Good drainage is essential. Raised beds should be constructed in areas where surface or internal drainage is inadequate. It is ideal to prepare the beds a month or more in adavance of planting the bulbs, to give their soil a chance to settle. If the soil is heavy clay, it should be loosened by tilling in gypsum or builder's sand. A mixture of organic materials such as peat, pine bark or compost can then be applied as the next step in improving a heavy clay, but should only be added once the drainage has been improved; otherwise, organic additives may only increase the bulb's tendency to rot. Generous amounts of organic material do improve sandy soils, though many fine displays of daffodils persist on land of very low organic content. Daffodils prefer a neutral pH in the range of 5.5 to 7.5.

Whether or not to chill daffodil bulbs artificially before planting is a subject about which experts disagree. Certainly, if planted in September or October, when our temperatures are still very warm, the bulbs are liable to rot. Yet imported bulbs arrive in garden centers at precisely that season, to be set out on open shelves at room temperature. For this reason, it is worthwhile to heed the advice of Dallas area daffodil experts. They suggest placing the bulbs in the lower part of the refrigerator in labeled paper bags and storing them there until the first cooling fall rains lower soil temperatures below 55 degrees F. This usually occurs in November through most of Texas and the Gulf South. If rains do not come in time, deep soaking can be a suitable substitute. After the initial planting, there is no longer a problem, since the bulbs remain in the ground all year, except when they are being divided every three or four years.

After their flowers have faded, it is always a temptation to tidy up by removing the daffodils' foliage. Resist this urge; controlled experiments have shown that cutting daffodil foliage shortly after blooming may kill the bulb, or at least weaken it so that it will bear fewer blooms in subsequent years. Next year's flowers begin to form in the bulb immediately after bloom, and by interrupting the growth cycle of the plant, the removal of the foliage at this critical time can abort the following season's bloom. If for any reason it should prove necessary to cut away the daffodil's leaves, allow at least six weeks after the last flowers have faded before doing so.

Most daffodils may be planted six inches deep (to the base of the bulb) and six inches apart. Small types and miniatures may be planted as close as one inch apart and covered with as little as an inch of soil. After planting, beds should be lightly mulched with pine or wheat straw, coastal Bermudagrass hay or similar material. This also keeps down weed growth and prevents dirt from being splashed on the open flowers.

High nitrogen fertilizers and fresh manures are not suitable for use with daffodils since they are sometimes associated with bulb rot. One to one-and-one-half pounds of low nitrogen fertilizer, such as 8-24-24, may be broadcast over every 100 square feet of bed right after planting or just as the first leaf tips begin to emerge from the ground. (A pint jar will contain approximately one pound of granular fertilizer.) Bone meal is a popular fertilizer for daffodils and other bulbs, though superphosphate is preferred by some daffodil experts. Both materials are good sources of phosphorous which may, however, be more economically available in a standard fertilizer mix. The best way to make sure you are giving your bulbs the nutrients they need, of course, is to test your soil every three to four years. For help with this, contact your County Agricultural Extension Agent.

Except in naturalized plantings where it may not be practical, daffodil bulbs should be dug from their beds every three or four years to keep them from overcrowding and decreasing in bloom. When the foliage has died down naturally, but not disappeared, dig the bulbs, remove the foliage and wash them with a hose to remove soil. After allowing the bulbs to air dry, place them in a mesh bag and hang them from the rafters of a well ventilated storage shed to cure. Inspect the bulbs after a couple of months and remove any that appear to have rotted or shriveled.

Forcing Daffodils

Bowl culture can be rewarding and easy with daffodils such as 'Paper-white' and 'Soleil d'Or.' To succeed with bowl-culture, select a large bowl or clay saucer and fill it with pebbles. Place the bulbs in the pebbles so that the pebbles support the bulbs. Then fill the bowl with water up to the level of the bulb's basal plate to initiate rooting. Once this process has begun, the bulbs must never be allowed to dry out. Place the bowl in a sunny window. They should immediately begin to sprout roots and foliage, and flowers should appear in 3–6 weeks.

After the blooms have faded, discard the bulbs since there is little chance they will be of further use in the garden.

Pot culture is another effective way to force daffodils. Place a few pieces of broken clay pots or large gravel over the drainage hole in the bottom of the pot. Partially fill the pot with a good mixture of garden soil, sand, and peat or a commercially prepared potting soil. Place as many bulbs as possible in the pot, but take care that the sides of the bulbs do not touch one another. Then fill the pot with soil, leaving just the tips of the bulbs exposed. Water thoroughly and regularly, so that the media doesn't dry out at any time during the forcing period. Label each pot with the variety and date of planting.

After planting, place the pots in cold storage at temperatures of 40–50° F. for a minimum of twelve weeks. The lower part of a refrigerator provides an ideal environment if you set the thermostat so the temperature won't drop below 40° F., or place the pots in trenches outdoors during late fall or winter and cover them with a heavy layer of mulch. After 12 or more weeks, roots should be coming out the bottoms of the pots, and leaf growth should have begun.

Naturalized Narcissus in East Texas

H. Brent Pemberton

At this point, move the pots to a semi-dark spot where the temperature remains cool, around 60° F. The new leaves will be pale and whitish, but they will green up quickly when you expose them to light. As soon as they do begin to show color, move the pots again, this time to a sunny location. Here the daffodils will quickly come into bloom. Bulbs forced in this manner may sometimes be salvaged for future use after the flowers fade by plunging the pot into the soil outdoors and allowing the foliage to mature. Plant the bulbs out in the garden and let them rest undisturbed for at least two growing seasons before using them for forcing again. Besides the fact that it allows a reuse of the bulbs, this method of forcing, unlike bowl culture, succeeds with many different daffodil cultivars. Generally, though, the earlier a cultivar flowers outdoors, the better it is for forcing. Pot culture works equally well for hyacinths, crocuses, and tulips.

Varieties Known to Naturalize in Texas and the Gulf South

There are many daffodils recommended for garden use in the northern half of Texas and the states bordering the Gulf of Mexico. The ones described in this section, though, are those few that are found marking old homesites, cemeteries and roadsides, varieties that are unsurpassed for their reliability as naturalizers. Some of them extend their range over the entire Gulf area.

Narcissus jonquilla is early flowering, has rush-like leaves, and prefers sandy, acid soils and abundant moisture. Its clusters of bright yellow flowers are tiny, but powerfully fragrant.

Narcissus jonquilla 'Golden Scepter' is a medium-large flowered, sweet smelling narcissus. One of the older jonquil hybrids, it is a proven performer in the middle and lower South. Since it is single-flowered, it offers an excellent substitute for the larger-cupped daffodils. 'Sweetness' is another desirable old yellow jonquil hybrid of considerable garden merit.

N. jonquilla x odorus 'Campernelle' is the most common yellow narcissus of East Texas, Central Texas, and the Deep South. This cultivar is well adapted to all Southern conditions, including the poorly drained soils of the coastal regions. Leaves of 'Campernelle' are rush-like and the flowers fragrant; an early bloomer, it often flowers by March 1. Though it first appeared as a natural hybrid in southern France, 'Campernelle' has been in cultivation since the 1600s.

N. jonquilla x 'Trevithian' is a more modern hybrid that is more refined and later blooming than 'Campernelle' (March 1–April 15). 'Trevithian' is dependable, graceful, and performs well even in heavy soils. It is considered by some to be the best yellow daffodil among the modern hybrids for mass color. 'Quail' is another choice, multi-flowered jonquil hybrid.

Narcissus jonquilla

A. Scott Ogden

A. Scott Ogden

Narcissus jonquilla 'Golden Scepter'

N. jonquilla x odorus 'Campernelle'—rushlike leaves and fragrant flowers

N. tazetta 'Pearl'—star-shaped flowers

N. tazetta 'Grand Monarque'

N. jonquilla x 'Trevithian'—dependable,
graceful, performs well in heavy soil

N. cyclaminius 'Peeping Tom'

N. cyclaminius 'Peeping Tom' is very early flowering (February 15), well adapted, and available. 'Peeping Tom' does best in sandy soils, and though not recommended for deep South Texas, this hybrid should prove very durable in the rest of our region. 'Auburn,' 'Bartley,' and 'February Gold' are other cyclaminius hybrids of value.

N. tazetta 'Papyraceus' is the dependable 'Paper-white' that seems to perform best in South Texas and other coastal areas. It blooms very early, sometimes in November and is well adapted to drier areas. The early flowers are subject to frost damage in northern parts of the region. It is very fragrant and among the earliest bulbs to bloom.

N. tazetta 'Constantinople' is another good narcissus for South Texas, early blooming and probably the most fragrant of all. It is the double form of the Chinese Sacred Lily, *N. tazetta orientalis*, which is also an excellent garden plant for South Texas. Plants of 'Constantinople' are large and lush, blooming in January, and naturalizing along the Gulf Coast. 'Constantinople' is known to have been in cultivation since the 1600s.

N. tazetta 'Grand Monarque' is superior in durability and adaptability to ordinary "paper whites." This hybrid blooms in late March. It is found in old gardens, cemeteries, and homesites in Texas and the South. For mass color it may be the best of all daffodils in Texas and the Gulf South. It is well-adapted to heavy soils, hardy throughout the region, and in cultivation since the 1600s.

N. tazetta 'Silver Chimes' is a modern hybrid that is widely available and very good for naturalizing. Thriving in heavy soils, this daffodil blooms late and sports a very lush, dark green foliage. 'Silver Chimes' is a hybrid of *N. triandrus* and *N. tazetta* 'Grand Monarque.' Some daffodil experts consider this well-adapted variety to be a "typhoid Mary" since it is often a carrier of fusarium disease, and they plant it only in isolated areas, if at all.

N. tazetta 'Pearl' has beautiful clusters of star-shaped flowers; petals are white and cups are citron yellow. They are often found around old homes in East Texas and are usually in bloom during February.

H. Brent Pemberton

Naturalized Narcissus found along roadsides

Summary of Daffodil Classification

The American Daffodil Society and the Royal Horticultural Society of Great Britain have developed a system of classifying daffodils that may be helpful in studying the many cultivars available. These divisions are briefly defined below. Listed along with each are some varieties of that class that are recommended as landscape material for the Dallas-Fort Worth area. For more detailed information, contact the American Daffodil Society or a local member.

In the descriptions of daffodil cultivars below, colors are abbreviated as follows: W—white or whitish, G—green, Y—yellow, P—pink, and O—orange. The color of the perianth (petals) is listed first, followed by the color of the corona (trumpet). The corona is divided into three zones: an eye-zone, a mid-zone, and the edge or rim. Colors are listed in that order, if they differ from the first color mentioned for the corona.

Division 1—Trumpet Daffodils: The trumpet (corona) is as long or longer than the petals (perianth). One flower per stem. Recommended varieties: 'Arctic Gold' y-y, 'Trousseau' w-y, and 'Cantatrice' w-w.

Division 2—Long-cupped Daffodils: The cup is more than one-third, but less than equal to the length of the petals. One flower per stem. Recommended varieties: 'Festivity' w-y, 'Butterscotch' y-y, 'Old Satin' w-y, 'Ceylon' y-o, and 'Daydream' y-w.

Division 3—Short-cupped Daffodils: The cup is not more than one-third the length of the petals. One flower per stem. Recommended varieties: 'Tranquil Morn' w-wyy and 'Aircastle' w-y.

Division 4—Double Daffodils: The flowers are either double or semi-double in the trumpet or petals. May have more than one flower per stem. Recommended varieties: 'Cheerfulness' w-wyy, 'Erlicheer' w-w, and 'Tahiti' y-yrr.

Division 5—Triandrus Daffodils: Usually more than one flower to a stem, head drooping, petals often reflexed. Recommended varieties: 'Tresamble' w-w, 'Liberty Bells' y-y, and 'Hawera,' miniature, y-y.

Division 6—Cyclamineus Daffodils: Narrow, pendant, usually single flower per stem and reflexed petals. Recommended varieties: 'Tete-a-Tete', miniature, y-o, 'Charity May' y-y, and 'Beryl' y-o.

Division 7—Jonquilla Daffodils: Small, fragrant flowers, 2–6 per stem, rush-like foliage, good for naturalizing in the Southwest. Recommended varieties: 'Stratosphere' y-o, 'Sweetness' y-y, 'Sun Disc', miniature, y-y, 'Suzy' y-o, and 'Quail' y-y.

Division 8—Tazetta Daffodils: Usually 2–6 sweet scented flowers to a stem, very short cupped, rounded petals. Recommended varieties: 'Golden Dawn' y-o and 'Geranium' w-o.

Division 9—Poeticus: One flower per stem, white petals and very small, buttonlike, red-edged cup. Late blooming. Recommended varieties: 'Actaea' w-grr and 'Cantabile' w-g.

Division 10—Species, Wild Forms and Wild Hybrids: Recommended species: 'Jonquilla' y-y, 'Bulbocodium' y-y and 'Cyclamenius' y-y.

Division 11—Split Trumpet Daffodils: The trumpet is split at least one-third of its length. Recommended varieties: 'Cassata' w-w and 'Baccarat' y-y.

Division 12—Miscellaneous Daffodils: Flowers not falling into any of the foregoing divisions (but not pinks or miniatures). Recommended varieties: None.

Nierembergia hippomanica
(ne rem BER gi a   hip o MAN ik a)
CUP FLOWER
Family: Solanaceae ○◗
Zone 8   6″–12″   Spring, Summer, Fall

Nierembergias are native from Mexico to Chile and Argentina. The most popular and widely available cultivar is 'Purple Robe.' One-inch flowers of intense violet nearly cover the finely textured foliage periodically from spring until fall. White flowering types as well as creeping and taller-growing forms are also available.

Cup flowers require a good, well-drained but moist soil and prefer partially shaded exposures. They are grown as perennials in Zones 8–10 and as annuals in colder climates. Propagation is by seed, division or from cuttings taken in the fall. Established clumps should be cut back severely after flowering is completed in the fall.

The rich violet color and dense flowering habit make nierembergias popular in borders and rock gardens. They tend to be short-lived in coastal areas and are better adapted to inland locations.

Oenothera missourensis
(ee no THER uh   miss oo ree EN sis)
OZARK SUNDROP, SHOWY PRIMROSE
Family: Onagraceae ○◗
Zone 5   1′   Spring

This is an interesting perennial that is native to alkaline, rocky soils of the Texas Hill Country. Large (4″), very showy, bright yellow flowers appear a few at a time on the spreading mounds of shiny, dark green foliage. *O. missourensis* is very drought tolerant, but will rot in wet soils. It prefers sunny sites, and blooms for a month or more each year in late spring. Propagation is by seed

Oenothera missourensis—Ozark Sundrop's showy, bright yellow flowers

Ozark Sundrops prefer sunny sites.

or cuttings and availability is better than that of most perennials native to our area.

O. speciosa, Showy Primrose, is one of Texas' most beautiful wildflowers, but an invasive pest in the garden where its running roots make it very difficult to control. It bears beautiful pink or white flowers, two inches across, in great profusion for several weeks each spring. *O. speciosa* grows in poor, dry soils, flourishing almost anywhere and is a beautiful plant, but it is best planted only where it cannot invade cultivated areas.

Ophiopogon japonicus
(oh fee o POE gon   ja PON i cus)
MONKEY GRASS, BORDER GRASS, MONDO GRASS

Family: Liliaceae   ○◐●
Zone 7   6"–12"   Evergreen

Ophiopogon japonicus and its cultivars are smaller plants, generally, than the liriopes to which they are frequently compared. Where foot traffic is light, ophiopogons are sometimes used as turf substitutes, especially in heavy shade, where true grasses will not survive. Because of their extreme shade-tolerance, ophiopogons furnish an invaluable ground cover for use beneath live oaks and magnolias where few other plants will grow. As with liriope, monkey grass forms such a dense turf that interplantings with bulbs and other seasonal color plants usually fail. The dense, dark green foliage is tough and drought tolerant, once established. It is especially attractive in combination with ferns in shady borders.

There are several useful, distinctive cultivars of *O. japonicus*. The common form is readily available in nurseries and garden centers and considerably less expensive than the others. When used as a border or

ground cover, it should be divided into uniform clumps containing three or four plants and spaced approximately six inches on center. Irregular sizing of divisions and spacing result in a patchy appearance that may take years to become uniform. An annual trimming in late winter or early spring with a lawn mower adjusted to its highest setting helps keep large areas of monkey grass uniform and neat. Monkey grass may be divided and reset at any time, but fall and spring plantings require the least amount of post-planting care.

O. japonicus 'nana' is a relatively new and dwarf form of monkey grass that is very useful in finely-detailed, small gardens or as a ground cover for specimens in containers. Although neater and more compact in growth than the species-type, this dwarf form is also slower growing and correspondingly more expensive.

Ophiopogon japonicus—Monkey Grass

Ophiopogon japonicus 'nana'—a dwarf form of monkey grass

O. planiscapus 'Arabicus' offers a striking combination of narrow, purple-black foliage and pink flowers. Because its foliage is so dark, this cultivar should be planted in a light-colored setting. Without this contrast, 'Arabicus' may go unnoticed. *O. Jaburan* is a large-growing plant with leaves up to 2' long and ½" wide. It is often confused with *Liriope muscari* and is sometimes sold as *L. muscari* 'Evergreen Giant.' Borne near the ground, the flowers of the common forms of monkey grass remain hidden among the foliage and are not nearly as showy as those of the liriopes. To protect monkey grasses from leaf scorch during the summer months, plant them where they will receive at least half a day of shade, preferably in the afternoon.

Both monkey grasses and liriopes develop onion-like sections on their roots that resemble bulbs, at least in appearance, but unfortunately, they will not give rise to new plants if removed and replanted. Nor are these fleshy swellings the symptoms of root knot nematodes or any other parasite or disease. They are storage organs, and a primary reason these plants are so drought tolerant.

Opuntia humifusa (O. compressa)
(oh PUN tee uh   hum ee FOO suh)

HARDY SPINELESS PRICKLY PEAR

Family: Cactaceae ◯◑
Zone 7   2'–3'   Yellow

This spineless selection of the familiar Prickly Pear is an interesting garden plant with large, smooth, pads of a rich green color. Its flowers are yellow and the purple fruit is marginally edible. This species is more prostrate than some and, since it has no significant spines (it may exhibit some of the small and less bothersome fine spines), it makes an attractive, practical addition to the arid landscape or border.

O. x 'Ellisiana' is a shrubby type of spineless prickly pear with pale green joints and apricot-yellow blooms, hardy north to Dallas. It is presumably a natural hybrid of *O. Lindheimeri* and *O. Ficus-indica*. Prickly Pears are very coarse-textured plants that are most useful as accents. They are easily propagated by partially burying individual pads in the soil. Flowers are showy during the summer, and are followed by colorful fruit.

Opuntia imbricata—Walking Stick Cholla

Opuntia humifusa—Hardy Spineless Prickly Pear

O. imbricata, Walking Stick Cholla, is hardy even in North Central Texas. It differs markedly in appearance from the Prickly Pears, being more tree or shrub-like with a woody trunk and typically 5'–6' tall. The 3" purple flowers are borne in profusion, making quite a spectacle on mature plants. Fruits are yellow and fleshy, about 1" long. Propagation is not quite as easy as Prickly Pear, but can accomplished with L-shaped cuttings taken in late spring. These should be planted right in the garden soil with one leg underground, the other left uncovered. *O. imbricata* is thorny and slow growing but quite beautiful when mature. It must have a sunny location and well-drained soil.

Ornithogalum umbellatum
(or ni THO ga lum　um bell LAY tum)
STAR OF BETHLEHEM
Family: Liliaceae　　　　　　　　　　　○◑
Zone 7　　1'　　Spring

A native of Europe and North Africa, *O. umbellatum* has naturalized in parts of the eastern United States and may sometimes be found at cemeteries and abandoned homesites in Texas and the Gulf South. It is a clump-forming, spring bulb that is nearly as prolific as the *Muscari racemosum* it resembles in bulb and foliage. A silver stripe marks the center of each leaf, and a green stripe marks the reverse of each petal; the white, star-shaped flowers measure about 1" across, and are borne 5–20 per stem from about mid-March into April. This species makes a good foil for larger bulbs.

O. narbonense is an unusual Star of Bethlehem from southern France that bears graceful wands of white star-shaped flowers on 18" stems. It is well-adapted to heavy black soils and naturalizes in North Texas. Blooms emerge in April on this rather homely but enchanting flower which is reminiscent of wild hyacinth (*Camassia*).

Ornithogalum umbellatum—Star of Bethlehem

O. narbonense is an unusual Star of Bethlehem from France.

Oxalis crassipes
(OX al is   KRA si pees)
PINK WOODS SORREL

Family: Oxalidaceae ○◐●
Zone 4   1′   Pink

Various forms of oxalis occur naturally both as annuals and perennials in Texas and the Gulf South. The annual forms are noxious weeds, but some of the perennials offer material for the garden. The best oxalis for landscape use is, in my opinion, an import from Argentina that has been popular in Southern cottage gardens for many years. Sometimes sold as *O. violacea*, *O. crassipes* is a long-flowering, hardy perennial that makes an excellent plant for a sunny or, preferably, partially-shaded location.

O. crassipes seems to thrive equally well over all parts of Texas and the Gulf South. I have seen them blooming in the fall as well as spring in West and Central Texas and northern Louisiana. Warm spells during the winter can also initiate flowering. Heaviest bloom begins in early spring and lasts until very hot weather. If growing conditions are good in fall, a repeat, but less spectacular, display occurs. The clover-like foliage sometimes dies down during the heat of July and August but remains evergreen under good growing conditions. Flower color varies from pale pink to rose, and includes a rare white form. During the spring season, plants may reach a foot or more in height.

Oxalis prefer rich, sandy soil, partial shade and copious moisture but will flourish in a variety of less ideal conditions. They are useful as an edging plant, for massing in front of shrubs or at the front of a perennial border. Spider mites can be a problem but may be controlled with insecticidal soaps or chemical sprays labeled for mite control. Fall division every 3 or 4 years is beneficial, since otherwise the clumps of small rhizomes may grow excessively dense, forcing themselves one atop the other. Division is not essential, however. *O. crassipes* is considered a minor bulb, but when used effectively in the landscape can create lasting impressions with a minimum of care.

Passiflora incarnata
(pass i FLOR uh   in car NAY tuh)
PASSION VINE

Family: Passifloraceae ○◐
Zone 7   15′–20′   Summer, Fall

Passion vines are root hardy in most of our region, although the vines freeze back to the ground with the first severe cold. The bright green leaves are three-lobed and serrated along their margins. Long, prominent tendrils act as hold-fasts for the fast-growing stems. The flowers are as exotic in appearance as the name suggests, about 3″ in diameter, pinkish-lavender in color with a fine, delicate fringe. They open in the morning to again close at night, and are reported to be symbolic of the Crucifixion.

Despite the tropical beauty of its bloom, *P. incarnata* is actually a rather common native. Several related species are foreign in origin, but are less cold hardy. The fruit of the Passion Vine is large, 2″–3″ in diameter, egg-shaped and reported to be edible. One species, *P. edulis*, is grown in the tropics as a food crop. Propagation of the Passion Vines is from seed, cuttings or the root sprouts, which are plentiful enough to become a nuisance in good soils. Passion Vines are easily grown and a good source of quick shade and exotic flowers for the southern landscape.

Oxalis crassipes—Pink Woods Sorrel

Oxalis crassipes 'album'—white blossoms

Pavonia lasiopetala—Rock Rose

Pavonia lasiopetala
(pa VON ee uh   las ee oh PET ah la)

ROCK ROSE

Family: Malvaceae ⦿◗

Zone 8   3′–4′   Spring, Summer, Fall

Pavonias are drought tolerant, shrubby perennials that are very useful in borders and masses. The five-petaled, single, rose-pink flowers are about 1½″ in diameter and they bloom in sufficient profusion to create a pleasant sprinkling of color. They close in the afternoon and open again the next morning.

Pavonias grow in light or heavy soils, but do not thrive where drainage is poor. The major cultural requirement is a periodic shearing, a treatment that keeps the plant compact and in flower. *P. lasiopetala* serves as an excellent subject for dry borders in arid regions. It also shows to good advantage in containers. Propagation is from seed, or cuttings taken during winter or summer.

Penstemon Cobaea
(PEN steh mon   koh BEE uh)

BEARD-TONGUE, WILD FOXGLOVE

Family: Scrophulariaceae ⦿◗

Zone 5   1′–2′   Spring

P. Cobaea is one of the showiest native perennials. It may be found growing naturally from Central Texas to Kansas, and prefers open, sunny areas having well-drained, alkaline soils. Flowers resemble snapdragons and emerge in mid-spring; usually lavender, they may also be white, purple, or any shade in the range between. The evergreen foliage forms small clumps of relatively large, simple leaves. Individual plants increase slowly, but may sometimes be divided in the fall or early spring. Seed propagation is reported to be successful, although my limited attempts have not been so. Wild Foxglove is

a plant of considerable landscape value, but a lack of commercial sources is limiting its use. Until a means is found to propagate it readily, its beauty will have to remain primarily a part of our beautiful natural landscape.

P. tenuis, Sharp-sepal Penstemon, Brazos Penstemon, is a small flowering species native to coastal areas of Texas and Louisiana. Individual flowers measure only about ¾″ but bloom profusely in loose, showy, terminal panicles from mid-spring until early summer. The only color I have grown is a lavender-pink, but pale-pink to dark-rose forms are reported in the literature. *P. tenuis* is a good garden plant that creates an almost ethereal effect

Penstemon Cobaea—Beard-Tongue, Wild Foxglove

D. Greg Grant

P. tenuis—a good filler in the border

White penstemon

Penstemon tenuis—Sharp-sepal Penstemon, Brazos Penstemon

for many weeks. The color is soft and it combines well with other perennials.

Mature height in flower is about 2′. When the blooms fade they should be cut back to near ground level, unless seed production is desired. They often respond to this pruning with another, but less showy round of blossoms. *P. tenuis* seems to prefer slightly acid soils but is not very particular about drainage. It is very easily grown and readily self-sows seed to produce plenty of new plants. Mature clumps may be divided in the fall or very early spring.

P. murrayanus, Cup-leaf Penstemon, is a brilliant red-flowering species native to acid sands of East Texas. Foliage is a distinctive blue-gray; 1¼″ flowers open in pairs on showy terminal panicles that may be 3′–6′ tall. Clumps of foliage may be divided in the fall but they have never become large enough to disturb in my garden. A better means of propagation is from seed sown in early fall. *P. murrayanus* is best grown in well drained, acid soils with low fertility. It may need staking but is a worthy candidate for the back of perennial borders.

I have been unable to identify a white penstemon given to me by a friend in Beaumont, Texas. Individual flowers are not as large as *P. Cobaea*, but considerably larger than *P. tenuis*. It appears to be very well adapted and performs well in my garden with a long bloom period in spring. *P. barbatus* and its many cultivars are among the most popular perennials in other parts of the nation, but will not survive our long, hot summers in Texas and the Gulf South. Penstemons are a useful and beautiful group of plants with considerable garden potential. Like many of our native perennials, they deserve much more study and trials than they have received in the past.

Perovskia atriplicifolia
(peh ROF ski uh   a tri pli ki FOE lee uh)
RUSSIAN SAGE

Family: Labiatae   ○◗
Zone 6   3′–4′   Summer

Russian Sage is becoming quite popular in the Southeast and seems to do well for us in Texas and the Gulf South. Foliage is cut-leaf, gray and quite attractive in itself. Spikes of lavender-blue flowers are borne during the long summer season. The plant may need pruning occasionally during the growing season to keep it shapely.

Russian Sage prefers a sunny, well-drained location. It should be cut back in winter or early spring, but will quickly grow back during spring and early summer. Cut foliage from Russian Sage contributes a cool gray to floral arrangements, and releases a light sage-like scent when handled. Propagation is primarily from cuttings, but also from division.

Perovskia atriplicifolia—Russian Sage

Phlox divaricata
(FLOCKS die VARE i kah tuh)
BLUE PHLOX, WILD SWEET WILLIAM
Family: Polemoniaceae ○◑
Zone 5   12″–15″   Spring

    P. divaricata is valuable for its long season of bloom, compact form, and ease of culture. Showy clusters of flowers stand on erect stems well above the foliage in March and April. In addition to the common blue-lavender form, a creamy white cultivar, 'Fuller's White,' and a violet-blue, 'Laphamii', are sometimes available. Foliage is a dense mass of opposite, linear leaves whose edges are lined with fine, sticky hairs. Leaves are a bright, light green in early spring, turning a much darker green during the summer. Blue Phlox are semi-evergreen in Texas and the Gulf South, although they are of little landscape impact when not in bloom.

    P. divaricata is native to the eastern U. S. and from Florida to East Texas. It grows best with morning sun and at least partial shade in the afternoon. Soil must be well-drained, and if the phlox are to thrive, it should contain large amounts of organic material such as composted pine bark, peat, or compost. Apply a balanced fertilizer immediately after flowering. Phlox are not very drought tolerant and benefit from a summer mulch and fairly frequent irrigation during dry spells. Propagation is by division, cuttings, or seed.

    P. divaricata will tolerate considerable shade and is an excellent plant for semi-shady borders. It combines well with spring flowering bulbs, and has an informal, loose appearance compatible with cottage and woodland gardens. The long bloom season and showy flowers make Blue Phlox one of the best spring-flowering perennials.

    P. subulata, commonly known as Moss Pink, is a matt forming, prostrate phlox to 6″, with exceptionally

Phlox divaricata—Blue Phlox, Wild Sweet William

showy spring blooms. Foliage is fine textured and mossy in appearance, evergreen and fairly drought tolerant. Excellent drainage is an absolute requirement of this plant, and in gardens close to the Gulf, where humidity and rainfall are high, Moss Pink often rots. This is a wonderful rock garden plant since it is very compact in form and creeps over rocks and edgings. The primary hue is a loud pink, although many other colors are available. I have found this pink sort to be the only one that lasts in my garden, although I have tried a half-dozen various colors. It is also the only one I have found in old gardens of Texas and the Gulf South. Phlox are rarely found in abandoned gardens and cemeteries since they degenerate unless divided every few years. They begin flowering with the first warm spells of late winter, bloom heavily in March, then scatter flowers until mid-May.

    Propagation of *P. subulata* is primarily by division, or by cuttings taken in mid-fall. Old clumps seem to die out, much like dianthus, making it advisable to divide

P. subulata—Moss Pink

Moss Pink is a wonderful rock garden plant for its compactness & characteristic creeping nature.

P. pilosa—Prairie or Downy Phlox

P. paniculata—Summer Phlox or Border Phlox prefer well-prepared garden soil.

mature clumps or start some new cuttings each fall. Moss Pinks prefer sandy, relatively poor soils. They tend to "move around" in the garden but are usually welcome wherever they go.

P. paniculata, better known as Summer Phlox or Border Phlox, bloom in summer and early fall. They are common in old gardens throughout the South and are well worth consideration for the perennial border. Summer Phloxes also come in many colors although a pink form, almost as bright as the common loud pink *P. subulata*, is the only one I find in old Texas and Gulf South gardens, with the rare exception of a pure white cultivar. *P. paniculata* prefers well-prepared garden soil, high in fertility and organic content, although they will grow fairly well, even if unattended, in less desirable surroundings. Protection from hot afternoon sun, a summer mulch, and frequent watering will result in a longer bloom and higher quality flowers.

Summer Phlox bloom for prolonged periods in the summer. If dead-heading is performed conscientiously, and the plants are kept well watered, they will often repeat in late summer and early fall. Staking is usually necessary since normal height is 3'-4' and stems tend to be weak. Summer Phlox are excellent for the middle or back of deep borders where their blossoms may be seen, but their leggy stems are partially hidden. Propagation is by division of clumps in fall and early spring, or from cuttings. Individual plants should be placed about 18" apart and clumps should be divided every third year.

P. pilosa, Prairie or Downy Phlox, is a species native to pine woodlands in the region. It is somewhat similar to *P. divaricata*, but bears pinkish-blue or, rarely, white spring flowers on 15" stems. Culture is similar to *P. divaricata*. All of the perennial phlox are winter-hardy.

Physostegia virginiana
(fie zoh STEE jah)

OBEDIENT PLANT, FALSE DRAGONHEAD

Family: Labiatae ◯◐
Zone 5   2'–4'   Late Summer, Fall

Few perennials are at their best in late summer and early fall, but several cultivars of the Obedient Plant do span that period with handsome spikes of snapdragon-shaped flowers. They were given the name Obedient Plant because the individual flowers are attached to the plant on a hinged stalk that holds its position if moved to the right or left.

The common form of *P. virginiana* is a rather loud lavender-pink. This begins flowering in late August or September and may continue through October. Cultivar 'Summer Snow' is pure white, blooms a month or more earlier, usually in late June or July, and is also less aggressive in the garden. 'Vivid' is more compact, usually limiting itself to a height of about 2', and starts blooming in September to carry on through the fall with attractive pink flowers. 'Variegata' is an excellent foliage plant, each leaf of which is evenly edged in white. Flowers of 'Variegata' are similar to the common form.

Physostegias like moisture and can tolerate fairly wet locations. They suffer, but usually do not die, during dry spells. If grown in the sun or filtered light they may not need staking. Tip-pruning in May or June helps keep the plants stocky. Clumps spread so rapidly in moist, fertile soils that they can become a nuisance. 'Summer Snow' and 'Vivid' are not nearly as aggressive as the common form. This vigorous increase of the plants does aid the process of propagation, which is achieved through division in early spring.

Physostegia virginiana—Obedient Plant

Physostegia variety 'Summer Snow'

Platycodon grandiflorus— Balloon Flower

'Obedient Plant' is common in country gardens of the South and may sometimes be found lingering on at abandoned homesites. It is very well adapted to the region, but needs sufficient moisture in late summer and early fall to produce a real show.

Platycodon grandiflorus
(pla tih KOE don)
BALLOON FLOWER

Family: Campanulaceae   ◯◑
Zone 4   1½'–3'   Late Spring

P. grandiflorus receives its name from the shape of its buds. It is marginally adapted to the Gulf South, succeeding much better in areas a hundred miles or more inland from the coast. Star-shaped flowers open from the round buds in blue, pink, or white. There are also handsome, semi-double forms, as well as dwarf and large-growing cultivars.

Though the Balloon Flower is a late spring bloomer, by removing spent flowers the gardener can extend its flowering into the summer. Well-drained and well-prepared soil is preferred, along with some protection from hot afternoon sun during the summer months. In wintertime, the Balloon Flower enters a deep dormancy from which it is slow to emerge in spring. Transplanting should be left to fall or early spring, with care being taken not to damage the plant's carrot-like tap root. This plant may be propagated easily from seed, and seedlings usually bloom the second year from sowing. Mature clumps may be divided, but it is not necessary to do so for the well-being of the plants.

Plumbago auriculata
(plum BA go a rik u LA ta)
BLUE PLUMBAGO

Family: Plumbaginaceae   ◯◑
Zone 9   3'–4'   Spring, Summer, Fall

Hot, dry, summer weather takes its toll on many ornamentals, but established plants of Blue Plumbago will keep on blooming through the dog days with a minimum of care. In the southern half of Texas and the Gulf South, Plumbago is a dependable perennial, but in northern areas it requires replanting each spring.

The major value of this plant is the almost continuous display of clusters of blue, phlox-like flowers it mounts from May until frost. Since flower color varies unpredictably from a clear, light blue to pure white, it is a good idea to select plants while they are in bloom if a particular hue is desired.

Blue Plumbago appreciates good drainage but will do well in fairly poor soils. Plants may be slow to start but are tough, drought tolerant, and long lasting, once established. Mass plantings are one effective way to use Blue Plumbago, but they serve also as cover for slopes and as background or filler plants in the border. The graceful, arching growth habit has a softness that blends well in a variety of settings.

Mature height is usually 3'–4' with a similar spread, but individual branches can become almost vine-like, climbing several additional feet if given support. Full sun or partially shaded exposures both suit equally well. If a heavy frost blackens the foliage, the whole plant should be cut back to ground level. A winter

Plumbago auriculata—Blue Plumbago

Plumbago's almost continuous display of blue flower clusters

mulch can often provide sufficient protection to extend the plant's territory through much of Zone 8. Plumbagos that are set out in spring usually have ample time to become sufficiently established to return the next year.

Propagation is from seed or cuttings. Seedlings often volunteer in the vicinity of established plantings, and mature specimens can be divided during the spring and early summer. It is not necessary, however, to divide Blue Plumbago to keep it growing vigorously. Small potted plants can be purchased economically, and are ideal for setting out in early spring, but gallon or larger container specimens are best for midsummer to early fall plantings. Since cold damage is likely in most parts of Texas, it is best not to set out new plants after October 1.

An outstanding summertime planting is the combination of Blue Plumbago with a white form of the annual Madagascar Periwinkle such as 'Little Blanche.' The effect is cool and refreshing, while the two plants share a near-invulnerability to heat and drought.

Polianthes tuberosa
(pol ee AN theez   too buh ROE suh)
MEXICAN TUBEROSE

Family: Agavaceae   ○◑
Zone 9   2'–4'   Late Summer

This is one of the most fragrant flowering plants of summer. Like corn and dahlias, tuberoses were domesticated by pre-Columbian Indians of Mexico and are not known as wild plants. Tuberoses are still popular in Mexican gardens, where they are called "Nardo" or "Azucena." *P. tuberosa* has been grown commercially for florists and bulb distributors in the San Antonio area for many years. They are also grown commercially in the south of France as cut flowers and as a source of perfume. Flowers are white, tubular, and loosely arranged on spikes that can reach 3'–4' in height. The season of

bloom is late summer to early fall. Foliage is long, slender, and grass-like, with little landscape value.

Nematodes can be a problem that limits the performance of affected plants. 'Mexican Single' performs best in hot climates; double 'Pearl' often fails to open properly except in cooler fall weather. *P. howardii*, with its red and green, unscented blooms, seems to resist nematode attacks and grows well in heavy alkaline soils.

P. tuberosa grows from elongated tubers that are planted in mid-spring. These may be left in the ground year-round when grown in sunny, well-drained areas of Zones 9 and 10, but in more northern locations the tubers should be lifted and stored like gladiolus after the foliage has yellowed. The tubers always show a point of green if they are alive and healthy. For a mass effect in the border, tubers should be planted 4"–6" apart and 2" deep in well-prepared garden soil. Sunny locations with some protection from hot afternoon sun are ideal.

Polianthes tuberosa—Mexican Tuberose

Poliomintha longiflora
(pol ee oh MEN thuh   lon gi FLOR uh)
MEXICAN OREGANO

Family: Labiatae ◯◗
Zone 9   2′–4′   Summer

Mexican Oregano is a beautiful plant with small, lance-shaped, aromatic leaves. Although not the plant most commonly grown as the pot herb oregano, *P. longiflora* has a similar scent and is often used for that purpose. The flowers are borne in clusters in summertime and are lavender-pink, tubular shaped, and about 1½″ long. As they age, the blossoms pale to a lighter lavender or white. Propagation is by cuttings of the somewhat brittle stems. Plants form fairly compact mounds and are pleasant in groups.

P. longiflora grows well in sun or partial shade, but must have porous, well-drained soil. It is fairly drought tolerant and blooms over a long period during the late spring and summer. Cold tolerance is questionable north of Central Texas.

According to Manuel Flores, a botanist and nurseryman from San Antonio, knowledge of the introduction of *P. longiflora* is sketchy but revolves around Kim Keeble and the Huntington Botanical Gardens in California. Its introduction can be traced back to the Black Sun Herb Farm and Rusty Crowley of the Casa Verde Growers near San Antonio. It was found growing wild in the mountains south of Monterrey, Mexico, and was used locally for flavoring meats such as *cabrito* (barbecued goat), and as a tea. It never seems to set seed in cultivation, possibly due to the lack of a proper pollinator.

Poliomintha longiflora—Mexican Oregano

Ranunculus macranthus—Large Flowered Buttercup

Ranunculus repens 'Flore Pleno'
(ra NUNK kew lus   REE pens)
BUTTERCUP

Family: Ranunculaceae ◯◗
Zone 5   1′   Spring

This plant has not bloomed as well for me as in photographs I have seen from other areas, but the foliage alone is worthwhile. Creeping Buttercup is a double flowering form of a colonizing European buttercup, though it has naturalized in some parts of the United States. Flowers are ¾″ across, green centered, very double, and waxy yellow. Leaves are three-lobed and triangular, and 3″–4″ across, somewhat resembling a dark, glossy green form of celery.

Creeping Buttercup has colonized a moist, fairly shady area in my garden where it has formed a loose ground cover. It spreads by stolons that root at each node as it touches to ground. This plant suffers greatly during

dry weather and should only be planted where moisture is abundant.

R. macranthus, Large-Flowered Buttercup, is native to damp places in Central Texas and in scattered locations along the Rio Grande River and Trans-Pecos areas. It produces waxy-yellow 2″ flowers in profusion on plants that can reach 2′ during March and April. Leaves are 5–7 lobed, handsome, and long-stalked. Although rarely available in the nursery trade, *R. macranthus* definitely has garden merit.

Ratibida columnaris
(ra tee BEE duh   ko lum NAR is)
MEXICAN HAT

Family: Compositae ◯◗
Zone 7   2′–3′   Summer, Fall

Though a Texas native, this flower is more often seen in European gardens than in Texas and the Gulf

South. The ray flowers are yellow-orange with a deep reddish-brown base that surrounds the prominent, greenish central cones. Mexican Hats are drought resistant, but also flourish in coastal areas where soils and moisture vary greatly. For this reason, the plant is compatable with a wide variety of garden perennials, many of which require more moisture.

Foliage is finely cut and has a light and airy appearance that blends well with other perennials. If spent flowers and stems are removed, flowering will often recur in late summer. Plants should be cut to the ground after the first hard frost. Ratibida grows easily from seed and often self-sows in the garden. Plants usually bloom the second year from seed. The annual form of this plant, *R. peduncularis*, is similar in appearance. Both forms set large quantities of seed.

Rhodophiala bifida
(roe doe FEE ah luh   BIF ih duh)
OXBLOOD LILY

Family: Amaryllidaceae   ○◗
Zone 8   10″−12″   Early Fall

R. bifida is an extremely well-adapted and interesting fall-blooming Amaryllid that was brought to Texas from Argentina early in the 20th century. It was introduced by a German plantsman and early colonist of Central Texas named Heinrich Oberwetter. Oxblood Lily blooms along with the lycoris and is often confused with it. It has settled very succesfully in Central and East Texas where large displays often mark old homesites. An extensive planting on the former site of old Allen Academy in Bryan, Texas, includes the rosy-pink form

Rhodophiala bifida—Oxblood Lily resembles a small red amaryllis with its strap-like foliage.

'Spathacea.' An orange cultivar, 'Granatiflora,' is also reported to exist.

Oxblood Lily seems equally well-adapted to heavy clay or deep, sandy soils. The flowers resemble small red amaryllises and are borne several to a stem. Foliage is strap-like and emerges after flowering, to flourish through the winter, and then yellow and disappear by summer. The best time to dig and divide *R. bifida* comes just as the foliage yellows. Bulbs set 6″−8″ apart and about 3″ deep create an effective display by the second year. The common form rarely sets seed in cultivation but offsets prolifically. Seed-bearing strains often vary in color.

Another common name for this interesting and well-adapted plant is "schoolhouse lily" because it usually blooms about the time school starts each fall. Flowering is triggered by the first soaking rain in late August or September, after which the flower stalks quickly spring forth to create their magical effect. *R. bifida* is most effective when planted in relatively large "drifts" but may also be used as a border.

Rosmarinus officinalis
(rose may REE nus)
ROSEMARY

Family: Labitae   ○◗
Zone 8   2′−4′   Late Spring

Many landscape plants suffer during the dry heat of August but Rosemary thrives on it. Although usually cold hardy in South Texas, some winter protection may be needed elsewhere in Texas and the Gulf South. Once established, Rosemary grows well even in poor, dry, rocky soils so long as the drainage is good. In fact, it is more cold tolerant in such situations than when grown in rich soils. There are many forms of *R. officinalis*, most of which are useful and attractive plants well-suited to planting with perennials.

The genus name *Rosmarinus* means dew of the sea, while the "officinalis" part of the name indicates that the plant was one used for medicinal purposes. Rosemary was an essential ingredient of early herb and kitchen gardens, and is almost always present in English cottage gardens. There it is often planted close to the front door, where people would brush against it as they passed, to release some of the foliage's clean, rich scent. The foliage is popular, fresh or dried, for seasoning. Reportedly, an aromatic oil used in perfumery and medicine is distilled from the Rosemary's fresh needles.

The evergreen character of the narrow foliage qualifies this as an especially ornamental plant, just as its many distinct horticultural forms make it an unusually versatile one. Prostrate selections furnish an unusual ground cover and make an attractive detail as they spill over retaining walls. Upright forms provide materials for a compact hedge or an elegant container-plant. Mature heights range from 18″ to 4′, depending upon the variety and growing conditions. Small lavender-blue flowers in spring and summer are attractive but not spectacular.

'Lockwood deForest' is an upright variety reported to tolerate cold particularly well. It bears dark blue flowers and tends to rebloom better than most cultivars. Said to be a hybrid of *R. prostratus* and *R. x* 'Tuscan Blue,' this like all Rosemarys thrives in dry, calcareous soils. 'Prostratus' is a low spreading form that rarely exceeds 2′ in height. It is not as cold hardy as the upright forms, but is worth moving or covering for a few nights each winter. 'Albus' is a white flowering cultivar; 'Tuscan Blue' an upright and rigid Rosemary with blue-violet flowers; and 'Collingwood Ingram' a bright, blue-violet flowering cultivar with graceful, curving branches. Mrs. Madelene Hill, a well-known herb authority from Cleveland, Texas, found a hardy rosemary in 1972 in Arp, Texas, that is said to be hardy to Washington, D.C. . The National Arboretum has given this plant the name *R. officinalis* 'Arp'. *R. corsicus* is pine-scented, but similar in its lack of cold hardiness to the prostrate forms.

Rosemary is propagated from cuttings. If pencil-size cuttings are taken in late fall or early winter, the leaves removed from the bottom half of the stems, and then stuck in moist garden soil, they will reliably root by summer. In moist climates, where rosemaries often prove short-lived, it is a good idea to root new plants periodically. If grown in containers, the plants may be moved to a more protected location during the coldest part of winter.

An interesting note concerning the landscape use of Rosemary comes from Miss Gertrude Jekyll in her book *Wood and Garden*:

> ". . . . . bushes of Rosemary, some just filling the border, and some trained up the wall. Our Tudor ancestors were fond of Rosemary-covered walls, and I have seen old bushes quite ten feet high on the garden walls of Italian monasteries. Among the Rosemaries I always like, if possible, to "tickle in" a China Rose or two, the tender pink of the Rose seems to go so well with the dark but dull-surfaced Rosemary (204–205).

Rudbeckia maxima
(rood BECK ee uh   MAKS ee muh)
CONEFLOWER, BLACK-EYED SUSAN

Family: Compositae   ○◑
Zone 7   5′–6′   Summer

Coneflowers are native to much of Texas and the Gulf South. They prefer dry, well-drained soils and sunny locations where they yield generous crops of 4″, black-eyed yellow flowers during June and July.

Rosmarinus officinialis—Rosemary

Rudbeckia fulgida 'Goldsturm'—Black-Eyed Susan

These blossoms are ray-type; the yellow petals center on the black cone that gives this flower its name. Foliage is a dense rosette of grayish-green leaves, 6″–8″ long, and 2″–3″ wide. Propagation is by seeds and division. Young seedlings may sometimes be found in the vicinity of parent plants, but *R. maxima* is not overly aggressive in the garden.

R. fulgida 'Goldsturm' is a compact selection of *R. fulgida* that is fast becoming a favorite in Southern gardens. It blooms from mid to late summer with masses of golden-yellow, black-eyed daisies and must be propagated by division since it does not come true from seed. Seedlings are likely to be good garden plants, but not exactly like the parent. Since it is very vigorous in most of Texas and the Gulf South, 'Goldsturm' may be divided each year in early spring or fall.

It performs best in sunny locations but, like all Rudbeckias, occasionally "melts" in Gulf Coast gardens.

R. grandiflora, Giant Coneflower, is a rhizomatous perennial native from Missouri and Oklahoma to Louisiana and Texas. It can reach a height of 3′ and bears large yellow flowers with brown-purple centers. Giant Coneflowers are usually found in low-lying areas, but adapt well to garden culture. Sunny or partially shaded locations are best. Propagation is by seed, or by division of mature clumps.

Ruellia Brittoniana
(roo EL ee uh   brit tohn ee AN uh)
MEXICAN PETUNIA

Family: Acanthaceae   ○◐
Zone 8   3′   Spring, Summer, Fall

This desirable plant is native to Mexico, but has escaped cultivation to naturalize in some areas of Texas

Ruellia "Blue Shade"

Ruellia malacosperma—Mexican Petunia variety

and the Gulf South. There are *Ruellias* that are native to our area, but these related species are nothing more than troublesome and persistent weeds. The Mexican Petunia, by contrast, is an extremely tough, drought resistant plant that blooms for a very long period and requires no maintenance. It grows in any soil, clay or sand, and tolerates wet or dry conditions. Flowers resemble lavender-colored petunias borne on tall stems. Leaves are narrow, in the case of *R. Brittoniana*, and broader leaves on the equally common and similar *R. malacosperma*. Clumps tend to surround themselves with shoots and can become invasive in good soils, if not controlled. *R.* "Blue Shade" is a low-growing form popular as a ground cover in the San Antonio area. It seldom exceeds 10″ in height, and grows best in partially shaded locations. Propagation is by seeds, cuttings, or division. Ruellias are among the most carefree perennials and can be attractive in the center or back of wide borders. They are often found marking abandoned homesites, and in older gardens of the region.

Salvia coccinea
(SAL vee uh   KOK sin ay uh)
SCARLET SAGE

Family: Labiatae   ○◐
Zone 8   1′–2′   Spring, Summer, Fall

Although native to sandy soils of Gulf South states, Scarlet Sage adapts well to a wide variety of cultural situations. Flowers appear on 2″–7″, spike-like racemes over a long period, and are fairly similar to the commonly sold annual form of *S. splendens*. Scarlet Sage tolerates full sun, but does best where it gets some afternoon shade. Propagation is by seed or cuttings. Only rarely available in nurseries, *S. coccinea* is a useful plant for massing in the perennial border. After hard frost, the foliage should be cut to the ground. Mulching is helpful in northern extremeties of its range to prevent excessive root damage.

Salvia elegans—Pineapple Sage

S. elegans, Pineapple Sage, is an interesting ornamental and culinary herb for gardens in our area. Dried and fresh leaves of *S. elegans* have a pineapple or fruity scent useful for seasoning. It is a brilliant red-flowering salvia native to Mexico that is usually grown as an annual. In Zones 9 and 10, however, it often survives from year to year as a perennial, and makes an interesting addition to the border or herb garden. Propagation is by seeds or cuttings. Plants should be cut back and mulched after the first frost.

S. farinacea is among the most useful perennials for our area.

In the southern half of Texas and Gulf South states, it returns reliably from the roots each spring. In other areas it is well worth planting as a long-flowering annual. There are relatively few blue flowers from which to choose, and this one is a dependable source of lavender-blue, purple, or white, depending upon the cultivar selected.

Blue Sage is native to alkaline soils of Central, West, and South Texas, but will adapt to almost any soil condition. It produces a more compact growth in sunny exposures, but will make a presentable display in partial shade. Propagation is from cuttings, seeds, or division of mature clumps. In addition to the common, native form, several cultivars are commonly available. 'Victoria' is a moderately dark blue-purple that tends to be more compact (about 18″) than the species. 'Blue Bedder' is a good medium blue. The only white cultivar of which I am aware is 'Porcelain', which is actually more of a grayish-white.

In normal landscape settings, Blue Sage tends to grow much more luxuriantly than it does in its native environment. To keep it looking neat and attractive, I find it helpful to prune the plants back heavily, at least once, in late summer. With a little supplemental watering they come back quickly to provide a wonderful fall display. Shearing old bloom spikes also helps to keep the plants neat and in good flower production. Plants should be cut to the ground after the first hard freeze. *S. farinacea* is a useful plant for massing in the perennial border. It is sufficiently versatile to thrive in low-water-use or conventional landscape settings.

S. Greggii is known as Autumn Sage or Cherry Sage. The name Autumn Sage conjures the image of a fall flowering herb. Some references describe *S. Greggii* as fall blooming only, which is far from true. My experience with the plant over a twenty-year period has been that it is almost constantly in flower from late spring until hard frost. The species name Greggii honors Josiah Gregg (1806–1850), an early American explorer and botanist. *S. Greggii* is native to dry sunny sites in southern and western Texas and New Mexico. It may also be found in

Salvia farinacea var. 'Victoria'

Salvia farinacea var. 'Porcelain'

S. Greggii—Autumn Sage or Cherry Sage

the Mexican states of Coahuila, Sonora, and Durango. It is actually classed as a sub-shrub, since it normally does not die back in the winter.

Although generally ignored by most nurserymen and home gardeners in this century, *S. Greggii* was a plant frequently found in the cottage gardens of early Texas. Once established, the plant usually thrives on existing rainfall. It does need at least tolerably good drainage, but succeeds in either full sun or partially shaded exposures. Thanks to an increasing awareness on the part of the gardening public, this plant is beginning to see more use.

In recent years, the development of a broad range of colors within the species has greatly increased its landscape value. Pure whites, rich reds, pinks, and salmons have now joined the more common purplish-red selection. Flowers borne in the terminal racemes are tube-shaped and two-lipped, about one inch long. Leaves are opposite, narrowly oblong with a blade length of ½″ to 1¼″. Foliage has a pleasant, spicy scent. Propagation is usually from cuttings taken during the growing season.

Landscape uses of *S. Greggii* are many. It is a natural for use in containers or massed in borders for low maintenance landscape color. In settings where a more refined look is desired, the plants respond very well to periodic shearings of old flower stems during the summer. Occasional light applications of a balanced fertilizer and irrigation during unusually dry periods will ensure repeat flowering from May through November in most of Texas and the Gulf South.

Little is known about this species' winter hardiness north of the Dallas-Fort Worth area, but West and South Texas are excellent locations. Well-drained sites in East Texas also produce handsome specimens. *S. Greggii* is a beautiful, practical source of landscape color in most of Texas and the Gulf South. It furnishes another example of the "rediscovery" of plants that were popular in the early gardens of our region but that have been ignored in the recent past.

S. guaranitica is another salvia, one that is interesting primarily for its magnificent dark-blue to violet-blue flowers. A native of Brazil, Paraguay, and Argentina, it is often cultivated as an annual since it is not very cold tolerant. Plants seldom exceed a height of 3′ and bloom over a long period during the summer and fall. *S. guaranitica* may have the richest colored blue flowers of any plant I know. It is propagated from cuttings, and grows best in well-drained soils in partial sun.

S. leucantha, Mexican Bush Sage, is a rather recent introduction to my garden, but one I plan to keep. Plants can become rather large 5′–6′ mounds, but are

S. guarantica—dark-blue to violet-blue flowers

S. leucantha—Mexican Bush Sage

S. leucantha with uniform deep rose-purple spikes and flowers

more typically 3′–4′. Foliage is large for a salvia and grayish-green. It blooms only in the fall, but is quite spectacular during late September, October, and November, when it sends up long, slender, rose-purple spikes studded with small white flowers. There are clones of this plant that bear flowers of other colors, my favorite being one that produces spikes and flowers of a uniform deep rose-purple. Mexican Bush Sage furnishes good cut flowers and is very drought tolerant. It is probably not reliably root hardy north of Zone 9. Propagation is from cuttings, or by division of mature clumps in the spring. Mexican Bush Sage is a spectacular plant for specimen or border use.

S. 'Indigo Spires' is a recent release from the Huntington Botanical Garden in California. It is reported to be a cross between *S. farinacea* and *S. longispicata*. Although I have grown it for only two years, I consider it the most beautiful and useful of all the salvias I know. 'Indigo Spires' much resembles *S. farinacea*, but the flowers are much larger (up to 15″ long), the color more intense (a rich blue-purple), so that the plant makes a more dramatic statement in the landscape. Cold hardiness is a major question, since we have not had a cold winter in the past two years. In good, well-drained soil and full sun, my plant has made a 4′ mound, blooming from spring until hard frost. Propagation is from cuttings taken during the growing season.

The salvias are a diverse and extremely useful group of plants for Texas and the Gulf South. If managed properly, they can be useful in both refined or naturalistic settings. Many perform well with little water. The keys to keeping them attractive are shearing, fertilizing, and watering during the growing season (though many perform well despite drought), and a cutting back after they freeze. Few plants offer so much color for so little care.

S. 'Indigo Spires'

Santolina virens—variety of Lavender Cotton

Santolina Chamaecyparissus
(san toe LIE nuh   ka mee SIH per ris us)
LAVENDER COTTON

Family: Compositae   ◯◖
Zone 7   1½′   Summer

Though actually a sub-shrub, Santolina is often planted with perennials. It is a fine textured, mounded plant that tends to be short-lived in the South. Yellow button-like flowers appear in summer if plants are not clipped. Santolina must have very well-drained soil and a sunny location. It is useful in dry landscapes and well-adapted to West Texas. Plants look better when clipped fairly often. Gray Santolina can make an impressive border or low hedge, but plants die occasionally, leaving conspicuous vacancies. Best use is probably as masses in dry land borders and as ground cover around green plants. *S. virens* is very similar but with deep green leaves of interesting texture. Flowers are creamy-chartreuse rather than bright-yellow. Santolinas are well-adapted to dry, alkaline soils, and are propagated by cuttings.

Saxifraga stolonifera
(saks ee FRA gah   stoe lon IF er uh)
STRAWBERRY GERANIUM

Family: Saxifragaceae   ◖●
Zone 6   4″–6″   Spring

Strawberry Geranium is a native of eastern Asia and used as ground cover for shady, protected areas or in shaded rock gardens. It burns easily in the hot summer sun of our region and must have shade for much of the day. Foliage is evergreen, in basal clusters, coarsely toothed and about 3″ across. Leaves are reddish on the underside, green and white with white veins above. The small, white flowers give a cloud-like appearance for a short time each spring. Strawberry Geranium likes moisture, but must have well-drained soil. Propagation is by division of rooted stolons. 'Tricolor' is an interesting pink-and-cream variegated cultivar that is sometimes available.

Saponaria officinalis 'Flore Plena'
(sap oh NAR ee uh)
SOAPWORT

Family: Carophyllaceae   ◯◖
Zone 7   1'–2'   Summer

Bouncing Bet is an interesting perennial that is well adapted to most of Texas and the Gulf South. It spreads by rhizomes, has lance-shaped leaves about 3"–4" long, and bears fragrant, double, pink, phlox-like flowers from late spring until fall. It is a tough plant that will tolerate a wide variety of growing conditions. I first saw it growing in a dry, rocky area on the former homesite of General Sam Houston at Independence, Texas. I have also seen it on an abandoned homesite near San Antonio. The foliage makes an attractive, dense ground cover, and the flowers are quite showy.

S. officinalis has long been used as a cleansing agent, for in addition to its supposed medicinal properties, the roots contain a lather that serves as a soap substitute. Propagation is by division, or by cuttings taken at almost any season. Bouncing Bet is a lush, green plant that is very drought tolerant, though the foliage burns in very sunny areas during the hottest days of summer. Flowers appear in abundance in late spring or early summer, to repeat occasionally during late summer and early fall. Shearing old blossoms and stems keeps the plants looking better, and stimulates rebloom later in the season. The plants appear to be resistant to insects and diseases. Bouncing Bet is native to Europe and Asia but is reported to have naturalized in North America. It grows well in dry or moist areas.

Saponaria officinalis 'Flore Plena'—Soapwort

Scilla hyacinthoides
(SILL uh   high a sin THOY dees)
HYACINTH SCILLA

Family: Liliaceae   ◯◖
All Zones   2'–3'   Spring

This tall, blue squill blooms around the end of April. Flowers are bell-shaped and appear in clusters on tall, leafless stalks. Leaves are strap-shaped, to 1½' long. *S. hyacinthoides* is a native of Yugoslavia that grows well from Central Texas east through the Gulf South. This is a worthwhile bulb that was common in old Southern gardens and cemeteries, and that now occurs sometimes in naturalized colonies along streams, but is rarely available in the nursery trade. Sometimes it is sold under the name of *S. natalensis*. Hyacinth Scilla is easily grown, but must have plenty of water during the late winter and spring growing seasons. Best landscape use is in drifts among other shrubs and perennials. Full- or partial-sun exposures and moist, well-drained soils are best. Mature clumps may be divided after the foliage yellows in late spring.

Sedum acre
(SEE dum   AK ruh)
STONECROP, GOLDMOSS

Family: Crassulaceae   ◯◖
Zone 8   4"–6"   Spring

Goldmoss is a useful sedum that offers the gardener ease of culture and a bright yellow-green foliage that will spread into a dense mat. Bright yellow flowers are borne in branched heads in March and April. The fine-textured, light green foliage provides an excellent contrast to darker greens. *S. acre* requires little soil to thrive, a fact that makes it a popular choice for rock gardens. Sunny or partially-shaded exposures seem to serve equally well, but well-drained soil is a necessity. All sedums are drought tolerant and very easily rooted from stem pieces.

To cover an area with this ground cover, till and rake the soil; then dot with small stem pieces of *S. acre*. After covering the sprigs with fine, loamy soil, water generously. Sedums are plagued by few insect or disease problems, but cannot compete successfully with weeds. Unfortunately, hand-weeding is the only solution, and weeds may prove difficult to remove from the sedum's matted growth. This plant is good for small, detailed areas where its texture and color can be contrasted with that of other perennials.

S. Morganianum, Burro's Tail, is a useful subject for hanging containers and as a ground cover in small areas, although it is cold hardy only in Zone 10. Foliage is an

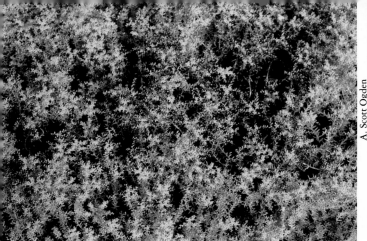

Sedium acre—Goldmoss

S. Palmeri—native variety of Mexico

S. spectabile

attractive gray-green and densely arranged on the trailing stems. Like all sedums, Burro's Tail has brittle, easily broken stems, and is readily propagated from stem cuttings.

S. *Palmeri* is native to Mexico and a useful ground cover in our region. It is a bit coarser in texture than S. *acre* and has yellow to orange-yellow flowers. It is hardy and easily grown.

S. *reflexum* is a fairly common gray-leafed cultivar with bright yellow flowers. Typical height is 6″ – 12″. S. *reflexum* blooms in summer and is sometimes eaten in soups or salads. Both crested and miniature forms are sometimes available.

S. *potosinum* is a species that I have known since a child, though I never learned its correct name until Scott Ogden identified it on a recent plant hunting expedition to Mexico. It is the smallest of all the sedums I know and has gray-green foliage. Flowers occur prolifically in spring, and are whitish and star-shaped. S. *potosinum* is an excellent ground cover for rocky areas, or under specimen plants in containers. It spreads fairly rapidly, and hangs over the edges of rocks, walls, and containers in an attractive manner. S. *potosinum* is fairly common in Texas

S. potosinum—white, star-shaped flowers

gardens. It is a native of the Sierra Madre Oriental, from the neighborhood of Monterrey south into the state of San Luis Potosi in Mexico. Other garden perennials native to this interesting area include S. *Palmeri*, *Setcreasea purpurea*, *Justicia incana*, *Salvia Greggii*, *Pavonia lasiopetala*, and *Echeveria Runyonii*, as well as the spineless prickly pears, Ghost plant (Graptopetolum), Mexican Oregano and shrimp plants.

S. *spectabile* is the only large flowering sedum I have observed thriving in Texas and the Gulf South. It has blue-green, roundish foliage, and bears bright pink flowers in round, flat heads in late summer. Established plants can be 18″–24″ tall. Most large flowering sedums melt in our heat and humidity, but this one seems to be well-adapted to most of our region. New plants are started from stem cuttings.

Sempervivum tectorum
(sem per VEE vum   tek TO rum)
HOUSELEEK, HEN AND CHICKENS
Family: Crassulaceae ◐
Zone 8   10″–12″   Spring

Silvery-blue rosettes of thick fleshy leaves on thick short stems characterize this favorite succulent of our area. Coral-pink flowers on wavy stems are showy, but do not appear until the plant is mature, or its roots restricted in a container. *S. tectorum* is of easy culture, but will not tolerate soggy soils or shady exposures. It is a traditional favorite as ground cover for small spaces, or more commonly, in containers. Propagation is by leaf or stem cuttings, both of which root very easily. *S. tectorum* is sometimes confused with the Ghost Plant, *Graptopetalum paraguayense*, another well- adapted succulent popular in our region. *Echeveria Runyonii* is a third succulent that may also be commonly known as Hen and Chickens.

Senecio Cineraria
(se NEE see oh   sin er RAY ree uh)
DUSTY-MILLER
Family Compositae ◐◐
Zone 8   2′–3′   Spring

There are several plants that are commonly known as Dusty-Miller; *Centaurea cineraria*, and several species of *Artemisia* share the name in our region. *S. Cineraria* is not very well-adapted to the heat and humidity of our coast. It has beautiful, thick, cut leaves covered with white, matted hairs that give the plant its distinctive silvery appearance. For inland parts of our region and in dry, sunny exposures, it is fairly satisfactory. Yellow to cream-colored flowers are daisy-like and appear in spring. *S. Cineraria* responds well to heavy shearing in late winter. Propagation is usually from cuttings taken during the growing season.

S. confusus, Mexican Flame Vine, is a showy, twining vine to about 10′. It is usually root hardy in Zone 9, and often evergreen in Zone 10. Flowers are daisy-like and borne in large clusters at the ends of stems. They are about 1″ in diameter, very bright orange-red with golden-yellow centers. Flowers occur all during the growing season. Culture is easy, with full sun or partial shade and light soils preferred. Propagation is by seed, division, or cuttings.

Setcreasea pallida—Purple Heart

Setcreasea pallida
(set KREE see ah   PA li duh)
SETCREASEA, PURPLE HEART
Family: Commelinaceae ○◐
Zone 9   12″–18″   Spring, Summer

Setcreasea is planted primarily for its rich purple foliage. It colors best in full sun, partially shaded areas tending to produce greener leaves. Flowers are white, pink or purple, and are borne over a long period, but make little visual impact. Propagation is from stem cuttings, or by division of the rapidly spreading clumps. Setcreasea is a good plant for ground cover in small to moderate-size areas or in containers. It freezes back with hard frost, but quickly returns the next spring in Zones 9 and 10. Leaves are lance-shaped and partially enclose the fleshy, purple stems. Well-drained soil and fairly dry conditions are ideal for this plant. Soggy soils promote rotting.

Solanum Rantonnetii
(so LAY num   ran ton NEH tee eye)
BLUE POTATO BUSH
Family: Solanaceae ○◐
Zone 9   5′–6′   Summer

Blue Potato Bush may be trained as a bush or a vine. It blooms almost continuously from late spring till frost, and can be quite striking in the landscape. To maintain a neat appearance, severe and fairly frequent pruning is usually necessary. Evergreen in mild climates, *S. Rantonnetii* defoliates in severe cold, and freezes back when exposed to temperatures in the low twenties or teens. It is easily propagated from cuttings.

The commonly cultivated form of this plant is reported to be the 'Grandiflorum.' This bears flowers about 1″ across (twice the size of the wild species), of a violet-blue with prominent yellow centers. Flowers are abundant through the warm seasons, leaves are up to 4″ long and bright green.

S. Pseudocapsicum, commonly known as Jerusalem Cherry, is commonly grown and naturalized in South and Central Texas and other areas in the Gulf South. It is sometimes sold as a florist pot plant because of its showy, round fruit, which is reported to be poisonous. Jerusalem Cherry is propagated from seed, and easily grown in sunny or partially-shaded locations. Compact and spreading forms are sometimes available. Typical height and spread is about 2′ by 2′, but plants twice that size may sometimes be found, especially in summers following mild winters. *S. Pseudocapsicum* is usually sufficiently winter hardy to use as a garden perennial in Zones 9 and 10.

Solidago altissima
(so li DAY go   al TISS si muh)
GOLDENROD

Family: Compositae ◯◐
Zone 4   3′–5′   Early to Late Fall

There are many Goldenrods common to our region, both in the garden and in the wild. For years they had a reputation for causing hay fever, but experts tell us that their pollen is heavy and not easily windborne. The culprit is usually the pollen of the far less attractive ragweed, which blooms at the same time. Goldenrods of this species grow larger and more vigorously in the garden than they do in their natural state, so allow them plenty of room. Some of the more dwarf cultivars are appealing, but even they border on the invasive in our climate.

Flower heads are large and pyramidal in shape, golden yellow in color. Leaves are lance-like and 3″–5″ long. Propagation is by seed, or by division of mature clumps, which should be cut back to the ground after the first hard freeze. Goldenrods prefer well-drained locations and full or nearly-full sun. They adapt to a wide range of growing situations, and provide color at a time of year when few plants are at their peak.

Sprekelia formosissima 'Orient Red'
(spreh KAY lee uh   for moe SISS si muh)
AZTEC LILY

Family: Amaryllidaceae ◯◐
Zone 8   1′   Spring, Fall

Aztec Lilies are native to the high mountains of Mexico, and flower best during cool spring and fall weather. Bulbs are hardy in the middle and lower South, and perform well in any well-prepared garden soil. Foliage is similar to daffodils. Dark crimson blooms have three erect segments and three lower ones that are rolled into a tube at the basal end. Bulbs are best set out in fall, 3″–4″ deep and about 8″ apart, in sunny, well-drained

A. Scott Ogden

Sprekelia formosissima 'Orient Red'—Aztec Lily

Solidago altissima—'Cloth of Gold' Goldenrod

Stachys byzintina—Lamb's Ears

Sternbergia lutea—Lily of the Field

A. Scott Ogden

locations. Sprekelias are best grouped for mass effects in the landscape, or planted in containers. They can bloom several times each year in the spring and fall. *S.* 'superba' is sometimes offered for sale, but blooms only in spring for our area, if at all.

Stachys byzintina
(STA kis by ZIN tin a)
LAMB'S EARS

Family: Labiatae ○◑
Zone 4   12″ – 18″   Summer

Silvery leaves and compact habit make Lamb's Ears a favorite perennial in much of the nation. It grows poorly in the heat and humidity of the immediate Gulf Coast, but can be useful for inland and arid parts of our region. It must have good drainage and a sunny exposure and rots under sprinkler irrigation.

Flowers are pink or purple in closely set whorls along the spikes. Propagation is by seed or division of established clumps every 3 or 4 years in early spring or early fall.

Lamb's Ears are effective edging for bearded iris plantings and the front of sunny perennial borders. Established plants should be pruned back in early spring.

Sternbergia lutea
(stern BER gee uh   loo TEE uh)
LILY OF THE FIELD

Family: Amaryllidaceae ○◑
All Zones   6″ – 9″   Fall

This plant bears its large, clear yellow flowers in mid-September, holding them just a few inches above the ground. Though sometimes called "Autumn Crocus," it is not actually related to the crocuses. *S. lutea* is fairly common on old homesites in the Dallas area. It is believed by many to be the lily-of-the-field referred to in

the Bible, and was introduced to the United States by Thomas Jefferson at his famous Monticello estate. Leaves are narrow and 6″ – 12″ long, remaining green from bloom time until midwinter. Bulbs should be planted in August or September and set about 4″ deep and 6″ apart in a sunny location. Mature clumps should be divided and reset in August only after they become crowded. *S. lutea* blooms at a time when its bright yellow flowers are particularly noticeable. It is a valuable addition to the rock garden, and is also attractive naturalized in drifts.

Stigmaphyllon ciliatum (*Mascagnia macroptera*)
(stig ma FIE lon   si lee AY tum)
BUTTERFLY VINE

Family: Malpighiaceae ○◑
Zone 9   10′ – 20′   Summer, Fall

S. ciliatum is distinguished by its fruit, which resembles 2″ – 3″ chartreuse butterflies. The vine flaunts clusters of small, bright yellow, orchid-like flowers from late summer through early fall. These mature into the unusual fruit, which is usually arranged one to three per stem. The chartreuse coloring of the "butterflies" changes to brown as they dry. They are beautiful and useful in dried arrangements and last for many months. Leaves are shiny, dark green, lance-shaped and about 3″ long. Stems are slender and twining.

Butterfly Vine is a vigorous plant that is usually contained by freezing temperatures. Once established, the plant returns reliably and promptly each spring, but a mulch should be provided and care should be taken to provide protection from winter winds. Sunny locations such as south or east exposures are best. *S. ciliatum* is rather drought tolerant, once established. It is fairly common in South Texas, the Rio Grande Valley, New Orleans and South Louisiana.

S. ciliatum—with fruit resembling chartreuse butterflies

Stigmaphyllon ciliatum—Butterfly Vine

Because of its tenderness to cold, this plant is sometimes cultivated in greenhouses and other enclosed structures outside its range. Most garden soils are adequate for Butterfly Vine, but extremely alkaline conditions result in yellowing from iron chlorosis. Propagation is from cuttings, seed, or the layers that spring up naturally in the vicinity of mature plants. Another easy technique for starting new plants is to bury a length of the vine, weighting it down with a brick or stone, but making sure to leave the vine's tip exposed. After several months, the buried portion of vine will usually have developed enough roots to be separated from the parent plant.

Butterfly Vine is an interesting, quick-growing cover for trellises, chain link fences and arbors. Flowering and fruiting often occur simultaneously and create considerable interest in the garden. Damaged portions of the plant should be cut back each spring as new growth appears.

Stokesia laevis
(stoe KEE zee uh   LAY vis)
STOKE'S ASTER

Family: Compositae
Zone 7   1′–2′   Spring, Fall

Sometimes known as "Cornflower Aster," *S. laevis* is native from South Carolina to Florida, and west to Louisiana. In her book *A Southern Garden*, Elizabeth Lawrence extolls its virtues, rating it "one of the best perennials for the South." Stoke's Aster occurs naturally on moist but well-drained soil. Flowers are many petaled, 2″–5″ across, and an unusual wisteria-blue. Foliage is smooth and of a medium texture, with toothed, medium-green leaves 2″–8″ long.

Stokesia prefer a sunny location but will tolerate filtered light. They are long-lived in well-drained soils

Stokesia laevis—Stoke's Aster variety 'Blue Danube'

and may develop into large clumps from Central Texas east, where they are best adapted. Several cultivars are available: 'Blue Danube' is a soft blue; 'Silver Moon' is not a pure white, but a nice color; and 'Blue Moon' tends to be more mauve. *S. laevis* blooms all summer in cooler climates, but for us it more often yields a heavy spring bloom, followed by a summer's rest, then sometimes a rebloom in fall.

Tagetes lucida
(ta JE tez   loo SEE duh)
MEXICAN MARIGOLD MINT

Family: Compositae   ○◗
Zone 8   2–3′   Fall

T. lucida is native to Mexico and Guatemala where its foliage is used for teas, seasoning and medicinal purposes. When not in flower, this plant would be difficult to identify as a marigold since it has simple, lance-shaped leaves with slightly serrated margins. Another important, if less visible, difference is that *T. lucida* does

Mexican Marigold Mint, impressive with asters

Tagetes lucida—Mexican Marigold Mint

not seem susceptible to spider mites, a pest that limits the use of common garden marigolds in our area.

Mexican Marigold Mint bears clusters of golden-yellow, single flowers that occur from mid-fall until frost. Plants form attractive many-branched mounds, if grown in well-drained soil and sunny exposures. The leaves have a distinctive and pleasing, anise-like scent and are popular as a substitute for tarragon in seasoning vinegars. New plants root readily from cuttings taken

during the growing season, and mature clumps may be divided in spring. Mexican Marigold Mint is impressive when combined with the fall blooming aster described in this text. It also contrasts pleasantly with *Eupatorium coelestinum*, the fall blooming Ageratum or Mist Flower. Although they freeze back in late fall, my plants have always returned in spring, bigger and better than before. *T. lucida* is a good plant for sunny exposures in South and West Texas, where it seems to be fairly drought resistant.

Thymus vulgaris
(TIE mus   vul GA ris)
GARDEN THYME

Family: Labiatae   ◑
Zone 5   12″–18″   Summer and Fall

Thyme has been an unobtrusive but persistent feature of American gardens since colonial times. It is planted mostly as a culinary herb, which may be used fresh or dry, but it can also add an attractive note to the landscape. As perennials, thymes are short-lived, requiring division every two or three years. Native from the western Mediterranean to southeastern Italy, this species doesn't like the intense heat and humidity that grips our

A. Scott Ogden

Tradescantia occidentalis—Spiderwort

Thymus vulgaris—Garden Thyme

region from July through September, and it requires shade for half the day to survive. With the arrival of cooler fall temperatures, thymes regain their vigor to grow well. Well-drained soil is a must, and an alkaline pH is preferred.

Thymes are available in a number of cultivars and a number of sizes and habits. Creeping types are attractive in containers and rock gardens, but the way they hug the hot earth in summertime makes them the least adapted to our area. The upright thymes reach a height of 12″–18″, and are useful as bonsai specimens or for mass plantings.

Among the many thyme cultivars is *T. x citriodorus*, which is better known as "Lemon Thyme." Tiny, dark green leaves cover this compact, lemon-scented herb, which is especially attractive when planted in a container. *T. x* 'Argenteus' is an attractive, silver-leaved form. Thyme flowers are small, usually lilac in color, and are borne in dense whorls that literally blanket the plant. Propagation is from stem cuttings or layers which root easily during the cool seasons.

Tradescantia occidentalis
(tra des KAN tee uh)
SPIDERWORT

Family: Commelinaceae   ◯◖
Zone 5   2′–3′   Spring, Summer

Spiderworts are native from Minnesota to Texas and are found in moist, fertile, soils. The garden hybrids offer somewhat larger flowers and a wider range of colors, although the native forms may also be useful. These plants are of exceptionally easy garden culture and available in a wide variety of colors, including blue, purple, white, pink, and rose. The stems are grass-like, with

long, lance-shaped, clasping leaves attached to the joints. Flowers are three-petaled, about one inch in diameter, and are borne from spring to early summer. As the summer heat becomes more intense, the blossoms open only for a few hours each morning, closing usually by noon.

Spiderworts grow well in sunny or partially sunny exposures. They provide color over a long period, but their display is not usually a major feature of the garden. Best use is in naturalized plantings and wet sites where they may be grown with Louisiana Iris and other moisture-loving perennials. Propagation is by division of mature clumps in the fall, or by stem cuttings taken anytime during the growing season.

T. flumensis is better known to gardeners in our area as "Wandering Jew." It is a tender, vining perennial for Zones 9 and 10, and prefers moist, fertile soils and full or partial sun. It spreads rapidly under ideal conditions. Propagation is from cuttings taken at any time and rooted in water or soil. The species has green foliage, but there are a number of hybrids with creamy-white or purple variegated leaves. The green form appears to be more cold hardy than the variegated cultivars, and light mulches can provide protection during moderate cold spells. Landscape uses include ground cover and hanging containers.

Tulbaghia violacea
(tool BOG ee uh   vee oh LAY see uh)
SOCIETY GARLIC

Family: Amaryllidaceae   ◯◖
Zone 8   2′   Spring, Summer, Fall

Society Garlic is an old favorite with Gulf Coast gardeners. It blooms almost continuously from spring

Tulbaghia violacea—Society Garlic

Tulbaghia variety 'Silver Lace'

Tulipa chrysantha

through fall, bearing umbels of bright, lilac-violet colored flowers. Leaves are flat, garlic-like and about 1' long. Variety 'Silver Lace' is striking with its white-margined foliage. *T. violacea* is native to South Africa and is very well-adapted to the Gulf South. Bulbs may be divided and reset from late fall through early spring in good, well-drained garden soil. Full or partially sunny exposures are best. Landscape uses include masses or borders in herbaceous or shrub plantings. Society Garlic is also a good container plant.

Tulipa clusiana
(TOO lip uh   cloo see AN uh)
LADY TULIP

Family: Liliaceae
Zone 9 north   1'   Spring

Most gardeners to our region have found hybrid garden tulips to be annuals. *T. clusiana* is a small, beautiful species tulip that naturalizes in all of our region, with the possible exception of Zone 10. The medium-sized flowers bloom about April 1. Exterior petals are a boldly colored red, and the inner petals white, a combination that results in a gay, candy-striped effect. Flowers exhibit daily sleep movement, expanding to flat white

Tulipa clusiana—Lady Tulip

stars at noon, but closing to tight red buds each evening. Best performance occurs in sunny exposures and well-drained soil. Clumps may be divided and reset after the foliage yellows in late spring.

T. chrysantha is similar to T. clusiana and blooms about two weeks later to bear somewhat smaller flowers of yellow and red. It is a native of Iran and thought by some to be merely a variety of T. clusiana. 'Cynthia' is a pale yellow hybrid between T. clusiana and T. chrysantha.

Typha latifolia
(TIE fuh ˉ la ti FOE lee uh)
CATTAIL

Family: Typhaceae ◯◗
Zone 7   4'–6'   Summer

Cattails are commonly found growing naturally in wet, open areas of Texas and the Gulf South. Foliage is flat, reedlike, may be 4'–6' tall, and is usually evergreen in our area. Flowers are tall, brown and look like a weiner on a stick. Cattails spread by underground roots, and can be invasive. They thrive in poorly-drained soils to create a distinctive and elegant, vertical accent. The cattails' invasive character may be controlled by planting the clumps in containers, and then submerging these in ponds.

Verbena x hybrida
(ver BEE nuh)
GARDEN VERBENA

Family: Verbenaceae ◯◗
Zone 8   1'   Spring, Summer, Fall

Although they are, in fact, perennials, verbenas are often replanted each spring as annuals. Though they will sometimes return from year to year, these flowers tend to

Verbena x hybrida—Garden Verbena

Typha latifolia—Cattail

Verbena x teasii

be short-lived, and require trimming, replanting, fertilizing, and an occasional top-dressing with fresh soil or compost to maintain a consistently good appearance. Flowers are most prolific in spring and show to best advantage tumbling over retaining walls or the edges of containers. Colors are vivid tints of red, pink, white, or purple. Flat clusters of individual flowers may be 2″–3″ across. Foliage of most garden verbenas is oblong to ovate and 2″–4″ long, but some types have finely cut leaves.

V. peruviana is native to Brazil and Argentina, and popular in Central and West Texas. It is very low-growing and a dwarf, although runners spread to cover the ground fairly rapidly. Flowers are usually bright scarlet.

V. rigida, Tuber Vervain, is more erect in form and has bright lavender flowers. It is native to southern Brazil and Argentina, but has naturalized from North Carolina south to Florida and west to Texas. There is a white form, 'Alba', and a lilac one, 'Lilacina,' that have been identified. *V. rigida* will flower the first year from seed, but is easily propagated by cuttings or division. Indeed, it is a bit invasive and may need to be controlled in the landscape. It is common along roadsides of East Texas.

The verbenas known as "sand verbenas" in Texas, sold under the trade name of "Tex-Tuf" by San Antonio-area nurseries, are well adapted to most of Texas and the Gulf South. They have finely-cut foliage and are available with flowers of bright pink, purple, white, and lavender. They are thought to be an early 1900s hybrid *V. x teasii*, which has extensively naturalized in Texas during this century.

Verbenas like fertile, well-drained soils; open, sunny areas; and occasional irrigation during dry periods. They profit from an occasional trimming to remove older, less vigorous growth; from fertilization; and from top-dressing with well-rotted organic material or topsoil. Propagation is by division, seed, or cuttings.

Viola odorata
(vee OH lah   oh do RAH tuh)
SWEET VIOLET

Family: Violaceae   ◑●
Zone 6   6″–12″   Winter, Spring

Violets were once considered indispensable perennials for the well-designed garden. Although there are several species of violets native to Texas, the violet of choice for most Southern gardens was *V. odorata*, which is of European, Asian and African origin. Dark blue or purple is this species' predominant color. Well into the early 20th century, violets were among the most popular

Viola odorata—Sweet Violet hybrid 'Royal Robe'

florist cut flowers. Their fragrance, rich colors, and relatively easy culture contributed to nationwide popularity.

Violets prefer a rich, moist, but well-drained soil high in organic content and slightly acid. Partially shaded locations are preferred, but full sun and full shade can also produce good violets. Their natural bloom period is late winter and early spring. Although evergreen, garden violets become semi-dormant during our long, hot summers. They can, however, endure considerable drought and heat stress, usually resumimg lush, healthy growth with the onset of cooler, more moist fall and winter conditions.

Landscape uses include borders and ground covers. Large container shrubs can often be enhanced by a mass of violets at their base, for they provide attractive foliage, fragrance, and color at a season when few other plants are at their peak. Mature height is usually 8″–10″. The rounded foliage is quite attractive even when the plants are not in bloom. Spider mites are an occasional problem, but may be controlled with insecticidal soaps or chemicals labeled for such use.

Propagation is usually by division of mature clumps during early to mid-fall. Seeds can also be used to produce new plants, but require considerable attention during the early stages.

Borders of garden violets may still be found in some of the old gardens of Central Texas and eastward throughout the region. They can be long-lived and relatively low maintenance perennials. Few plants perform as well in shady areas or offer color and fragrance from December-March.

The hybrids found in old gardens in our area include 'Royal Elk', with long stemmed dark purple flowers; 'Royal Robe', a garden favorite in the South with dark purple flowers; and 'Charm' which is a white cultivar. Violets naturalize well in wooded gardens. Violets native to our region are many and include *V. pedata*, Bird-Foot Violet, *V. primulifolia*, Primrose-leaf Violet, *V. affinis*, Brainard Violet, and *V. Walteri*.

Wedelia trilobata
(wa DEL ee uh   try low BAH tuh)
WEDELIA
Family: Compositae   ○◐
Zone 9   12″–15″   Spring, Summer, Fall

Wedelia is a fast-growing tropical ground cover that is becoming popular in those areas where it does not winterkill. It is not fully hardy in Zone 9. It bears yellow daisy-like flowers throughout the warm seasons, but its bloom never makes a major impact. Foliage is lush, dark green up to 4″ long, and rather thick, with a rough upper surface.

Wedelia likes plenty of moisture and loose, well-prepared soil. Propagation is from cuttings, which root readily at almost any season. It is not a plant of refined appearance, but in naturalistic settings it can be effective.

Westringia rosmariniformis
(wes TRIN jee uh   roz ma RIH nih for mis)
WESTRINGIA
Family: Labiatae   ○◐
Zone 8   3′–6′   Spring, Summer

Westringea is native to southeastern Australia. It is relatively new to Texas, but appears to have considerable merit. Light, well-drained soil and sunny exposures are preferred. It is very wind and salt tolerant. Leaves are medium to gray-green above and whitish beneath, somewhat similar to Rosemary, but lighter and airier in appearance. Small white flowers open from late winter through summer. Propagation is from cuttings taken during the growing season. Westringia supplies a useful color and texture to combine with other low-water-use perennials. Flowers are attractive, but secondary to the overall color and texture of the plant.

Yucca filamentosa
(YUK kuh   fill uh men Tow suh)
ADAM'S NEEDLE
Family: Agavaceae   ○◐
Zone 7   3′–4′   Spring, Summer

The Yuccas best suited for use in perennial borders are almost trunkless and form mounding rosettes of a pointed-leaf foliage that is flexible and not a major danger to passersby. *Y. filamentosa* is native from South

A. Scott Ogden

Yucca pallida—North Central Texas native

Yucca filamentosa—Adam's Needle

Carolina to Mississippi and Florida on dry, infertile soils. It is fairly common in the nursery trade, although there is some speculation that the species offered under that name is really *Y. Smalliana*. Foliage is gray-green and flexible. Flowers make a real spectacle in the landscape. Fragrant, white, pendulous blossoms cluster in large masses atop slender spikes 4'–8' tall. Yuccas do best in sunny exposures with well-drained soil. Once they are established, irrigation is rarely necessary.

Propagation is from seed, by division of offsets, or from root cuttings. Trunkless yuccas are not easily transplanted and are best purchased as container plants. They are valuable as specimens in containers or masses in the border. Europeans value them highly, and some of the best English borders utilize yuccas.

Y. pallida is a North Central Texas native often found in old gardens of the region. It is esteemed for its compact rosettes of wide, glaucous leaves, and spring-blooming spikes of white drooping flowers. *Y. rupicola* is similar but has bright green foliage.

Zantedeschia aethiopica
(zan tay DES key uh   ee thee OH pi kuh)
CALLA LILY

Family: Araceae
Zone 9   2'–3'   Spring

Calla Lilies prefer semi-shaded locations having rich, moist, well-drained soil that is slightly acid. They also prefer morning sun, afternoon shade, and a location adjacent to the south side of a structure. Callas are not very cold hardy and may be lost during cold spells, even in Zone 9.

Foliage is large and heart-shaped, borne on long stems, and rich, dark green in color. Flowers are large, creamy-white, semi-funnel-shaped spathes with prominent yellow centers. Callas are traditional flowers of New Orleans and other Gulf Coast areas. Other species are *Z. albomaculata*, with white spotted foliage; *Z. Elliottiana*, with yellow flowers and white spotted foliage; and *Z. Rehmannii*, a dwarf plant that produces small, pink flowers.

Zantedeschia aethiopica—Calla Lily

Callas grow from thick, tuberous roots that should be planted in early spring. They are often cultivated in containers, where they should be allowed to go semi-dormant during the winter and put on a low-water, low-fertilizer diet. Container-grown specimens bloom better after becoming somewhat crowded and root-bound. Callas are elegant as cut flowers or in the garden. They require a special location and attention to reach perfection.

Zephyranthes grandiflora
(ze fee RAN theez)

RAIN-LILY

Family: Amaryllidaceae ◯◐
Zone 7   1′   Summer

The flowering bulbs we call rain-lilies actually belong to two genera, *Zephyranthes* and *Habranthus*, but all are beautiful, tough, and useful garden plants. *Zephyranthes* literally means "flower of the west wind." *Z. grandiflora*, sometimes sold as *Z. robusta*, is one of the largest and showiest of the rain-lilies. Although its origins are obscure, it is known to have been introduced very early to gardens in warm countries and has escaped frequently throughout the subtropics.

Rain-lilies are useful in the landscape for border or mass plantings, and require little attention, once planted. Sunny locations are preferred, and a well-prepared soil and heavy feeding encourage better growth and flowering. Bulbs of rain-lilies may be planted at any time, with fall being ideal. Seeds of rain-lilies, like other Amaryllids, should be sown as soon as they are gathered.

Z. atamasco is sometimes known as Atamasco Lily or Wild Easter Lily. It is a beautiful Southeastern native and differs from other rain lilies by prefering shady, woodsy places, and by blooming early in the spring. Its large, funnel-shaped, white blooms put on a good show, and are compatible with acid loving plants such as azaleas and Louisiana phlox. *Z. atamasco* spreads rapidly to produce clumps of grassy foliage in the winter, and falls dormant with the advent of summer heat. Mature clumps may be divided and reset at that time.

Z. citrina is the most common yellow rain-lily in cultivation and is often sold as *Z. sulfurea*. It bears golden-yellow blooms prolifically from midsummer into the fall, and may be quickly increased by seed. Reportedly, it is a native of countries bordering the Caribbean. *Z.* sp. 'Valle's Yellow' is similar, but paler yellow and more everblooming. Both species thrive in rich soil, abundant sun, and moisture.

Z. candida, the White Rain-Lily, is sometimes erroneously called "Autumn Crocus," and because of its attractive foliage can be a most useful landscape plant. The winter growing foliage of *Z. candida* is dark green

Z. atamasco—"Atamsco Lily" or "Wild Easter Lily"

Zephyranthes grandiflora—Rain Lily

A. Scott Ogden

Z. citrina—Yellow Rain Lily

and at first glance looks somewhat like monkey grass (*Ophiopogon japonicus*). It is excellent as a border plant for sunny areas and is easily propagated by division. White Rain-Lilies are native to the shores of Rio de la Plata, the River of Silver in Argentina, which takes its name from this white-blooming Fairy-Lily. Flowers appear from late summer well into the fall, usually beginning with autumn showers.

Z. Drummondii (Cooperia pedunculata), the Giant Prairie-Lily, is a large, white-flowered native of Central Texas that produces primrose-scented evening blooms from April through midsummer and sporadically into the fall. Its big, black-coated bulbs grow well in rocky, arid soils as well as rich loams. The Giant Prairie-Lily is a favorite garden subject throughout the Southern states.

Zephyranthes of nearly any type are worthy of trial in Southern gardens. Hybridizers have created many breathtaking combinations among these diminutive amaryllids. Choice clones include 'Ruth Page'-deep rose, 'Ellen Korsakoff'—a peach blend, 'Capricorn'—burnt orange, 'Grandjax'—a vigorous pale pink, 'Aquarius'—creamy yellow, and 'Prairie Sunset'—an everblooming orange blend. These varieties are only rarely available

Z. candida—White Rain-Lily

Z. sp. 'Valle's Yellow'

Zephyranthes hybrid 'Ruth Page'—deep rose

A. Scott Ogden

Habranthus tubispathus v. *texanus*—Copper-Lily

from hobbyists and specialty bulb dealers. Interested gardeners, however, may wish to try their own luck at creating hybrids.

Habranthus tubispathus v. *texanus,* Copper-Lily, is commonly native of Texas and Argentina and very easily grown, blooming in late summer and fall. It performs best in areas that do not receive excessive irrigation. A better garden border subject is *H. robustus*, whose large, pink funnels make spectacular displays through the summer. *H. brachyandrus,* with its dark, purple-throated blooms, is also a good performer along the Gulf Coast.

H. brachyandrus—dark purple-throated blooms

'Ellen Korsakoff'—a peach blend

H. robustus with large pink tunnels

'Aquarius'—creamy-yellow

PART THREE

Old Garden Roses and Companion Plants

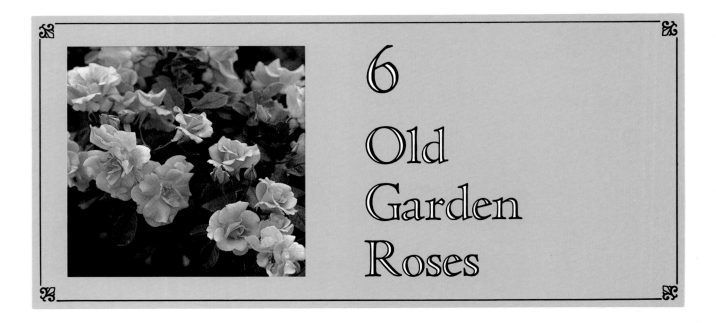

6
Old
Garden
Roses

Long before its extensive hybridization, the rose had survived cheerfully in the gardens of history. Early rose cultivars retained the resilience and fortitude programmed by nature, but these qualities have sometimes been neglected in modern hybrids developed primarily for showy blooms. Unlike most modern roses, which grow poorly without many hours of devoted attention, many old roses are remarkably self-reliant. These historic cultivars will give today's busy homeowner an appreciated rest from much of the spraying and nurturing demanded by their younger cousins. Some of them actually prefer a minimum of pruning, and as specimens found in old cemeteries and abandoned homesites attest, many have survived even without care from human hands.

The definition of an old rose is a bit nebulous. The American Rose Society considers any rose introduced before 1867 to be classed as such, but most collectors consider any rose 75 or more years old, and having typical "old rose" characteristics, to be eligible. One telltale sign is the unforgettable "true rose" perfume that lives on in its undiluted form in old roses. These flowers have a richness and diversity of fragrance lacking in the majority of modern roses. Modern roses are hybridized primarily for their striking colors and "ideal" bloom forms, and the shape of the plant itself is not outstanding, especially if judicious pruning is not practiced. Old roses have an inherent beauty of form, a quality which does not diminish over the years, making them particularly useful as landscape plants.

Another proof of an old rose lies in the blossom's color. The old rose colors tend to be more muted and pastel than those of modern hybrids, and many collectors

A bouquet of old roses shows a collector's preference for their softer hues.

acquire a preference for these softer hues. Many old rose varieties also display handsome foliage, while others set attractive hips in the fall which can be harvested for their vitamin C content.

Overshadowed by modern hybrids, old roses have been neglected in this century, but now there is a movement afoot to restore them to their rightful place in the garden. Their historic interest, color, fragrance, and form make old roses as indispensable to today's gardens as they have been for centuries and, as many gardeners will affirm, the best thing about old roses is that they provide all these landscape values without becoming a maintenance burden.

Rachel's Garden at "The Hermitage" features mixed borders.

HISTORICAL PERSPECTIVE

The rose has been "Queen of the Flowers" through the ages—yet where did it originate? Some roses are native to the United States, but the majority come from Europe and the Orient. Species roses native to the temperate zone were long ago cross-pollinated in nature—and later in gardens—to bring about new varieties.

In the late 1700s and early 1800s, European botanists explored the world in search of new plants of garden value and discovered roses in China and the Far East which bloomed year-round (Chinas and Teas). Crosses between these Oriental roses and their European cousins (the once-blooming Gallicas, Musks, Centifolias, and Damasks) gave rise to the Noisettes, Bourbons, Portlands, Hybrid Perpetuals, Polyanthas, and Grandifloras. As roses became increasingly popular in this century, the Hybrid Teas replaced nearly every other class because of their classic bud form and unusual colors.

While the modern hybrids won the praise of many, there were some rosarians who maintained a preference for the older varieties. The renowned English gardener Gertrude Jekyll extolled the beauty and landscape value inherent in many of the old cultivars. Vita Sackville-West's famous garden at Sissinghurst Castle featured many of the once-blooming and prized old varieties. In America, dedicated rosarians Ethelyn Emery Keays and Roy Shepherd advocated collecting and growing historic roses.

In the 19th century, old roses were highly prized as landscape plants and were found in the gardens of virtually every home, whether mansion or modest cottage.

These shrub and rambling roses, propagated from cuttings shared among friends and relatives, produced copious displays of flowers and required little attention other than the winter application of barnyard manure.

Interest in old roses is increasing today, as Americans are searching them out in historic cemeteries and abandoned homesites, where the plants have endured in spite of years of neglect. Rose books written during the last century are being republished, public gardens established, and organizations formed to provide educational information on this fascinating and diverse group. Interest has been further stimulated by the naming of the rose as our national flower by Congress during 1986. The genus *Rosa* contains many exciting plants that are worthy of much more extensive use in American gardens.

Roses in Early Texas Gardens

When the appeal of new lands and fresh beginnings lured Americans from the Southeast to Texas in the colonial period from 1822–1846, these families loaded their belongings onto ox wagons for the difficult journey. Many a pioneer wife, looking at the home of her youth perhaps for the last time, dug a piece of a rose her mother had planted as a bride, and carefully tended and transported this living reminder of loved ones to her new home in the wilderness.

Early on, Texas was a land of contrasts. Towns and plantations were oases of civilization and refinement amid the chaos of the wilderness. One such plantation

A Texas cottage garden featuring roses

belonged to Texas patriot Lorenzo de Zavala, the first vice president of the Republic of Texas, and his wife Emily. A granddaughter, Adina de Zavala, described in detail Emily's garden at Lynchburg (near Houston) for the *San Antonio Express* of December 2, 1934. Roses had been her grandmother's favorite flower, Adina recalled. Emily had admired the great gardens of France while at the Court of St. Cloud (her husband, Lorenzo, served as minister to France when Texas was still a part of Mexico). Several of the roses in the Lynchburg garden were presented to de Zavala when he left France to return to his Texas home.

Sited on a bluff of the San Jacinto River, the de Zavala garden included many China, Tea and other roses known to us today. Among these were 'Louis Phillipe' and 'Cramoisi Supérieur,' which graced many of the early gardens of Texas and can still be found today. 'Cherokee,' 'Lady Banksia,' Moss, and Cabbage roses were also mentioned. In her later years, Emily de Zavala added 'Catherine Mermet,' 'Paul Neyron,' and 'Maréchal Niel.' Rose hedges, arches and arbors helped shape the garden which also included extensive use of annuals and perennials. The overall design would be considered that of a cottage garden.

In 1934, when she wrote of the old family garden, Adina de Zavala was the president and historian for the Texas Historical and Landmarks Association, and Texas was gearing up for its Centennial. The following quotation is from her article:

> Nearly three thousand years ago the rose was styled by the Athenians "Queen of Flowers," and few today will dispute that this title was fittingly bestowed.
>
> Texas is a land of flowers, a land of such varied soil and climate, that nearly everything grows. Why not, now, as a preparation for visitors during the Centennial Year, plant more roses of all sorts, so that every vacant spot shall produce a rose plant? Visitors will then exclaim over the quantity and beauty of our roses, and name us—the State of the Roses—The Lone Star State.

The descriptions of other Republic gardens are few. Englishman William Ballaert, visiting East Texas about 1843, wrote of the roses on an old pioneer's grave. Mary Austin Holley, a cousin of Stephen F. Austin, visited her brother's plantation "Bolivar" in 1835, and remarked on the "monthly roses" on the graves of her nieces who had succumbed in the terrible cholera epidemic of 1833. Mrs. Holley also mentioned a bank of "multiflora roses," no doubt one of the double pink varieties popular at this time, used as a fence at Bolivar. Most likely, the roses Ballaert and Holley described were 'Old Blush,' an original pink China, which had been imported to America by

1800 and had become popular all over the Southeast. The settlers called it "Pink Daily," "Old Monthly," and "The Daisy Rose," referring to its almost perpetual habit of flowering.

Surviving at Amon Underwood's East Columbia plantation (built in 1839), our rose society "rustle" in 1982 found the 'Chestnut Rose,' a double dark rose colored form of *Rosa roxburghii* (1814), and 'Fortuniana,' a white double climber (1850).

The most famed of Texas roses is still a mystery to horticulturists and historians. "The Yellow Rose of Texas" is believed by some to be the climbing yellow Banksia (1824) which prospers well in the South, bearing clusters of straw-yellow flowers in early spring. Others believe the yellow rose was 'Harison's Yellow' (1830), a very thorny, chrome-yellow shrub rose with about a dozen petals and yellow stamens. It was sold to pioneers moving west, and so lines the routes to the West where they passed.

'Fortune's Double Yellow'

ROSE CLASSES AND VARIETIES

Of the thousands of old roses introduced over time, many are lost forever, but many are still in cultivation. Roses are usually divided into classes that might be compared to breeds of animals. Some of the best classes have been almost abandoned by the nursery trade primarily because they are not sufficiently cold hardy to survive in northern climates where most of the roses are shipped. Fortunately for those of us in the South, some of the best of these less cold hardy roses are coming back into production and are once again available to us, even if on a limited scale (refer to the list of suggested sources in the appendix).

I have also included instructions for rooting your own roses, since this is the time-honored method for handing down roses within a family or among friends. It is also the way many fine roses have been rescued from extinction by old rose collectors in recent years.

Since there are so many fine old roses, it has been especially difficult to select the ones for this book. Those chosen are among the very best for Texas and the Gulf South. They are grouped according to class, and with each class is included a brief outline of its history, landscape uses, hardiness factors, flowering habits, and other cultural information. Following these introductions to the various classes are more specific descriptions of each variety they comprise. Generally, the classes and their varieties are presented in approximate chronological order of appearance, to provide a sense of evolution within the sphere of old roses. Because the pronunciation of French names does not come naturally to most of us, I

have included a syllable-by-syllable approximation. Near the end of the section on old roses is information on their culture as well as landscape use lists.

Species Roses and Related Hybrids

Species roses may be defined as those growing in wild populations in nature. Most of the roses listed below are species, the remainder being hybrids that retain many species characteristics. All those included tend to be of excellent vigor and are for the most part disease resistant. They are good choices for naturalizing and will often grow well without attention if planted properly and given minimal care during the first year or so. Species roses are particularly valuable for use with native perennials since both groups of plants tend to thrive with minimal attention.

Species roses can impart a natural elegance to the landscape and fit well into a wide variety of settings. Although many are climbers, with a minimum of pruning and training they can be grown as hefty shrubs.

Rosa moschata
'MUSK ROSE'

Species   1540   6' – 10'

The aroma of beeswax and honey distinguishes this climber or lax shrub which presumably originated in India or southern China and then spread west to southern Europe and northern Africa. It came to England via

Spain in 1521 and was in America by 1800. Musk roses prosper only in warm, humid climates where they can become large and everblooming. Cream-colored, medium-sized flowers appear in large clusters. The sweet fragrance is free in the air and more noticeable in the evening hours. The 'Musk Rose' is a parent of both the Noisette and Hybrid Musk classes and has only recently been identified and once again made available. Charles Walker, President of the Heritage Rose Foundation, has both the double and single forms of this plant at his garden in Raleigh, North Carolina. These are among the most fragrant roses I have experienced. The long bloom season, wonderful fragrance and ease of culture should once again make this a popular rose for locations that can absorb a fairly large specimen.

Rosa eglanteria
'SWEETBRIER'

Species   possibly prior to 1551   8′ – 10′

Clusters of single pink flowers occur in spring and are followed by orange-red, edible hips. 'Sweetbrier' is useful as a large shrub or climber, and is known for its apple-scented foliage. The fragrance is especially strong immediately following a warm rain.

Rosa palustris scandens
'SWAMP ROSE'

Species   1726   5′ – 6′

The 'Swamp Rose' is native from Louisiana eastward to Florida, occurring along streams and in marshes. This ability to tolerate wet, poorly-drained locations is rare among roses and adds to the value of the plant. The form most often found in old gardens in the South is double or semi-double and blooms in mid to late spring. Its stems are almost thornless, and the plant has a neat, weeping appearance that makes it attractive even when not in bloom. This form was in Empress Josephine's collection at Malmaison and was painted by Redoute, as *R. hudsoniana scandens*. Fragrance is excellent and the soft pink flowers can nearly cover the gracefully arching limbs for several weeks each spring.

Rosa moschata—'Musk Rose'

Rosa palustris—soft, fragrant, pink flowers

Rosa palustris scandens—'Swamp Rose'

Rosa laevigata—'Cherokee Rose'

'Cherokee Rose'—a climbing variety

Rosa multiflora 'Carnea'

Rosa laevigata
'CHEROKEE ROSE'
Species   1759   5′–15′

Georgians may be well aware of their state flower, but the 'Cherokee Rose' is little known elsewhere in the South. This disfavor derives from an unfortunate confusion of the 'Cherokee Rose' with the 'Macartney Rose' (*R. bracteata*), a distinct species that is a true pest to Southern stockmen and farmers. The 'Cherokee Rose' is a climber to 15′ or more, with neat, dark green leaves. In the spring it blooms profusely, bearing flowers of 5 pure white petals that soon drop cleanly to disclose the star-shaped sepals. It makes a good hedge, climber or pillar and is valuable for its ease of growth and disease resistance, although the stems are quite thorny.

Rosa multiflora 'Carnea'
'CARNEA'
Species   1804   15′–20′

This is an early parent of many of the rambler roses. It reached England in 1804 via the East India Company and has clusters of small, double, pink flowers. Although it blooms only in spring, it creates quite a display, throwing waves of pink blossoms over buildings, banks, dead trees, or fences—any place it can ramble.

Rosa setigera—'Prairie Rose'

Rosa setigera
'PRAIRIE ROSE'

Species   1810   4–6'

This is one of the roses native to Texas and the South. The arching branches, clusters of single, bright pink flowers that open in late spring, and the handsome red hips that follow them characterize this easily-grown plant. A thornless form of *R. setigera* 'Serena' is sometimes available in the trade. The plant does not sucker, but branch tips will root readily when they touch the ground. The 'Prairie Rose' is very drought and cold tolerant, and especially appropriate for low maintenance plantings.

Rosa roxburghii
'CHESTNUT ROSE'

Species   prior to 1814   5'–7'

The 'Chestnut Rose' is truly distinct. The double pink form was introduced from a Chinese garden to England in 1820. It has been found persevering in neglect at a number of old Texas and Southern gardens. Flowers occur primarily in May and June and are followed by bristly hips that resemble chestnut cases and fall off while green. Flaking, light brown bark on older plants, and leaves composed of a great many leaflets (up to 15), make the 'Chestnut Rose' easily remembered. Although not particularly fragrant, the flowers are quite beautiful, occur over a long period, and the plant is very disease resistant.

Rosa multiflora 'Platyphylla'
'SEVEN SISTERS'

Hybrid Multiflora   1817   15'–20'

Like many of the other roses described in this book, 'Seven Sisters' thrives only in the South where winters are relatively mild. There is much confusion concerning the identity of this rose, but the real 'Seven Sisters' is an impressive once-blooming rambler with large clusters of small flowers in shades of pink, mauve, and purple.

Rosa banksiae 'Lutea'
'YELLOW LADY BANKS'

Species   1824   10'–20'

The Yellow Banksia is an outstanding climbing rose for the South. The date of introduction given is when the plant was discovered in China and imported to England. It was named for the wife of the Royal Horticultural Society's president. Although usually treated as a climber and provided with structural support, it does fine with no support at all. Grown this way, Banksias require a great deal of space and can easily reach 15' in diameter and height. The only real enemy of this plant is severe

'Yellow Lady Banks'—close-up of the straw-yellow blooms

Rosa roxburghii—'Chestnut Rose'

R. banksiae 'Alba Plena'—'White Lady Banks'

cold. During the disastrous winter of 1983–84, Banksias and some other tender roses were damaged as far south as Central Texas. The flowers are very double, about 1″ in diameter, and last 3–4 weeks in early spring. The graceful arching habit of its thornless canes, its vigor, and its drought tolerance place this among the most useful of all old roses. The white form of this species, *R. Banksiae* 'Alba Plena' (1807), is rarer and much more fragrant. The scent is sometimes described as reminiscent of violets. Otherwise, the plants are quite similar, except for an occasional thorn on the white form.

Rosa anemoneflora
'WHITE CAROLINA CLIMBER'
Species   1844   10′–15′

This hybrid species was discovered by the great plant hunter Robert Fortune in China. When it was shipped home to England, it was generally panned by everyone who saw it. Then someone had the bright idea

Rosa banksiae 'Lutea'—'Yellow Lady Banks'—a climbing rose

that *R. anemoneflora* might be sulking in the cool, wet English climate and sent it to the American South where, like its Banksia cousins, it responded wonderfully. Somewhat like 'White Lady Banks,' it is covered in the spring with 1″ white flowers; the outer petals are smooth, but the centers are tufted and shaggy. It has a fragrance and an early spring bloom time like that of the Banksias.

Rosa x odorata
'FORTUNE'S DOUBLE YELLOW'
Miscellaneous Old Garden Rose   1845   6′–10′

This rose bears the name of its finder, Robert Fortune, a young Scottish undergardener who discovered it in the newly-opened China of 1845. Other names for this rose are "Beauty of Glazenwood" and "Gold of Ophir." Fortune's personal account of the event is as follows: "On entering one of the (mandarin's) gardens on a fine morning in May, I was struck with a mass of yellow flowers which completely covered a distant part of the wall. . . To my surprise and delight I found that I had discovered a most beautiful new yellow climbing rose" (52). Actually, the color is more buff-apricot with rose-colored penciling on the outer edges of the petals. Slender, apple-jade foliage lends a delicate appearance. Gertrude Jekyll praised it as being "indispensable on account of its grace and beauty" (264). 'Fortune's Double Yellow' blooms for several weeks in spring, and like many of the other old roses, it flowers more prolifically after several years' growth.

Rosa x odorata—'Fortune's Double Yellow'

'Fortuniana'

'FORTUNIANA'
Miscellaneous Old Garden Rose   1850   6′–10′

This rose is another of Robert Fortune's discoveries. Its advantages are its ability to thrive in poor, dry, sandy soils and its disease resistance, making it popular as an understock in Australia and parts of Florida. 'Fortuniana' is closely related to the Banksias, having the same cascading habit and similar leaflets, but its blooms are larger and in white only. Some experts speculate that it is a cross between *R. laevigata* (Cherokee Rose) and *R. banksiae* 'Alba Plena', and characteristics of both species appear obvious when the plant is examined closely. It has sometimes been sold erroneously as White Banksia. Fragrance is good, but the real value is in the ease of culture and graceful effect from this plant, which blooms about the same time as the Banksias each spring.

'ANEMONE ROSE'
Hybrid Laevigata   1896   6′–10′

"Pink Cherokee" is another name for this unusual rose that is a cross between the 'Cherokee Rose' and a Tea. Somewhat like a clematis in appearance, with large, pink flowers touched with rose blush, it blooms very early in the spring and grows rapidly. Because of the tender types in its family tree, it is not dependably cold hardy beyond North Texas.

'MERMAID'
Hybrid Bracteata   1918   10′–20′

'Mermaid' is reported to be a cross between *R. bracteata* (Macartney Rose) and an old yellow Tea rose. It is very vigorous and thorny, but also beautiful and fragrant. Sprinkled among the shiny, healthy foliage, the flowers bloom from late spring until frost. They are large, single, sulfur-yellow in color, with petals that shed cleanly. 'Mermaid' is very popular in England where it is used extensively as a wall rose in the gardens of Hampton Court, Hever Castle, and countless other

Hybrid *Bracteata*—'Mermaid'

R. foliolosa x R. rugosa—'Basye's Purple Rose'

'Mermaid' is a good wall rose.

estates. Jack Harkness, a past president of the Royal National Rose Society, gives 'Mermaid' his five-star rating and lists it among the ten finest roses of all time. It thrives in Texas and the South and is only occasionally damaged by cold in those areas.

R. foliolosa x R. rugosa
'BASYE'S PURPLE ROSE'
Shrub   1968   5'–6'

'Basye's Purple Rose' is a cross between *R. Foliolosa* (native to Arkansas) and *R. rugosa* (native to Japan). It was bred by Robert Basye, a retired university professor and active rose breeder from Caldwell, Texas, in his search for hardy, drought tolerant, disease resistant cultivars. 'Basye's Purple Rose' met all these criteria, yet he rejected it as a "jewel in the rough." The ravishingly fragrant, large, single flowers appear in profusion during the spring on a large, healthy shrub. Mr. Basye considers this rose to be a truly unusual color; royal purple with prominent gold stamens. When grown on its own roots it does sucker and can spread rather rapidly. It was given to me by Mr. Basye in 1983. I gave stock material to the Antique Rose Emporium at Brenham where it has been propagated and distributed.

China Roses

As early as a millennium before the birth of Christ, the Chinese had bred their single-flowering native roses into true garden types. The revolutionary characteristic of these roses was that they were everblooming. The everblooming quality of modern roses can all be traced back to these early Chinas.

Individual blossoms of most Chinas are not spectacular. These roses will never win "Best of Show," but their profusion of flowers, disease resistance, and typically long, healthy life more than compensates. It is not unusual to find specimens of China roses 100 or more years old surviving entirely without human care in cemeteries and abandoned homesites in Texas and the South. Bloom season is heaviest in mid-spring, with sprinklings of flowers all summer. Another heavy bloom in fall usually follows the first good rains in September or October.

Chinas are useful as hedges, specimen plants, or borders. If pruned severely, most of them can be easily maintained as small, rounded plants. When allowed to grow with only dead or weak wood removed, they slowly attain large size.

Dean S. Reynolds Hole, English rosarian and cleric who is credited with the formation of the Royal National

Rose Society, summed up his praise for the China Roses in his book *Our Gardens* published in 1899. "There is no other claimant to the title of Semper florens, bestowed by an ecumenical council of botanists upon the China or monthly roses—'Semper, ubique, ab omnibus'—always, everywhere, for all" (167).

'OLD BLUSH'

1752   5–6'

Other names for this rose are "Parsons' Pink China," "Old Pink Daily," "Common Monthly," and "Daisy Rose." This thrifty rose is one of the most common—yet pleasant—of the old roses. It bears medium, semi-double, light pink blossoms in many-flowered clusters, which often blush a dark rose on the outer edge of the petals in strong sun. 'Old Blush' is constantly in flower, with a really heavy flush in the spring. The bush is upright in habit and may bloom 11 months of the year in the Gulf South.

'CRAMOISI SUPÉRIEUR'

(krah mwah ZEE   Soo pay ry UHR)

1832   4'–6'

Another commonly used name for this rose is "Agrippina." It is said to greatly resemble the original red China, *R. chinensis* 'semperflorens'. 'Cramoisi Supérieur' has velvety, rich crimson flowers with a silvery reverse in a double, cupped form, and, like all Chinas, is very nearly

'Old Blush'

'Cramoisi Supérieur' resembles the original red China rose.

'Cramoisi Supérieur'—excellent for hedges

everblooming in this climate. The leaves are small, dark green, and very healthy. It is excellent for hedges, at the back of the flower border, as a shrub, or equally well suited as a pot rose. One of Gertrude Jekyll's favorites, it is a valuable and beautiful landscape plant that provides almost continuous color.

'LOUIS PHILIPPE'
(loo-WEE   fee-LEEP)

1834   3'–5'

One of the first Texas plantings of 'Louis Philippe' was at the Lynchburg home of Lorenzo de Zavala, Texas'

'Archduke Charles' is a more refined rose than most Chinas.

minister to France in 1834, who brought this and other roses back with him from the Court of St. Cloud. His homesite and cemetery are now swallowed by the industrial development along the Houston ship channel. The double, cupped flowers of 'Louis Philippe' are dark crimson, with blush edges on the center petals. Constant flowering occurs from early spring until winter—and even an occasional bloom occurs during winter warm spells.

'ARCHDUKE CHARLES'
prior to 1837   3'–5'

The best description of 'Archduke Charles' comes from the premier American old rosarian, Ethelyn Emery Keays, who said, "The full, lasting flower with outer petals of deep rose-red opens in a cupped shape, enclosing in the cup smaller petals of whitish pink to real white. . . The rose color gradually creeps in and over the pale center so entirely that the flower becomes a rose colored bloom" (96). She adds: "A fine old rose, much admired in the past." 'Archduke Charles' has a more refined flower than most Chinas. A single bush may appear to bear blooms of several different colors simultaneously, because the flowers' colors change rapidly as they age.

'Archduke Charles'

'Hermosa'

'Green Rose'

'HERMOSA'

1840   3'—4'

The famous Southern nurseryman Thomas Affleck of Natchez, Mississippi, and Gay Hill, Texas, said of 'Hermosa' in 1856, "Still one of the best!" A gracious, blue-green bushy plant of moderate growth, 'Hermosa' bears full, medium-sized flowers in clusters of a subtle old rose shade and is nearly always in bloom. William Paul, in 1848 noted, "'Hermosa' is good for mass plantings or as a pot rose." It is sometimes classified as a Bourbon.

Rosa chinensis 'Viridiflora'
'GREEN ROSE'

prior to 1845   3'—4'

Rosarians may argue whether or not this flower is beautiful, but all agree the 'Green Rose' is truly different. British rose authority Jack Harkness describes it as an "engaging monstrosity." Flower arrangers find the bronzy green "flowers" useful and long-lasting subjects. It is found in many old gardens in Texas and the South.

Rosa chinensis 'mutabilis'
'MUTABILIS'

prior to 1896   4'—6'

This most interesting rose of unknown origin grows to about 6' and has bronzy young growth. The single flowers open buff-yellow, changing to pink and finally crimson; often flowers of all three colors appear simultaneously. It is sometimes called the "Butterfly Rose,"

'Ducher'

Rosa Chinensis mutabili—'Mutabilis' This flower changes from buff-yellow to pink to crimson.

'Mutabilis' grows to a medium-sized shrub.

because its blooms resemble those graceful insects. 'Mutabilis' is a useful but twiggy shrub that is recommended as a wall plant by some experts. Although the plant is normally grown as a medium-sized shrub, a magnificent specimen at Kiftsgate Court, Gloucestershire, England, is described in Gault and Synge's *Dictionary of Roses in Colour* as covering a wall 20' in height and as wide. Although occasionally bothered by powdery mildew during the spring, 'Mutabilis' can be a fine addition to the Southern garden.

'DUCHER'

1869   3'–4'

This is the only white China rose I know, and for that reason it is valuable as a landscape plant. The flower is rather full and more refined than most Chinas, except perhaps 'Archduke Charles.' The flowers are fragrant, creamy white, profuse and frequent.

"MARTHA GONZALES"

a found rose   2'–3'

Miss Pamela Puryear, historian and rosarian from Navasota, Texas, found this beautiful rose growing as a hedge in the Navasota garden of Martha Gonzales. It has been given to the Antique Rose Emporium and San Antonio area nurseries for possible introduction. There is some evidence that the true identity of "Martha Gonzales" is 'Fabvier' an old, single or semi-double red China. "Martha Gonzales" is a very compact growing plant ideal for low hedges (18"–24"). It is disease resistant and almost constantly in flower with 2" bright red blooms.

Tea Roses

Tea roses are exceptionally well-suited to the southern climates and are often found as large bushes marking old homesites where they have cheerfully survived with no care whatsoever for decades. They are large and

"Climbing Lady Pamela," with its characteristic tall, narrow bush, is an exquisite example of a Tea Rose.

'Bon Silène'

'Satrano'

memorable roses, the kind people speak of with nostalgia and family remembrance.

Many old Tea roses resemble in form the typical high-centered Hybrid Teas of today, so they are appreciated as cut flowers as well as landscape plants. This class, bred in Europe from tender rose hybrids of China, was very popular from the 1830s until its own more cold-hardy descendents, the Hybrid Teas, superseded it at the turn of the century.

As a rule, Teas have an upright habit, forming tall and sometimes narrow bushes with bronzy-red new foliage. In the Southern states, they bloom profusely in the spring and fall, with scattered summer flowers. Blossoms are spectacular and large in pastel pinks and yellows, with some reds and a few whites. Fragrance is distinctive, cool and somewhat like dried tea leaves. Most Teas have good resistance to blackspot and seem to thrive in the heat of Texas and the Gulf South. They are tender and are occasionally damaged by cold in Central and Northern Texas. Tea roses bloom until very cold weather. Accounts of early Texans gathering bouquets for Christmas and other midwinter events indicate that they were

considered an essential part of the garden at that time. The flower stems are weak and often bow gracefully with the weight of the large flowers. This was considered an elegant trait during Victorian times and is still appreciated by those who enjoy the many distinctive and easily grown roses that comprise the Tea class.

'BON SILÈNE'
(BOHn   see LEHN)

prior to 1837   4'–6'

'Bon Silène' is an old favorite that bears blossoms of a color unusual in a Tea rose. The deep rose-colored buds are profuse and well-scented. This is one of the oldest Teas and still among the best.

'DEVONIENSIS'

1838   8' – 10'

An extremely beautiful rose sometimes known as the "Magnolia Rose," 'Devoniensis' flowers are creamy white, very double, and large. Occasionally there is a blush of pink. 'Devoniensis' is somewhat like a climbing form of 'Souvenir de la Malmaison.'

'SAFRANO'

1839   5' – 7'

A large specimen of 'Safrano' in the beautifully restored kitchen garden of the Mordecai House in Raleigh, North Carolina, fits in beautifully with the herbs and perennials. Bright apricot buds open to large, semi-double flowers of fawn or buff-tinted saffron. Mature plants assume a handsome mounded form, often as wide as they are tall.

'SOMBREUIL'
(sohm BRUH ee)

1850   6' – 10'

The strong Tea fragrance, shiny, dark green foliage and spectacular creamy white flowers make this one of the most beautiful and useful of all roses. 'Sombreuil' is a rather mannerly climber, sometimes reaching 8'—10'. The flowers are often tinted with pink and are very double and formal, almost like an 'Alba Plena' camellia. Stems are very thorny, but the foliage is beautiful and unusually disease resistant. Heavy spring bloom with some summer flowers and a good profusion in the fall is typical for well-established plants.

'Sombreuil' has dark green foliage and creamy white flowers.

'Sombreuil' is a mannerly climber.

'Belle Portugaise' (Belle of Portugal)

'Monsieur Tillier'

'Duchesse de Brabant'

'Catherine Mermet'

Belle of Portugal is draped across a trellis for a picturesque effect.

'Mrs. B. R. Cant'

'Mrs. Dudley Cross'

'GLOIRE DE DIJON'
(glwahr   duh   dee ZHOHn)
1853   10'–15'

This is a magnificent rose with flat, quartered, peachy pink blooms tinged apricot in the centers. This is a favorite among the clergy in England, where 'Gloire de Dijon' has graced the south walls of homes and churches for over a century. It is excellent as a pillar or on a fence or trellis, but is not as blackspot resistant as some of the other Teas.

'DUCHESSE DE BRABANT'
1857   3'–5'

Tulip-shaped pink-rose flowers of medium size occur all season on a bush that is fairly small for a Tea rose. Fragrance is excellent although powdery mildew does find its foliage and buds irresistible, especially during the spring season. 'Duchesse de Brabant' was a favorite rose of Teddy Roosevelt, who wore a bud or flower frequently as a boutonniere. A white sport of this variety, 'Mme Joseph Schwartz,' is equally valuable and has pink tints on the edges of the petals.

'CATHERINE MERMET'
(kah tuh REEN   mehr MAY)
1869   3'–4'

This is one of the best Teas for cut flower use. Healthy and flowering profusely in our summer heat, 'Catherine Mermet' bears large, pink blossoms all during the warm seasons.

'MARIE VAN HOUTTE'
1871   4'–6'

'Marie van Houtte' epitomizes the unique, subtle color combinations that can occur in old Tea roses. The flowers are large, globular, and lemon yellow. The color is deeper in the center with pinkish-lilac tips washing the edges of the petals. The foliage is a rich, dark green that provides good contrast for the light-colored flowers.

'PERLE DES JARDINS'
(pehrl   day   zhar DEHn)
1874   3'–5'

The canary-yellow flowers are large, full and well-formed. Stems are stronger than on most Teas, which made 'Perle des Jardins' one of the most popular cut roses of its time.

'GENERAL SCHABLIKINE'
1878   3'–5'

Salmony-beige flowers with outer petals edged in carmine appear continuously from spring till fall on one of the finest of all Teas. Said to have more cold resistance than most in its class, 'General Schablikine' seems to have everything but a pronounceable name.

'MONSIEUR TILLIER'
1891   3'–6'

Full, fragrant flowers on fairly compact plants occur throughout the growing season. The most distinctive characteristic of this rose is its color: carmine, fading to brick red. Even fully open flowers are more handsome than those of most Teas.

'MRS. B.R. CANT'
1901   5'–7'

This is the most prolific flowering and vigorous Tea rose I have grown. The large flowers have pale silver-rose petals tipped with dark rose. They are very full, quartered, and fragrant. It has good resistance to blackspot but some temporary attacks of mildew may occur. 'Mrs. B.R. Cant' is among the best old roses for cutting.

'BELLE PORTUGAISE' (Belle of Portugal)
1903   15'–20'

This is a once-blooming rose that is spectacular for a few weeks each spring. The buds are long and beautiful, a rich, soft pink, opening to huge, blowsy, semi-double flowers. *R. gigantea* is a large-flowered species from China and an ancestor of the Tea class. This cultivar is one result of recrossing *R. gigantea* with the Teas. It is among the most tender of roses and is of little value in cooler climates. 'Belle Portugaise' is a very fast and rampant grower that can create quite a picture when covering parts of buildings, trellises or pergolas. Disease resistance is good.

'MRS. DUDLEY CROSS'
1907   4'–6'

This is a favorite of Tea rose connoisseurs. The full, pale yellow flowers are usually tinged with pink. The stems are thornless or nearly so and the foliage is exceptionally healthy and disease resistant. Color and flower shape are somewhat similar to the more modern 'Peace' rose, but 'Mrs. Dudley Cross' is smaller and daintier in size. This is one of the Tea roses most often found thriving in old or abandoned gardens. The flowers are excellent for cutting.

'Lady Hillingdon'

'LADY HILLINGDON'

1910   4'–6'

The beautifully pointed buds of rich apricot yellow and the young purple shoots and foliage are distinctive features of this lovely rose, while the sepals' ornamented edges add a note of elegance. Flowers are semi-double and occur throughout the growing season. It is less disease resistant than most Teas.

'ROSETTE DELIZY'

(roh ZEHT   duh lee ZEE)

1922   3'–4'

The small but perfectly formed flowers are an ochre yellow edged with brick red. Although a latecomer to the Tea class, 'Rosette Delizy' is distinctive and vigorous, but compact and modest in size.

Early Hybrid Teas

Early crosses between Teas and Hybrid Perpetuals resulted in the first Hybrid Teas. As *R. foetida* was brought into the breeding, new yellow, red, and orange colors were added. *R. foetida* is also credited with high susceptibility to black spot disease, which has made the class more vulnerable to that major fungal problem. The Tea roses used in the breeding contributed disease resistance and repeat flowering. A few Hybrid Teas that have stood the test of time are included for your information.

'LA FRANCE'

1867   5'–6'

'La France,' the very first Hybrid Tea, has the classic long-pointed bud typical of its Tea ancestry. Flowers are silvery-pink with darker reverse. There is a swirling characteristic to the center petals that is distinctive to 'La France.' The plant is vigorous, although susceptible to black spot in some locations.

'RADIANCE' (Pink Radiance)

1908   4'–6'

This is a famous rose bred by John Cook of Baltimore in 1904 and introduced by Peter Henderson in 1908. This original form is a warm pink in color. Although there are only about two dozen petals, the flowers are large, rounded and impressive, as well as very fragrant. 'Radiance' is one of the most popular roses of this century and well worth having if a good, vigorous clone is available.

'RED RADIANCE'

1916   4'–6'

This is a sport of 'Radiance' that is dark rose, not red, in color. It is very similar to its parent in every way except in color, and it probably became even more popular.

'CLIMBING ETOILE DE HOLLAND'

1931   10'–12'

Well-formed blooms of about 35 petals and unfading scarlet-crimson color make 'Climbing Etiole de Holland' one of the most popular roses of all time. Flowers can sometimes measure 5"—6" across. This is a climbing sport of the bush form which was introduced in 1919.

'CRIMSON GLORY'

1935   5'–6'

A Wilhelm Kordes introduction, 'Crimson Glory' is the red rose to which all others are compared. It is a deep, velvety maroon-red with petals of excellent substance and unforgettable fragrance.

Noisette Roses

The Noisettes, a group of graceful, repeat-flowering shrubs and climbers, were the first class of roses to originate in the United States. Early Noisettes have clusters of small flowers while the later ones have larger blossoms, with fewer per cluster. These later varieties resulted from crosses with roses from the Tea class.

John Champneys, a rice planter from Charleston, South Carolina, raised the first Noisette by crossing the Musk Rose known in Shakespeare's day with 'Old Blush.' He named it 'Champneys' Pink Cluster'. A few years later, Philippe Noisette, a florist from Charleston and a friend of Champneys', raised a seedling from Champneys' rose. In 1817, Noisette sent his rose to his brother Louis in Paris, who named it 'Blush Noisette.' The French eagerly received and expanded the new rose class because of its heavy clustering bloom, musky scent, and strong, healthy growth. Although considered more tender to cold than most classes, the Noisettes were immensely popular, and are well adapted to the Southern states. As a rule, however, they are not as resistant to black spot and mildew as the Teas and Chinas.

Many of the Noisettes have the ability to create a landscape effect unique among roses. Whether grown on walls, fences, arbors, or even on trees, the climbing varieties are indispensable to gardens where a period effect is desired.

'CHAMPNEYS' PINK CLUSTER'

circa 1811   4′–8′

This is a very fragrant rose that bears 1½″–2″ double pink flowers in large clusters throughout the season. It is effective when used against a fence or wall, or as a single specimen. With age, it can become a large and handsome upright shrub.

'BLUSH NOISETTE'

1817   3′–5′

From its Musk grandparent, 'Blush Noisette' inherited a tolerance for cold that was, unfortunately, lost in the later Noisettes; like all of its class, 'Blush Noisette' also duplicates the Musk Rose's ability to produce a fall bloom. The small, white blooms open from pinkish buds after every summer rain and put on a good display into the autumn. Blooms are continuous during the growing season, and have excellent fragrance.

'AIMÉE VIBERT'

(ehm MAY   vee BEHR)

1828   6′–10′

A vigorous climber or large shrub, 'Aimée Vibert' has enjoyed wide popularity in England and France. The dark green foliage is a perfect foil for the clusters of medium-sized, pink buds that open to pure white and have typically rich Noisette fragrance. 'Aimée Vibert' was a favorite of Gertrude Jekyll and appears in several photographs in her book *Roses for English Gardens*.

'Lamarque'—fragrant, double flowers, white with yellow centers

'Lamarque'—a fine noisette climber

'Champney's Pink Cluster'—a noisette rose

'LAMARQUE'

1830   8' – 10'

'Lamarque' is a fine climber and is a result of a cross
between 'Blush Noisette' and 'Parks' Yellow Tea-Scented
China'. The double flowers are moderate in size, and
white with yellow centers. Blooms occur in clusters and
fragrance is excellent. A specimen of 'Lamarque' found
by Extension Horticulturist Greg Grant in San Antonio
has been verified to be 97 years old. Several very large
and handsome specimens may be found tumbling over
garden walls along Church Street in the restored area of
Charleston, South Carolina. The foliage of 'Lamarque' is
unusually dark green and healthy.

'JAUNE DESPREZ'

(zhohn   day PRAY)

1830   15' – 20'

The medium-yellow, quartered blooms of 'Jaune
Desprez' have green centers and are wonderfully fragrant.
They were much admired in Charleston, South Carolina,
during the 1840s. It is another distinctive climber that
can create a beautiful garden picture. It blooms heavily
in spring and fall with scattered flowers throughout the
summer.

'Jeanne D'Arc'—a pure white rose with an outstanding fragrance

'Jaune Desprez'

'Céline Forestier'

'Jeanne D'Arc'—flowers with fruit

'JEANNE D'ARC'

(zhahn   dark)

1848   5' – 8'

The flowers of this rose are pure white, and like
most other Noisettes, outstandingly fragrant. If the
faded blooms are allowed to stay on the plant and mature, they ripen into large clusters of handsome red fruit.
Sometimes in late fall, both flower and fruit appear
together and make an impressive combination.

'CÉLINE FORESTIER'

(Say lean   Fohr res tee ay)

1858   10' – 15'

Strong, spicy scent accompanies the lovely quartered, flat, creamy-yellow flowers of 'Céline Forestier.'
It is sometimes slow to establish, but mature plants can
be spectacular.

'Maréchal Niel'

'Rêve d'Or'

'MARÉCHAL NIEL'
(mah ray SHAHL neel)
1864   10′–15′

This magnificent rose was legendary during the last century and early part of this one. The full, quartered, buttery yellow blossoms have a unique fragrance that is memorable. 'Maréchal Niel' is very tender to cold and difficult to establish. It appears to have degenerated over the years or perhaps acquired a virus that has weakened the plant. Until a vigorous source for propagation material can be assured, 'Maréchal Niel' will probably have to remain only in the memory of those of us who have seen and experienced its beauty and fragrance. Considered by many to be the finest yellow rose ever created, it is a moderate climber that blooms prolifically all season.

An apparently vigorous specimen of 'Maréchal Niel,' verified to be more than 50 years old, has recently been located in a Central Texas garden. Budwood and cuttings are currently being evaluated in several locations throughout the South to see if it retains the legendary vigor.

'RÊVE D'OR'
(rehv dohr)
1869   10′–12′

Being nearly thornless, 'Rêve d'Or' is especially useful in close quarters. The pendulous, globular flowers are beige-yellow and are produced all season.

'MADAME ALFRED CARRIÈRE'
(kah ree EHR)
1879   15′–20′

The buds on this vigorous plant are large and similar to typical Hybrid Teas. The flowers open pale lavender-pink, but quickly fade to white. It is famous in England for the displays it creates on walls.

Rosa moschata 'Nastarana'
'NASTARANA'
1879   3′–4′

Large clusters of medium-sized, pure white, fragrant flowers are produced almost constantly on this upright, 3′–4′ plant. 'Nastarana' is reported to have originated in Iran and was known to be popular in old Persian rose gardens. The fruit is red-orange when ripe and occurs in large clusters. Although susceptible to mildew and black spot, 'Nastarana' is a tough and attractive rose.

'CLAIRE JACQUIER'
(zhock YEHR)
1888   15′–20′

This is a vigorous climber with clusters of yolk-yellow buds that open to blowsy, double, cream-colored blooms. It has good fragrance and reblooms in the fall.

'MARY WASHINGTON'

1891   6'–8'

'Mary Washington' is more like some of the early, small-flowered Noisettes with its semi-double, pale pink flowers on a neat attractive plant. It may be used as a small climber or shrub. It has outstanding fragrance and is one of the most profuse bloomers to be found.

Bourbon Roses

Bourbon roses resulted from a natural cross between 'Old Blush' and 'Autumn Damask,' both planted as hedges on the French island then called Bourbon, now Reunion. An alert resident sent the plant to France where breeders further perfected the class. The first cultivar was painted by Redoute in 1817. There are about forty varieties still in commerce today.

Bourbons have some of the most beautiful flowers ever developed. They often have old-fashioned cupped or quartered blossoms, generally in pastel pinks, on large, robust plants. Due to their Damask influence, Bourbons tend to be more cold hardy than Chinas or Teas. Only a few varieties reliably repeat-flower in summer and fall in Texas and the South. These roses also tend to be more susceptible to black spot and mildew than Chinas or

Teas. Bourbon flowers tend to be highly fragrant and beautifully formed, which accounts for their popularity in spite of their spray requirements and sometimes sparse bloom.

'SOUVENIR DE LA MALMAISON'

(soov NIHR'd   la   mahl meh ZOHn)

1843   3'–4'

Malmaison was Empress Josephine's country place outside Paris. This rose did not grow there, amid her fine collection, but was introduced after her death and named in honor of her garden. 'Souvenir de la Malmaison' produces large, flat, quartered blossoms with thick petals, in a beautiful tint of pink. Fragrance is fine and the bush tends to be compact and attractive. It is the most reliably repeat-flowering Bourbon I have grown, and the only one I have found surviving in old Texas gardens. Thomas Affleck, the great nurseryman and writer said of 'Souvenir de la Malmaison' in 1856, "How I envy the grower who first saw that plant bloom, the seed of which he had sown, feeling that such a gem was his!"

'LOUISE ODIER'

1851   4'–6'

The very full, medium-sized, camellia-shaped blooms are a beautiful tint of light rose or deep pink inside. They have a delightful fragrance, but infrequently rebloom after the first long and impressive show in spring.

'ZÉPHIRINE DROUHIN'

(zay fih REEN   droo EHn)

1868   6'–15'

This mannerly climber is a treasure in the garden for its unusual, semi-double cerise flowers and thornless

'Souvenir de la Malmaison'—a Bourbon rose

'Zéphirine Drouhin'—a popular wall rose in England

'Louise Odier'

'La Reine Victoria'

'Madame Isaac Pereire'

'Variegata di Bologna'

stems. It is sometimes used as a large shrub and is one of the most popular wall roses in England. It has done beautifully in my Texas garden and finally, several years after planting, offered a few fall flowers in addition to the magnificent show in spring. It is very fragrant.

'LA REINE VICTORIA'

1872   5'–6'

The cupped, pale lilac-rose flowers of 'La Reine Victoria' are truly distinctive. The bush is rather tall and narrow, often with many canes. It has not been recurrent in my garden, and tends to black spot badly.

'MADAME ISAAC PEREIRE'
(pehr REHR)

1881   6'–7'

This is a very full and sumptuous rose. The flowers are a subtle, bright rose-madder with perhaps the strongest rose perfume extant. The plant is vigorous and thorny, but quite susceptible to black spot. Described as a good fall bloomer in the literature, like many of the Bourbons grown in the Deep South it rarely flowers after a long and plentiful spring season.

'MADAME ERNEST CALVAT'

1888   5'–7'

Actually a sport of 'Madame Isaac Pereire,' 'Mme. Ernest Calvat' produces dozens of quartered, full, rich pink flowers each spring. It may be grown as a shrub or trained on a wall, pillar, or fence.

'VARIEGATA DI BOLOGNA'

1909   4'–6'

The distinctively striped flowers of 'Variegata di Bologna' make it a popular choice in the garden or for cut flowers in the home. The very round flowers are 3"–4" across and appear in clusters of three to five. The white blossoms are streaked, flecked and splashed with pale purple and are well-scented.

Hybrid Perpetuals

Although the Hybrid Perpetual class contains some of the most beautiful of all the old roses, the "perpetual" part of the name is a bit of a misnomer. It was wishful thinking on the part of the Victorian nurserymen who developed these roses, for they are remontant rather than perpetual. Most varieties bloom heavily in spring, rest during summer, then bear scattered flowers in fall. The class has been interbred with almost all types of garden roses, but is perhaps closest to the Bourbons and Damasks.

The Hybrid Perpetuals were forerunners of the modern Hybrid Teas and have some similar characteristics. They are not as disease resistant as the Teas and

Chinas, but probably are less prone to black spot and mildew than the Bourbons.

An interesting way to grow Hybrid Perpetuals is to "peg" them. One method of pegging is to fasten the ends of the canes to the ground with stakes or wire pins; the lateral buds will break from the canes and provide a beautiful fountain effect. Another form of pegging is to secure the entire canes as closely as possible to the ground, so that the plant actually becomes a ground cover. The most popular way to grow Hybrid Perpetuals is as chunky shrubs with little trimming.

'Geant des Batailles'—a Hybrid Perpetual

'GEANT DES BATAILLES'
(zhay AHn   day   bah TY)

1846   4'–6'

This has been one of the best of the class in my garden. 'Giant of Battles' produces flowers of medium size in a beautiful red-purple color. They are highly fragrant and recurrent and produce a handsome shrub useful in border or mass plantings.

'GÉNÉRAL JACQUEMINOT'
(zhay nay RAHL   zhock mee NOH)

1853   4'–6'

Known affectionately as "General Jack," this rose was immensely popular for many years. The dark red flowers have good fragrance and were sold commercially as cut flowers by florists.

'Souvenir du Docteur Jamain'

'REINE DES VIOLETTES'

1860   4'–5'

This is one of the thornless or nearly thornless roses. The flowers are flat and an interesting muted cerise-lilac in color. It is a vigorous grower with attractive, glossy leaves.

'SOUVENIR DU DOCTEUR JAMAIN'
(soov NIHR   doo   doc TUHR   zhah MEHn)

1865   5'–6'

The neat, quartered blooms of this rose are deep crimson-maroon, aging to almost purple. The color is truly distinctive, as is the fragrance. Ancestry is legendary and includes the famed 'General Jacqueminot' (1853), 'Victor Verdier' (1859), and 'La Reine' (1843).

'BARONESS ROTHSCHILD'

1868   4'–6'

This rose was introduced by the famous French firm of Pernet and has huge blooms of light pink with exceptional fragrance. The flowers are of the cabbage type and are cupped.

'Paul Neyron'

'PAUL NEYRON'
(Pohl   nay ROHn)

1869   5'–6'

The huge, fragrant, rose-pink flowers often reach 6"–7" in diameter and are the epitome of old rose blossoms for many people. With its thornless stems and attractive foliage, a good flower of 'Paul Neyron' is a joy to behold. It has rebloomed well in my garden during all but the very hottest time of the summer and is a personal favorite.

'Climbing American Beauty'

'Ulrich Brünner Fils'

'Marquise Boccella'

'AMERICAN BEAUTY'

1875   4'–5'

'American Beauty' is a legendary rose worthy of its fame. It is remembered for its name and the dark, rich, pink color of its blossoms. The 3"—4" globular blooms have excellent substance and strong, heavy rose scent. The stems have few thorns and the plant tends to re-bloom well.

'CLIMBING AMERICAN BEAUTY'

1909   12'–15'

This deep rose, large-flowered climber is not a sport but a result of a series of crosses between 'American Beauty,' the species *R. wichuraiana*, and a Hybrid Tea. Still found in some of the old gardens of Texas and the South, it is quite spectacular in the spring but has not rebloomed in my garden.

'ULRICH BRÜNNER FILS'

1881   4'–6'

This has been one of the most profusely flowering and dependable rebloomers of all the Hybrid Perpetuals I have grown. The flowers are large and fairly full in an intense bright rose-red on a big, healthy bush. Fragrance is good, and the size and form of the plant make it useful as a hedge or specimen.

'MARCHIONESS OF LONDONDERRY'

1893   5'–6'

The flowers of this variety are often referred to as "Cabbage Roses." Actually, roses in the Centifolia class correctly carry this title but they do not generally thrive in Texas and the Deep South. The huge flowers of 'Marchioness of Londonderry' are white, tinged pale pink, and are reminiscent of the artificial flowers sometimes found in Victorian millinery.

'GEORG ARENDS'

1910   4'–6'

This rose is considered by some authorities to be the most beautiful pink rose ever raised. Fragrance is excellent. 'Georg Arends' is a result of a cross between 'Frau Karl Druschki' (1901) and 'La France' (1867).

'MARQUISE BOCCELLA'

1842   3'–5'

This rose is sometimes listed in the Portland class, of which there are few remaining members. It is also known as "Jacques Cartier" by some authorities. By any name or class, it is one of the finest old roses available, blooming almost constantly with medium-sized, button-eyed, bright pink, powder-puff flowers. The blooms have numerous tiny petals which reflex to give this charming effect. One blossom's light, sweet, Damask fragrance can fill a room. It is a very distinctive flower and plant that, once grown, is never forgotten.

Polyanthas

Polyanthas are hardy, sometimes disease resistant, and very floriferous. The plants are often dwarf and compact, lending themselves well to low borders, mass plantings, and container use. Their small, perfectly-formed buds are ideal for boutonnieres.

The Polyantha class was created by crossing the Chinas with the rambling Japanese Multiflora rose. The Chinas gave their everblooming characteristic and shrub shape to some of the roses in this class. Since both parents were from the same area in the Far East, some Polyanthas occurred naturally. The French breeders used them after their importation in 1865.

Although there are exceptions, my experience indicates the earlier members of the class to be more valuable in the garden. Some of the later Polyanthas appear to be highly susceptible to mildew.

'CÉCILE BRÜNNER'
1881   3'–4'

One of the most beloved roses of all time, this was created in France by Joseph Pernet-Ducher, who crossed 'Mignonette' and a Tea rose named 'Madame de Tartas.' The flowers are lightly fragrant and are like perfectly formed miniature Teas, the exquisite pink buds opening to 1½" reflexed flowers. 'Cécile Brünner' blooms heavily in spring, followed by continuous flowering until freezing weather. It is long-lived and has healthy foliage. Although this rose is often referred to by the masculine name Cecil, research by old rose authorities confirms that it was named for a lady and is properly called Cécile.

'CLIMBING CÉCILE BRÜNNER'
1894   10'–20'

The climbing sport of 'Cécile Brünner' is vigorous and fine, reaching 15'–20' on a trellis, fence, or wall. I

'Climbing Cécile Brünner' is a vigorous polyantha. It bears a delicate pink bloom.

have also seen it growing without support in an umbrella shape 8' – 10' feet across. Most of the old plants found in cemeteries and gardens are the climbing form, which attests to its unusual stamina and adaptibility to a wide range of growing conditions. Although more spectacular during spring and fall than the dwarf form, 'Climbing Cécile Brünner' tends to bloom less during the summer months.

'PERLE D'OR'
(pehrl   dohr)

1884   3'–4'

This rose is very similar to the dwarf form of 'Cécile Brünner' but with a slightly more salmon to orange-toned bloom. 'Perle d'Or' is lightly fragrant, with beautifully formed buds, and is effective in masses, hedges, specimen or container plantings.

'Perle d'Or' has a salmon to orange-toned bloom.

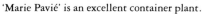

'Marie Pavié' is an excellent container plant.

'MARIE PAVIÉ'
(pahv YAY)

1888   2'–4'

This is one of the most useful roses I know. The pale pink buds occur in medium-size clusters and open to semi-double, blush white flowers. 'Marie Pavié' is intensely fragrant, usually thornless, and has dark, healthy foliage with small prickles on the midribs. Blooms occur all during the warm seasons in abundance. It is excellent in containers and as a 3'–4' hedge.

'CLOTILDE SOUPERT'
(kloh TIHLD   soo PEHR)

1890   3'–4'

The individual flowers of 'Clotilde Soupert' are unlike any other Polyantha—large and full, sometimes quartered, with over 100 neatly layered pale-pink petals. Fragrance is excellent, but mildew and black spot are especially troublesome during spring and fall. It is never out of bloom until hard frost.

'Clotilde Soupert'

'Marie Pavié'

'The Fairy' with tiny, double pink buds

'La Marne'

'LA MARNE'

1915   4'–6'

'La Marne' is an excellent landscape rose, quite effective as a hedge. The 10-petaled flowers with pink edges and cream-white centers are borne in clusters. Specimens of 'La Marne' are fairly common in old cemeteries throughout Texas and the South. Although susceptible to mildew, especially in spring, completely neglected plants often survive and look good for much of the year. The fragrant flowers are at their very best during the cooler parts of the blooming season.

'MEVROUW NATHALIE NYPELS' ('Nathalie Nypels')

1919   2'–3'

'Nathalie Nypels' is very similar to 'La Marne.' The foliage is dark green and glossy. Clusters of loose, semi-double, bright pink flowers occur continuously and are slightly larger than those of 'La Marne.' Fragrance is vague but the flowers and shrub are choice.

'THE FAIRY'

1932   3'–4'

Sprays of tiny, double, rose-pink flowers against petite, dark green leaves combine to make 'The Fairy' a tidy, handsome, and useful shrub. Flowering begins later than most roses, usually by mid-May. Summer heat turns the flowers nearly white, but the blooms continue as long as some moisture is available. Stems are thorny and the flowers have little fragrance, but the glossy foliage, compact form, and masses of pink flowers ensure the continued popularity of this fine rose. It is excellent for hedges, mass plantings or container use.

'JEAN MERMOZ'

1937   1'–2'

The flowers of 'Jean Mermoz' are long lasting and of great substance. They occur in clusters of six to nine and are a beautiful clear pink. Fragrance is minimal, but the compact form and beautiful flowers are sufficient to recommend this rose for low masses and containers.

Hybrid Musks

The Hybrid Musks include some of the most useful roses for landscape purposes. The first varieties were created by the Reverend Joseph Hardwick Pemberton (1850–1926), an East Anglian cleric who bred a possible hybrid of *R. moschata* with certain Hybrid Teas and Polyanthas to establish this distinctive rose class.

In the South, the Hybrid Musks tend to bloom heavily in the spring, followed by scattered summer

'Trier'

'Prosperity'

'Vanity'

flowers and then a delightful display in the fall that can last until very cold weather. Hybrid Musks may be used as shrubs, mannerly climbers, pillars, or hedges. The colors are beautiful pastels and blends, the fragrance outstanding, foliage handsome, and disease resistance good. Some varieties even bear handsomely ornamental fruit.

As landscape plants they are among the best roses available. In addition to being long-lived and easily grown, Hybrid Musks reportedly tolerate more shade than most roses.

'TRIER'

1904   5'–7'

This white rambling rose is important as one of the ancestors of Pemberton's and Bentall's Hybrid Musks. 'Trier' is lax in growth habit with small, blush-white blossoms showing yellow at the base of each petal. The small, red fruit is plentiful and attractive.

'DANAË'

1913   4'–5'

Exceptionally dark, shiny foliage and yolk-yellow buds that fade to creamy white characterize this Pemberton creation. The medium-sized orange-red fruit is attractive in the fall.

'PROSPERITY'

1919   4'–6'

Dark green foliage and sweetly fragrant, double flowers of ivory white with touches of pink describe this versatile plant. One of the few Hybrid Musks found in old Texas and Southern gardens, 'Prosperity' is sometimes trained as a climber. Red fruits provide an extra color accent.

'VANITY'

1920   6'–7'

Cerise-pink flowers recur throughout the season on this beautiful and unusual shrub of lax habit, that often spreads as wide as it is tall. The color is striking in the garden and useful as a background for perennials or lower, more compact-growing roses or shrubs. Fall brings large, orange hips.

'PENELOPE'

1924   4'–5'

The most popular of the Pemberton Musks, 'Penelope' is a dense, twiggy bush five feet high and even wider across. Vigorous and large leaved, it bears dense

'Penelope' with a salmon pink bloom and pink rose hip

'Penelope'—its dense, twiggy bush

corymbs of very pale salmon-pink flowers of strong aroma, followed by a winter crop of unusual pink hips. It is excellent as a hedge or shrub.

'CORNELIA'
1925   5'–6'

'Cornelia' has a subtle scent and a luscious color unique among the Hybrid Musks. The flowers are small, semi-double, and pale coral with gold stamens that show well against the dark green foliage. It is useful as a large shrub, specimen, or easily managed climber.

'BISHOP DARLINGTON'
1926   4'–6'

Coral-pink buds open to large, creamy, semi-double flowers imbued with true Musk fragrance. An upright form makes 'Bishop Darlington' useful for hedges.

'AUTUMN DELIGHT'
1933   5'–6'

After the Reverend Pemberton's death, his nursery manager, John A. Bentall, introduced this and other roses based on his breeding. 'Autumn Delight' is almost single flowered. The large, spectacular blooms are off-white and have prominent stamens.

'SKYROCKET'
1934   4'–6'

'Skyrocket' blooms in flushes with huge clusters of true red flowers covering a husky plant that can reach six feet tall and wide. One of the few Hybrid Musks found

'Cornelia'

in Texas and Southern gardens. A very useful variety and unusual color for the class. It was created by Wilhelm Kordes of Germany.

'BELINDA'
1936   4'–8'

This is a latter-day Hybrid Musk introduced by Ann Bentall, the wife of the Reverend Pemberton's former nursery manager. 'Belinda' matures into a rounded bush, bearing fragrant, soft pink flowers with a white eye and about ten petals each. It repeats well and bears clusters of red fruit. Ann's granddaughter was named for this rose.

'BALLERINA'
1937   4'–6'

'Ballerina' originated as a chance seedling discovered by Ann Bentall. An outstanding landscape plant

'Belinda'

'Skyrocket'—it can be a massive bush

'Ballerina' with ornamental fruit

'Ballerina'—single light pink flowers with white eyes

'Ballerina'—its fountain-like character

'Buff Beauty'

'Erfurt'

'Will Scarlet'

with dense, healthy, vigorous growth, 'Ballerina' lends itself especially well to group or mass plantings. The small, single flowers are light pink with white eyes and occur in large clusters throughout the growing season. The small fruits resemble nandina berries and are probably the most ornamental of the class. Mounded form and fountain-like character make 'Ballerina' an unusually attractive and useful plant.

'BUFF BEAUTY'

1939   4'–6'

The 2″ blooms of 'Buff Beauty' are muted apricot, blending beautifully with other old rose pastels. Its habit is a spreading bush, and its unbelievable flush of spring and fall bloom make it a favorite in the class. Like most other Hybrid Musks, 'Buff Beauty' is a shy bloomer the first year it is planted and tends to increase in floral display each year.

'ERFURT'

1939   5'–6'

The deep rose-colored, semi-double blooms are creamy white at the base of the petals and have gold stamens and a strong musk fragrance. This cascading bush reblooms well and was created by Wilhelm Kordes of Germany.

'WILL SCARLET'

1948   5'–7'

A sport of 'Skyrocket,' 'Will Scarlet' produces abundant clusters of medium-sized, fragrant flowers intermittently through the growing season, followed by profuse quantities of medium-sized, orange-red fruit. The scarlet flowers make 'Will Scarlet' a popular choice among those seeking a good low-maintenance shrub or climber.

'WIND CHIMES'

circa 1949   6'–7'

Single, rosy pink flowers paling toward the center in large sprays, followed by red fruit, characterize this later addition to the Hybrid Musk class. Fragrance is good and the plant is vigorous and thorny.

Assorted Roses of Merit from Various Classes

Included in this section are roses from a variety of classes that are worthy of consideration for landscapes in Texas and the Gulf South.

R. gallica versicolor
'ROSA MUNDI'
prior to 1581   3'–4'

This is the oldest striped rose on record and a sport of the Red Rose of Lancaster, *R. gallica officinalis*. It is a once-bloomer for a fairly long season in the spring, and is useful as a low-growing rose in front of taller roses or other plants. The semi-double blooms are a striking combination of red stripes over a pink background, with yellow stamens in the center. It is lightly fragrant.

'ROSE DU ROI'
Portland   1815   3'–4'

The Portlands are important as parents of the Hybrid Perpetuals. This is a semi-double flower, compact growing and very fragrant rose. The color is an intense, bright red. A long flowering season adds to the value of this historic rose.

'Harison's Yellow'

'Russell's Cottage Rose'

R. damascena bifera
'AUTUMN DAMASK'
prior to 1819   4'–5'

Also known as the "Pompeii Rose," the origins of this plant are lost in antiquity. Richly fragrant flowers occur in abundance in spring, and in a scattering through summer and fall. This was probably the first remontant (flowering more than once) rose in Europe and created quite a stir before the more everblooming China roses appeared.

'HARISON'S YELLOW'
Hybrid Foetida   1830   6'–10'

Pioneers moving westward often took 'Harison's Yellow' with them, and it persists in old California gardens today, testifying to the transcontinental trek to new frontiers. Some historians consider 'Harison's Yellow' to be the 'Yellow Rose of Texas.' The flowers are a deep, pure, golden yellow, semi-double, with gold stamens. The shrub is thorny with dark green foliage. George F. Harison was a New York lawyer and amateur rosarian who apparently bred this rose in a suburban garden and sold it to a retailer, who popularized it. Spring blooming only, it is better adapted to areas at least one to two hundred miles inland from the Gulf Coast.

'RUSSELLIANA,' 'RUSSELL'S COTTAGE ROSE'
Hybrid Multiflora   prior to 1837   5'–6'

This rose is occasionally found at old homesites or cemeteries in Texas and the Gulf South. Although only a once-bloomer, it is very tough and disease resistant. The medium-sized, double flowers occur in mid-spring and are a rich purple, changing to lilac as they age. The fragrance is Damask-like. It is a useful plant for the background or as a specimen. The hips are orange and fairly large.

'SALET'
Moss   1854   3'–4'

The Moss Roses are well known for mossy glands on their calyxes and stems that secrete a resinous odor, causing the cut bloom to perfume the hand that holds it. The mossy sepals enclose beautifully formed clear pink buds and open flowers that have many closely packed petals. Salet reblooms as well as a modern Hybrid Tea, but is better adapted inland from the Gulf Coast at least a hundred or more miles.

'COMTE DE CHAMBORD'

Portland   1860   3'–4'

The double flowers of this rose are bright pink fading to lilac-mauve. They have the typical fine fragrance of the Portland class. The bush is compact and flowers occur over a long season. It is a very elegant rose and a favorite of many rose growers.

'GRÜSS AN AACHEN'

Floribunda   1909   3'–4'

'Grüss an Aachen' is generally considered to be the first Floribunda Rose, and by some to be the best of the class. The flat three-inch flowers are a beautiful shell pink tinted with salmon. The bush is compact growing and replenishes itself constantly with the beautiful and fragrant blooms.

'SILVER MOON'

Large-Flowered Climber   1910   10'–20'

'Silver Moon' is a vigorous, healthy, once-blooming rose that may be used as a large mound or climber. The foliage is a dark, shiny, green and the flowers are loose, semi-double, pure white with showy yellow stamens. It is very thorny but also nicely fragrant.

'Comte de Chambord'

'NEW DAWN'

Large-Flowered Climber   1930   10'–20'

'New Dawn' claims the distinction of being U.S. Plant Patent No. 1, the first rose patented under federal regulations. It is an everblooming sport of the well known 'Dr. W. Van Fleet' and exceeded the popularity of its parent. The foliage is dark, shiny green and typical of *R. wichuraiana* hybrids. Flowers are pale pink and fairly double. Although considered an everblooming rose, it tends to bloom heavily in spring, rest during the summer, and repeat with a good fall show. A massive grower, 'New Dawn' is useful as a large hedge or climber.

'GENE BOERNER'

Floribunda   1968   4'–6'

In spite of its relatively modern date, I cannot ignore the beauty and usefulness of this rose. It would be just about perfect if it had more fragrance, but for landscape effect it is as good as any rose I know. Beautiful buds open into large clusters of clear pink roses from mid-spring until freezing weather, and the plant is exceptionally healthy, disease resistant and vigorous. It is a strong grower and can reach six feet or more in a season. I have grown this rose as a grafted plant and from rooted cuttings, both with success. At one time, 'Gene Boerner' was one of the most popular roses in the South. For landscape use, it should still be.

'CANTERBURY'

Shrub   1969   4'–6'

This rose is an introduction of David Austin in England. A vigorous grower and dependable recurrent bloomer, its flowers are rosy-pink, semi-double, of medium size, and very fragrant. It is another good choice for use at the back of the border.

'Gene Boerner'

'Silver Moon'

ROSE CULTURE

Roses are amazingly versatile plants that respond favorably to a wide variety of growing conditions. There are a number of characteristics known to produce healthy plants and prolific blooming. The most important of these cultural practices are selecting a good site, soil preparation, proper planting, application of fertilizers, dealing with insects and diseases, watering, and pruning. Tips for handling roses as cut flowers are also included in this section.

Selecting a Site

Roses are sturdier and produce more flowers in full or nearly full sun. A site with at least five or six hours of direct sun is desirable. Early morning sun is especially good since it quickly dries any moisture on the plants, which reduces disease problems.

Good drainage is essential for all but a few varieties of roses. If water tends to stand in the root zone for extended periods, either choose another location or raise the planting bed enough to improve the drainage. Good air circulation is helpful in the prevention of diseases, but extremely windy sites may require windbreak protection for good flower and foliage quality.

Soil Preparation

Roses can thrive in a wide variety of soils, although some may require modification. Clay soils are preferred. These can be improved by incorporating four to six inches of compost, pine bark, peat moss, or similar organic material into the upper foot of soil. Agricultural gypsum incorporated into heavy, alkaline clay can also improve soil texture. Sandy soils require even larger amounts of organic material to help hold water and nutrients necessary for good growth and flowering.

Roses prefer a slightly acid soil (pH 6.0–6.8). Soil pH can usually be raised about one point by adding five pounds of ground limestone per 100 square feet of soil area. To lower pH or make the soil more acid, incorporate three pounds of iron sulfate or one pound of ground sulfur per 100 square feet. It is highly desirable to prepare beds or holes several months prior to planting. This allows organic materials and nutrients to become more available to the plants.

Planting

To plant only a few roses, dig individual holes for them. Holes should be at least 12″ deep and 18″ wide. Mix about one-third organic material (peat, pine bark, or compost) with some of the soil from the hole, along with a gallon or two of well-rotted cow manure, if available. A half-cup of bone meal or superphosphate thoroughly mixed with the soil is also a good idea. A similar amount of agricultural gypsum is beneficial for heavy, alkaline clay soils. Soil preparation can be done just prior to planting but is more effective if completed several months before planting.

Spacing of the plants will vary with varieties. Some Polyanthas can be planted as close as 18″, while Chinas, Bourbons, Teas, Hybrid Perpetuals, Hybrid Teas, and Hybrid Musks are best at 3′–5′ spacing, depending on the variety. Climbers and ramblers need more space to develop their potential. Eight to ten feet is appropriate for most, but under good growing conditions Banksias, Cherokee, and certain others could be spaced at intervals of 15′ or more.

Bare root plants should be set out as soon after receiving them as weather and time allow. If a delay of more than a few days is necessary, remove the plants from the shipping bag and "heel them in" by covering the roots and part of the top with loose soil. Container-grown plants may be set out at any time, but most rose growers avoid the hot summer months, when extra irrigation and care may be necessary to ensure success.

Prune tops back an inch or two, cutting just above a live and healthy bud on each cane. Trim back canes or roots damaged in shipping or handling to healthy tissue. Dig the hole large enough to accommodate the natural spread of the roots and fill with soil mixture described earlier. Firm the soil well around the roots and water thoroughly to remove air pockets and settle the soil. Plants should be set at approximately the same level at which they have been growing, or slightly deeper.

Fertility

For everblooming types, fertilizers should not be applied until the first set of flowers begins to fade; in the case of once-blooming roses, eight to ten weeks after planting. A heaping tablespoon per plant of a complete fertilizer such as 6-10-4 or 8-8-8 may be applied every four to six weeks until about two months prior to the average date of first frost. Application after that time can promote soft fall growth that may result in freeze damage.

Roses are heavy users of nutrients and respond favorably to the frequent application of fertilizers. To determine fertility of existing soil, it is a good idea to contact your County Extension Agent for instructions on submitting a soil sample.

The time-honored fertilizer and soil-conditioner for roses is well-rotted cow manure. Since manure is often unavailable today, however, commercial fertilizers have become popular. Phosphorous is the material that helps plants develop strong, healthy roots and prolific flowering. Superphosphate is usually available and can be applied at the rate of three to four pounds per 100 square feet. Since phosphorous is not very mobile in the soil, it should be well-mixed during preparation.

Nitrogen is easily and quickly depleted from the soil and needs to be applied periodically during the growing season. It is necessary for more and bigger canes, stems, and leaves.

Potassium is needed for promotion of new growth, disease resistance, and cold tolerance. All three nutrients (nitrogen, phosphorous, and potassium) are included in balanced fertilizers, which many rose growers apply every four to six weeks through the growing season.

Watering

Many old roses are drought resistant and can exist on rainfall alone in much of Texas and the South. Most modern roses require watering. Supplemental irrigation is also encouraged for old roses, however, to develop more attractive plants and much greater volume and quality of blossoms. Water can be efficiently applied with soaker hoses, drip irrigation, or specially designed automatic sprinkling devices, keeping in mind that most rose varieties are less disease prone if their foliage remains dry. Deep watering at weekly intervals is far superior to frequent light sprinkling.

Mulches can help conserve water while moderating soil temperatures during extremely hot weather. Bark, pine needles, or even coastal bermudagrass hay applied several inches deep to beds or individual plants is an excellent practice. The mulch can be supplemented with well-rotted cow manure during the winter, thus adding organic material as well as some fertility to the soil.

Insects and Diseases

Some gardeners choose to grow old roses because they are often more resistant to insect and disease problems, but this varies considerably among varieties. Roses grown in open, sunny areas with good air circulation tend to be freer of such pests.

Insecticides such as Malathion, Diazinon, or Orthene can be effective in controlling aphids, thrips and other insect pests. Miticides are used to control spider mites.

The major pest of roses in most of Texas and the South is a fungal disease called black spot. If left unchecked on susceptible varieties, it can cause the plant to lose most of its leaves. The disease appears as circular black spots frequently surrounded by a yellow halo. Infected leaves yellow and drop off prematurely. Benomyl, Funginex, or Maneb used according to label instructions is effective in the control of black spot disease.

Powdery mildew is another disease that is a problem on some varieties, especially in the spring and fall. It appears as white powdery spores, similar in appearance to flour, on young shoots and buds and can cause distortion of foliage and flowers. Materials such as Funginex applied according to label instructions usually control the problem.

Pruning

The traditional heavy pruning practices may be appropriate for Hybrid Teas, but most old roses require less severe methods. Diseased or dead canes should be removed or cut back to healthy tissue any time during the year. General thinning of weak or crowded growth can best be accomplished in February or early March in most of Texas and the South. Shaping the plants and shortening the vigorous canes by one-fourth to one-third of their length can result in more attractive plants. Care should be taken to prune most climbers and one-time bloomers *after* they flower in the spring so as not to reduce their seasonal show.

It should be kept in mind that most old garden roses are attractive landscape plants with a pleasing natural form, which should still be apparent after pruning. In addition to late-winter pruning, some rosarians cut their plants back moderately in mid-August. This practice along with a light application of fertilizer and a thorough watering, if needed, can promote an excellent fall floral display in many varieties.

Hybrid Teas, Floribundas, and Grandifloras are usually pruned heavily in late winter (down to 18″–24″ from the ground). Miniatures are pruned to a few inches above the ground at this time.

Cutting Flowers

Improper cutting of flowers can injure the plant and decrease its vigor. It is best to cut few, if any, flowers during the first blooming season after planting. By removing only the flowers and no stem the plants will develop into larger bushes by fall, at which time some flowers and stems may be cut. Early removal of flowers with foliage and long stems reduces the food manufacturing capacity of the plant and subsequent bloom yield.

When cutting, use sharp tools and allow at least two leaves to remain between the cut and the main stem.

Use sharp shears or a knife just above the topmost leaf. Roses that are cut just before the petals begin to unfold will open normally and remain in good condition longer. Late afternoon is the best time of day to cut roses.

Plunge the stems immediately into warm water (about 100 degrees F.) and recut the stems an inch or so from the base. Add flower preservatives according to label instructions if maximum life is desired. Research has shown that the useful life of roses and many other flowers can be doubled by floral preservatives which can be purchased from retail florists or from floral concessions in supermarkets. A mixture of 7-Up drink (not the diet type) mixed equally with water has been shown to be an effective preservative. It is important for the mixture to stand long enough for most of the air bubbles to disseminate.

A good pure water source is as important as the use of preservatives. Rain water or distilled water should be used when arranging flowers, since sodium and other materials in most tap water can shorten their life. Place the flowers in a cool draft-free area until ready to use. High temperatures and direct sun quickly take their toll on cut flowers.

PROPAGATING ROSES FROM CUTTINGS

One of the joys of growing old roses is the fact that most of them thrive as own-root plants; that is, they will grow as well—or better—from cuttings as when grafted onto a rootstock the way most modern roses are grown and sold. Rooting cuttings is a relatively simple matter. It is the way most old roses were handed down from one family member or friend to another, and the way many old rose collectors prefer growing them today. Fortunately for us in Texas and the Gulf South, most of our better adapted old roses are particularly well suited to growing on their own roots and can be successfully propagated by anyone interested in making the effort. Remember that roses still under patent (17 years from date of introduction) cannot be legally propagated without paying a royalty to the holder of the patent.

Some old roses, like those in the Gallica and Rugosa classes, tend to sucker badly and may spread into areas where they are not welcome. If this is a concern, varieties that sucker may be grafted or budded onto a rootstock that does not have this characteristic, such as 'Fortuniana,' *R. multiflora*, or 'Dr. Huey.'

The following suggestions for rooting rose cuttings are not likely to result in 90–100 percent rooting, but neither do they require special structures, watering systems, or daily supervision. Success will vary because of the large number of variables involved, but many people

Old Garden Roses and landscape plants

"Seguin College Pink"—roses and perennials garden design by William Welch and Nancy Volkman

report 50–75 percent of the cuttings they treat in this manner develop into usable plants.

When to Take the Cuttings

Roses may be rooted at any time of the year but, for home gardeners, success is much more likely during the cool months from November through February. Late fall is a favorite time because there are usually a few blossoms still remaining on everblooming types to identify them.

How to Take Cuttings

The easiest part of the rose to root is the tip of a stem that has recently bloomed. Ideally, these tips have withered flowers or hips beginning to form. The flower heads or hips should be removed down to the first set of healthy leaves. Cuttings should be 6″–8″ long and should be cut from the parent plant with a sharp knife or pruning shears at about a 45 degree angle. It is important that the cuttings not be allowed to dry out or be exposed to extreme heat or cold. Experienced old rose

D. Greg Grant

Rose cuttings with heads and hips removed

collectors often carry ice chests, plastic bags, a small amount of water, and ice if they are likely to be in very hot conditions before getting the cuttings to the rooting area. Cuttings may be stored for several days in this manner, if necessary, but the sooner they are stuck, the better.

Preparing the Cuttings

The use of rooting hormones has been shown to increase the percentage of cuttings that root and the number of roots per cutting, but it is not necessary for success. Materials such as Rootone are commercially available in powder form and are popular with some rose growers. Others also like to use a concoction called "willow water." This is derived by taking approximately one-inch sections of cut branches from willows, splitting them and setting them to soak in a pan of water that has been brought to a rolling boil. (Rain water is ideal.) Allow the willow pieces to steep in the water overnight. It should look like weak tea. Remove the willow pieces and soak the bases of the rose cuttings in the concoction for several hours, or overnight. It is helpful to recut the rose cuttings about a half-inch from the ends before placing in the willow water. Willow water may be prepared in advance to facilitate the process. It may also be used for the initial watering of the newly stuck cuttings. Although it sounds a bit far out, research at the Ohio Agricultural Research and Development Center has shown that willows (apparently any species of *Salix*) contain substances that can induce rooting. These substances can be successfully removed from the willow wood by the method described and have been shown to improve the percentage of cuttings rooting in controlled experiments.

Selecting the Location and Sticking the Cuttings

Selecting the site for sticking the cuttings is very important. Roses prefer a sunny location, but for rooting purposes it is usually best that they be shielded from the hot afternoon sun. Bright light but not direct sunlight is ideal. It is also good if a location can be chosen where the soil is sandy and well-drained, and where drip from the roof helps to keep the area moist. An east- or north-facing flower bed against a house or other structure is usually a good choice. The sand or sandy soil should be amended with one-fourth to one-third peat moss, composted pine bark or similar material. The cutting bed should be well-tilled or spaded to insure a good blend of the soil and organic materials.

Before sticking the cuttings (setting them into the cutting bed), remove all foliage from their lower halves, but leave that of the upper halves in place. If a powdered rooting hormone is to be used, this is the time to apply it. Tip some of the hormone compound from its container onto a sheet of paper and roll or dip into it the basal end of each cutting. After treatment, tap the cuttings lightly to shake off any loose powder. Use a wooden pencil or dibel to make a hole for each individual cutting, since this will protect the cutting from damage as it is stuck, and should prevent the removal of the rooting hormone. The cuttings should be stuck several inches or

Rooting hormone

Rooted cuttings

Rooted plant ready to set out

about half the length of the cutting into the media, and placed 6″−8″ apart in rows. Label each row with a permanent marker stating the variety, if known, or the site where collected, and include the date on which the cuttings were stuck. Be sure to firm the soil carefully around each cutting and water thoroughly.

Care During the Rooting Period

It is especially important early in the rooting period of the cuttings that they not be allowed to dry out. This may require watering every other day or so if rain does not occur. It should not be necessary to provide cold protection to the rooting cuttings in most of Texas and the Gulf Coast, but extreme cold can cause damage that could have been prevented by covering for a few hours or days.

During the first month or two after being stuck, the cuttings begin to develop what is called callus tissue, a swelling on the cutting base where roots are to develop. As the winter begins to turn to spring, the cuttings will sprout roots and new growth. This is a critical time for the new plants and it is important that they not be allowed to dry out. Although the young plants are usually well rooted by late April or May, it is best to leave them in place until the next fall or winter. They are extremely vulnerable to stress the first summer and should be allowed to develop a good root system, undisturbed.

Transplanting to a Permanent Location

By late fall or winter, the young plants should be ready to move to a permanent location in the landscape. They will be small, but most varieties grow quickly and produce a fair quantity of flowers by the next spring. To protect them from wind damage, it is usually a good idea to prune back any tall shoots and thin the plants as needed at the time they are being transplanted. During their naturally dormant period in late winter, the plants may be dug either with a ball of soil or bare root. For best results, plant in well prepared soil in locations receiving at least a half-day of sun. A regular fertilizer program may be started by mid-spring.

Hinckley's Columbine with roses

SUGGESTED ROSES FOR VARIOUS LANDSCAPE NEEDS

ROSES USEFUL AS HEDGES (1'–3')

'Cécile Brünner'   'Grüss an Aachen'
'Cramoisi Supérieur'   'Hermosa'
'Ducher'   'Marie Pavié'
'Louis Philippe'   'Martha Gonzales'
'Old Blush'   'Perle d'Or'
'The Fairy'

ROSES USEFUL AS MEDIUM HEDGES (3'–6')

'Archduke Charles'   'Gene Boerner'
'Ballerina'   'Hermosa'
'Belinda'   'La Marne'
'Bishop Darlington'   'Louis Philippe'
'Blush Noisette'   'Mary Washington'
'Buff Beauty'   'Mrs. B. R. Cant'
'Champneys' Pink Cluster'   'Old Blush'
'Climbing Cécile Brünner'   'Penelope'
'Cornelia'   'Radiance'
'Cramoisi Supérieur'   'Red Radiance'
'Ducher'   'Russell's Cottage Rose'
'Danaë'   'Skyrocket'
'Mrs. Dudley Cross'   'Vanity'
'Duchesse de Brabant'   'Wind Chimes'
'Erfurt'

ROSES USEFUL AS LARGE HEDGES (6'–8')

'Canterbury'   'Mutabilis'
'Chestnut Rose'   *R. palustris scandens*
'Climbing Cécile Brünner'   'Trier'
'Cornelia'   'Ulrich Brünner Fils'
'Madame Isaac Pereire'   'Zéphirine Drouhin'

ROSES OF OUTSTANDING VIGOR

'Cherokee Rose'   *R. banksiae banksiae*
'Mermaid'   'Fortuniana'
'New Dawn'   'Silver Moon'
R. banksiae 'Lutea'

ROSES HAVING ATTRACTIVE HIPS

'Ballerina'   'Prosperity'
'Belinda'   'Russell's Cottage Rose'
'Danaë'   *R. eglanteria*
'Jeanne d'Arc'   *R. setigera*
'Nastarana'   'Trier'
'Old Blush'   'Wind Chimes'
'Penelope'

ROSES OF OUTSTANDING FRAGRANCE

'Aimée Vibert'
'American Beauty'
'Autumn Damask'
'Basye's Purple Rose'
'Blush Noisette'
'Buff Beauty'
'Céline Forestier'
'Climbing Etoile de Holland'
'Crimson Glory'
'Champneys' Pink Cluster'
'Clotilde Soupert'
'Comte de Chambord'
'Devoniensis'
'Duchesse de Brabant'
'Fortuniana'
'Gloire de Dijon'
'Geant des Batailles'
'Grüss an Aachen'
'Jaune Desprez'
'Jeanne d'Arc'
'Lamarque'
'La Reine Victoria'
'La France'
'Louise Odier'
'Madame Isaac Pereire'
'Maréchal Niel'
'Marquise Boccella'
'Mme. Alfred Carrière'
'Marie Pavié'
'Mary Washington'
'Mrs. B. R. Cant'
'Mme. Ernst Calvat'
'Paul Neyron'
'Radiance'
'Red Radiance'
'Rêve d'Or'
R. moschata
R. multiflora 'Carnea'
'Russell's Cottage Rose'
'Sombreuil'
'Souvenir du Docteur Jamain'
'Ulrich Brünner Fils'
'Zéphirine Drouhin'
'Rose du Roi'
'Salet'

SUGGESTED ROSES FOR VARIOUS LANDSCAPE NEEDS

THORNLESS . . . OR NEARLY THORNLESS ROSES

'Mrs. Dudley Cross'
'Reine des Violettes'
R. banksiae 'Lutea'
R. banksiae banksiae
'Marie Pavié'
R. setigera serena
R. palustris scandens
'Rêve d'Or'
'Zéphirine Drouhin'

ROSES FOR PERGOLAS, PILLARS, GAZEBOS, AND POSTS

'Anemone Rose'
'Belinda'
'Ballerina'
'Belle Potugaise'
'Claire Jacquiere'
'Céline Forestier'
'Champneys' Pink Cluster'
'Cornelia'
'Climbing Cécile Brünner'
'Climbing American Beauty'
'Climbing Etoile de Holland'
'Devoniensis'
'Erfurt'
'Fortune's Double Yellow'
'Fortuniana'
'Gloire de Dijon'
'Harison's Yellow'
'Jaune Desprez'
'Jeanne d'Arc'
'Maréchal Niel'
'Mme. Alfred Carrière'
'Mermaid'
'New Dawn'
'Rêve d'Or'
R. moschata
R. laevigata
R. multiflora 'Carnea'
R. multiflora 'Platyphylla'
R. banksiae 'Lutea'
R. banksiae banksiae
R. anemoneflora
R. eglanteria
'Sombreuil'
'Silver Moon'
'Trier'
'Variegata di Bologna'
'Zéphirine Drouhin'

DARK ROSE AND RED ROSES

'American Beauty'
'Bon Silène'
'Climbing American Beauty'
'Climbing Etoile de Holland'
'Cramoisi Supérieur'
'Crimson Glory'
'Geant des Batailles'
'General Jacqueminot'
'General Schablikine'
'Louis Philippe'
"Martha Gonzales"
'Mrs. B. R. Cant'
'Monsieur Tillier'
'Red Radiance'
'Rose du Roi'
'Skyrocket'
'Souvenir du Docteur Jamain'
'Ulrich Brünner Fils'
'Will Scarlet'

PINK AND PURPLE ROSES

'Ballerina'
'Basye's Purple Rose'
'Baroness Rothschild'
'Belinda'
'Canterbury'
'Catherine Mermet'
'Cécile Brünner'
'Climbing Cécile Brünner'
'Clotilde Soupert'
'Comte de Chambord'
'Duchesse de Brabant'
'Erfurt'
'Gene Boerner'
'Georg Arends'
'Grüss an Aachen'
'Jean Mermoz'
'La France'
'La Marne'
'Marie Pavié'
'Marquise Boccella'
'Mevrouw Nathalie Nypels'
'New Dawn'
'Paul Neyron'
'Radiance'
'Reine des Violettes'
'Russell's Cottage Rose'
'Souvenir de la Malmaison'
'The Fairy'
'Ulrich Brünner Fils'
'Wind Chimes'

ROSES HAVING WHITE OR WHITE-BLEND FLOWERS

'Aimée Vibert'
'Autumn Delight'
'Ducher'
'Fortuniana'
'Jeanne d'Arc'
'Lamarque'
'Mme. Alfred Carrière'
'Mme. Joseph Schwartz'
'Nastarana'
'Penelope'
'Prosperity'
R. banksiae banksiae
'Silver Moon'
'Sombreuil'
'Trier'

ROSES HAVING YELLOW OR YELLOW-BLEND FLOWERS

'Buff Beauty'
'Céline Forestier'
'Claire Jacquiere'
'Harison's Yellow'
'Jaune Desprez'
'Lady Hillingdon'
'Maréchal Niel'
'Marie van Houtte'
'Mrs. Dudley Cross'
'Perle des Jardins'
'Rêve d'Or'
'Safrano'

7

Companion Plants for the Perennial Garden

Perennials and old garden roses are the most likely candidates for the herbaceous border or cottage garden, but reseeding annuals, small flowering trees, flowering shrubs, and vines were historically present and are still well worth considering. Each of these three categories of plants will be briefly discussed in this section. Also included will be suggestions of a few sample species from each group.

RESEEDING ANNUALS

Annuals that reseed and return year after year can be as valuable as perennials to the garden. There is something special about these plants that like your garden so well they choose to come back each year for another visit. In addition to convenience and economy, reseeding annuals add an informal, spontaneous charm to the garden, since they frequently come up in places where we have not planted them.

Since seed was a valuable commodity and money sometimes scarce, early Southern gardeners often saved seeds of favorite annuals from year to year rather than gamble on the generosity of Mother Nature. Trading seed was a popular custom among friends, and families often handed down particular annuals, vegetables, and herbs from one generation to another. Seed can be saved just as successfully today, to be sown in pots or trays indoors or in the greenhouse, so that seedlings may be later set out when and where desired in the garden.

Whether seed is collected and stored or allowed to fall and naturally germinate in the garden, it is important to remember that modern hybrid varieties often do not come true from seed. Since they are not open-pollinated by commercial growers, seed saved from many of these modern types may produce flowers that bear little resemblance to the parent. Large and double flowers may return as smaller single types, and once-bright colors may be more muted.

If you hope for your annuals to propagate in this manner, you must let the plants mature their seed. Obviously, this cannot occur if you pick the seed before it ripens or, worse yet, if you destroy the plants before they have had a chance to complete their growing and fruiting cycles. Sometimes this will mean tolerating plants for several weeks after they have passed their peak and are slipping into an unattractive senility.

Most seed keeps well in storage if allowed to dry for a few days, packed in airtight jars or self-sealing plastic bags, and placed in the lower part of the refrigerator (where the temperatures should range from about 40–45 degrees F.). Be sure to label the seed, since it may not be recognizable several months later when the time comes to plant it. If the seed is not to be stored but rather allowed to germinate naturally in the garden, it is helpful to shake the seed pods or the entire plant upon picking to make sure the seed is properly scattered and not thrown into the compost along with the dead plant.

Since most annuals require cultivation and fertilization to thrive, it may be necessary to work the soil and add organic material and fertilizer after the seed has fallen. This cultivation process may destroy some of the seeds by planting them too deeply, but usually a sufficient number remain to provide plenty of plants for the next season.

A frequent problem with reseeding annuals is overgermination. The seedlings may sprout up in such numbers and so close together that the plants cannot grow or flower properly. To combat this requires careful observation on the part of the gardener, regular checks of the young seedlings so that when they reach a size large enough they may be transplanted or thinned. Most young seedlings may be successfully transplanted when they put on their second set of leaves. Some annuals such as poppies and larkspur are difficult to transplant,

Viola tricolor—Johnny-Jump-Ups

however. Their seedlings should be thinned but the remainder allowed to mature where they germinated.

Young seedlings of flowering annuals may be difficult to distinguish from weeds because often they bear little resemblance to the mature plants. Distinguishing one from the other requires practice and patience, until the young seedlings of desired annuals become familiar. This also prohibits the use of most pre-emergent herbicides and heavy mulches in areas where reseeding annuals are desired. The mulches and herbicides are just as effective in controlling the desirable annuals as the weeds. Mulches can be applied after the seedlings have sprouted, but should be removed before it is time for the germination of the next year's crop.

The following annuals are separated into warm and cool season plants. Remember that because of our long warm season, many of these plants may be resown after the completion of their spring and early summer flowering for an additional late summer/fall bloom.

Cool Season Annuals That May Reseed

Viola tricolor
JOHNNY-JUMP-UPS

Johnny-Jump-Ups are among the most delightful reseeding annuals. The only one that has reliably returned each year in my garden is the common purple and yellow form with flowers about one-half to three-quarters of an inch across. Like miniature pansies, Johnny-Jump-Ups can cover the ground with their neat foliage and small, fragrant blossoms. Since this plant is very cold tolerant, its bloom often begins in December or January and continues until late May or early June. It is not uncommon for Johnny-Jump-Ups to move into lawn or other areas adjacent to where they were originally planted. They prefer full sun or partially shaded locations. A good way to introduce Johnny-Jump-Ups into your garden is to purchase started plants the first year. If conditions are right, they will reseed each year thereafter.

Alcea rosea
HOLLYHOCKS

Hollyhocks are one of the plants often associated with old-fashioned gardens. Although often listed as a perennial, in most of Texas and the Gulf South they are annuals. In alkaline soils, they are very susceptible to cotton root rot, a disease that quickly kills plants at their peak, and for which there is no practical cure. Spider mites are another problem that discourages some from growing Hollyhocks. In the Gulf South, it is important

Alcea Rosea—Hollyhocks

Ipomopsis rubra—Gilea, Standing Cypress

Gilea and Petunias

to start Hollyhocks in the fall or very early spring. They like full sun and well-drained soil. The old-fashioned single types are still available from a few seed sources. They often reach 5′−7′ tall and can make quite a picture in the garden. By early summer, Hollyhocks are ready to call it quits in our area. They do often reseed, with small plants sprouting in the fall after the first good rains. These seedlings may best be transplanted when several inches tall.

Ipomopsis rubra
GILIA, STANDING CYPRESS

Standing Cypress is among our most spectacular wildflowers. Its spikes of tubular red flowers can reach 6′ in height but are very narrow and are most effective in masses. Native to sandy, alkaline soils of Central Texas, Standing Cypress is sometimes biennial in habit. Dainty

rosettes of finely textured foliage appear in late summer and fall, but give little clue concerning what is to come. Sometimes the plants bloom by late spring, but occasionally they will wait until the second year to flower.

A vivid coral-red color coupled with their immense height make Standing Cypress one of the most spectacular plants in the landscape. Hummingbirds are attracted in droves to the bright, tubular flowers. Starting new plants from seed is not difficult and, once established, they often reseed freely.

Lupinus texensis & *L. subcarnosus*
BLUEBONNETS

Recent years have seen the availability of bluebonnets as fall bedding plants along with pansies and snapdragons. This is an ideal way to use them, but you may prefer growing your own plants from seed. To insure even germination, commercial bedding-plant growers treat the hard-coated seed with sulfuric acid for periods of 30 minutes to one hour. This can be a dangerous process since the acid is highly toxic. Another way to get through the seed coat is to file it down or rub the seed over sandpaper. Seed should be planted in September or October for best results. Bluebonnets normally reach about 1′ – 1½′ in height and width.

Delphinium grandiflorum
LARKSPUR

Larkspur is a wonderful, old-fashioned annual that produces beautiful spike flowers of pink, purple, white, and mauve. They do not like transplanting, but with care this can be done in late fall or winter. Double-flowering forms often revert to singles in a year or two. They reseed so prolifically that thinning is usually necessary. If

Delphinium grandiflorum—Larkspur combined with dill

thinned to about 1′ apart, Larkspur produce a full and impressive mass of color. Seed should be sown in September or October, in fully or partially shaded soils that have been well-worked and fertilized.

Antirrhinum majus
SNAPDRAGONS

I have only had modest success in persuading snapdragons to reseed, but they will sometimes produce a few plants in the vicinity of last year's display. In Zones 8 and 9, plants may be set out in September or October with a reasonable chance of their making it through the winter unharmed. Unfortunately, there are few nurseries currently handling snapdragons in the fall, and it may be necessary to grow your own from seed. Mature height is 18″ – 24″. By pinching the terminal growth during midwinter, plants can be made to grow fuller and more productive. Snapdragons are among the most impressive spike flowers we can grow, and they thrive in a wide range of soil types so long as they find sufficient moisture, fertility, and sunlight.

Chrysanthemum parthenium (Matricaria capensis)
FEVERFEW

Feverfew reseeds prolifically in my garden and is most welcome. The clusters of small, daisy-like flowers

Chrysanthemum parthenium—Feverfew

Antirrhinum majus—Snapdragons

Lobularia maritima—Sweet Alyssum

Papaver somniferum—Poppies

Old-fashioned Poppies

Petunia hybrida—Petunia

are perfect for cutting and combining with old roses and perennials. The single-flowering type is the only one that reseeds for me. Seedlings emerge in late fall and bloom by early spring. Pinching them back makes for better and more compact displays. Sun or partial shade is preferred.

Centaurea Cyanus
CORNFLOWER

Cornflowers are known as "Bachelor's Buttons" in some parts of the country, but most of us in Texas and the Gulf South reserve that name for *Gomphrena globosa*, another good reseeding annual. Cornflowers are available in white, pink, lavender, and purple-flowering forms, and have naturalized along roadsides in North Texas and other areas of the South. They are excellent for cutting and return reliably each year to well-prepared soils. Full sun is the best location for Cornflowers. They usually reach a height of 18"–24".

Papaver somniferum
POPPIES

Poppies were grown in most 19th century gardens of our region. Single-flowered purples and pinks were most common, although double-flowering types have also been around for a long time. Poppies definitely resent any disturbance after they germinate in the fall. They like rich soils and full sun. Seed may be scattered on top of prepared soils and lightly raked in. The seed was used in cooking by our ancestors, and is still popular in German and Czech communities of Texas.

Lobularia maritima
SWEET ALYSSUM

Sweet alyssum is a low-growing annual that covers itself with white, pink, purple, or lavender flowers during spring and early summer. These blossoms are highly fragrant, and reseed readily in open, sunny areas. Sweet alyssum is excellent as an edging plant or filler in the herbaceous border or cottage garden.

Petunia hybrida
PETUNIA

If you have not tried the old-fashioned single-flowering petunias, you are in for a treat. Colors tend to be in the purple, lavender, white, and pink range, all blending beautifully with each other. Fragrance is outstanding, especially in the evening. If you cannot beg a few plants from someone in your community, try planting a package of mixed colored, single-flowering

Old-fashioned Petunias

petunias. If a few harsh colors appear, weed them out, and in a year or two you will have a good stand of the old-fashioned type. Petunias are quite cold hardy and usually can be planted safely from early to mid-fall. They are wonderful fillers in the cottage garden, where they generally reseed prolifically. Young seedlings transplant readily. Old-fashioned petunias tend to be more heat and disease resistant than the modern hybrids in my garden.

Phlox Drummondii
DRUMMOND PHLOX

This native phlox reseeds readily in sandy soils and is spectacular during early to mid-spring. Colors range from dark red to pink, buff, and rose. Mature height is about 12″–15″. Seed should be sown in September or October. Young seedlings maybe easily transplanted during late fall and winter.

Borago officinalis
BORAGE

Borage is an attractive annual herb, once popular in Texas and the Gulf South. The flowers and leaves are sometimes used to flavor drinks. The drooping, bluish flowers and hairy foliage are handsome in spring and reseed readily, once established. I have found Borage in a number of old Central Texas gardens where it fits in nicely with other spring blooming annuals.

Anethum graveolens
DILL

Dill is one of those plants that was always present in the gardens of our ancestors. It is handy to have around for use as a culinary herb, and for the fine texture of its foliage and handsome heads of white flowers. Mature plants can reach 3′–4′. They prefer sunny locations and well-drained soil.

Anthemis nobilis
CHAMOMILE

Chamomile is best known as an herb, but it is quite useful as an ornamental. The flowers are small, daisy-like, and white with yellow centers. Foliage is bright green and of very fine texture. Chamomile reseeds prolifically and blooms all through the spring months. Sometimes seedlings that germinate in early fall bloom before winter.

Althea zabrina
FRENCH HOLLYHOCK

A. zabrina seems to be better adapted to our area than the common Hollyhock. It is somewhat smaller, with a mature height of 2′–4′. Flowers are striped purple and white, although a solid purple occasionally makes an appearance. *A. zabrina* is available from some of the large seed companies and should be started in the

Althea zabrina—French Hollyhock

Borago officinalis—Borage

French Hollyhock's striped purple and white flowers

fall or very early spring. It is reported to be a very old garden plant. I have found *A. zabrina* in the gardens of elderly people who received it from their ancestors. Sunny locations and well-drained soil are preferred. It is reported to have been grown by Thomas Jefferson at Monticello.

Warm Season Annuals That May Reseed

Zinnia elegans
ZINNIA

Zinnias are sometimes known as "Old Maids" in the South. When at their peak in late spring and early summer, they can be very colorful. Zinnias are favorites as cut flowers, and come in numerous flower and plant sizes, colors, and forms. They prefer sunny, well-drained, and well-prepared soils. Seed may be collected and saved, but often revert to single flowering types. The size known as "Liliputs" reaches 18"–24" and bears 1½"–2" pompon-type flowers in a wide variety of colors. Giant flowering types are also popular. The very dwarf types are not as well-adapted to the Gulf South as the larger ones.

Ocimum basilicum
BASIL

Basil reseeds profusely in the garden and is welcome for spring and summer seasoning of vegetables. It is moderately ornamental and easily grown in almost any well-prepared garden soil.

Tagetes spp.
MARIGOLD

Marigolds are available in a wide variety of forms and colors. The large, double flowering types were once popular in our area but have lost much of their appeal because they attract spider mites. Seed of marigolds may be collected and saved for next year but can vary greatly. Marigolds are at their peak in late spring and early summer. They may be replanted in late summer for a good fall display.

Catharanthus roseus
MADAGASCAR PERIWINKLE

Periwinkles seem oblivious to our summer heat and humidity. Some of the new prostrate-growing forms are particularly ornamental in the mixed border. Though seed collected from hybrid types seldom comes true, the

Celosia cristata—Cockscomb

results are usually welcome and attractive plants. Periwinkles reseed prolifically, and should be thinned to 12"–16" apart for best results.

Portulaca grandiflora
PORTULACA

Portulaca is sometimes known as "Moss Rose" in our area. It thrives in our heat and humidity to bloom from late spring till fall. As the days become longer, Portulaca flowers open only during the mornings and for a short time in the afternoon. They usually come in mixed colors, but favorite selections may be quickly rooted from stem cuttings. Portulaca rarely exceeds 6" in height, and should be spaced 6"–8" apart.

Celosia cristata
COCKSCOMB

The crested or "Cockscomb" forms of *C. cristata* were prized by our ancestors. They are excellent for drying and using in winter bouquets. Both crested and feathered forms come in several colors of purple, pink, yellow, and white. They grow readily from seed and often reseed prolifically in the garden.

Gomphrena globosa
BACHELOR'S BUTTONS

Bachelor's Buttons were a favorite in old gardens of our area and are enjoying a renewal of popularity. Like periwinkles, they seem oblivious to the heat and humidity of our long summer season. Colors include dark red-purple, white, and lavender-pink. New compact forms reach about half the typical 2' height and spread of the common species. Another name for this plant is "Globe Amaranth." They are excellent as summer filler in the mixed border. Seedlings emerge in late spring but do not really begin to produce significant numbers of flowers until midsummer. Thereafter, they usually remain attractive until November.

Bachelor's Buttons are also excellent for drying. If cut at their peak and hung upside down in a dry, well-ventilated area for several weeks, they are ready to be arranged. By spring, the colors are beginning to fade and the old blossoms may be shredded and replanted for the coming summer. This is truly a recyclable plant!

Dolichos lablab
HYACINTH BEAN

Hyacinth Bean is a beautiful, fall flowering vine that mounts an impressive display of sweet pea-like flowers in late summer and fall. It is probably of Old World

origin, though Thomas Jefferson grew it on interesting overhead structures made of tree limbs at Monticello, his Virginia home. Leaves are light green and divided, fan-like, into three leaflets. The stunning flowers are followed by velvety, $2''-3''$ pods of dark purple. In mild areas the vines are perennial, but are usually treated as annuals and used primarily for fast summer shade on trellises, pergolas and arbors. Seed may be easily saved and planted the next spring, although seedlings often return in the vicinity of last year's plants.

Cleome Hasslerana
SPIDER PLANT

The lavendar-pink form of *C. Hasslerana* is most common, but the pure white cultivar is preferred by

Bachelor's Buttons—a good summer filler for the mixed border

D. Greg Grant

many. Spider Plant is another annual that thrives on our summer heat and humidity. It reseeds prolifically and should be thinned to about 1′ apart. Mature height ranges from 2′–4′.

Cosmos bipinnatus
COSMOS

C. bipinnatus is a delightful annual whose flowers come in beautiful blends of purple, pink, and white. Mature height is 2′–4′. C. sulphureus is a yellow or orange form from Mexico that is more robust, sometimes to the point of being a pest. Mature height is 4′–6′ and plants can sometimes spread 2′–3′. Cosmos are useful as filler in the summer border.

Cosmos bipinnatus—Cosmos

Gomphrenia globosa—Bachelor's Buttons

Dolichos lablab—Hyacinth Bean

Cleome Hasslerana—Spider Plant—White Garden, North Carolina State Arboretum

Cassia alata—Candlestick Plant

Ipomea alba

Ipomea purpurea—Morning Glory

Cassia alata
CANDLESTICK PLANT

C. alata is a big, dramatic plant best reserved for the back of large borders. In fall, large, spikelike racemes of golden flowers appear at the end of each branch. Individual plants may reach 6′–8′ in height and width. Seed planted in mid-spring can be very large by fall. If winters are sufficently mild, *C. alata* can become a perennial. The large pods contain seeds that may be easily stored over winter and replanted the next spring.

Ricinus communis
CASTOR BEAN

Castor Beans are traditional plants of rural Texas and Gulf South gardens. The large, tropical foliage may be bronze-red or green and mature plants may measure 6′–8′ tall and wide. Castor Beans are useful for quick shade and screening during the summer months. Where winters are mild the plants may survive to become almost tree-like. Both seeds and foliage are poisonous if taken internally, and can also cause contact allergies.

Ipomea Quamoclit
CYPRESS VINE

Cypress Vine is native to the tropics, but widely naturalized throughout the South. Foliage is pinnately cut and flowers are bright red and 1½″ long. *I. Quamiclit* is useful for providing shade or screening during the summer months and may reach 20′ in a single growing season.

Ipomea purpurea
MORNING GLORY

Morning Glories are among the most easily grown plants. They can also be spectacular. Various colors are available, but the deep blue, large-flowering types are most common. Morning Glories are useful for providing fast shade on arbors and screens.

Impatiens Wallerana—Impatiens

Ipomea alba is known for its fast growth and luminous, large white flowers that bloom in the night. Their fragrance is outstanding on a warm summers' night.

Impatiens Wallerana
IMPATIENS

Impatiens are among the few flowering plants that thrive in shady locations. They like rich, well-drained soil and lots of water. A wide variety of flower colors is available. Impatiens reseed prolifically, although hybrid types usually revert to more common forms. Some of the newer selections have interesting variegated foliage and larger flowers. Impatiens may be readily propagated from stem cuttings during the growing season.

Impatiens Balsamina
GARDEN BALSAM, LADY-SLIPPER

The old-fashioned Garden Balsam reseeds prolifically and comes in a variety of flower-colors. Both double and single flowering forms are common. They thrive during late spring and early summer in sunny or partially shaded locations. Mature height is 12″–15″.

SMALL FLOWERING TREES AND SHRUBS

Small flowering trees are appropriate to use in cottage gardens and mixed borders since they are in good scale with such plantings. They can help to make a visual transition between the house and garden while providing seasonal color. Large shade trees were rarely seen in the cottage gardens of our ancestors, but fruit trees and some of the following suggested species were frequently present.

FLOWERING TREES

SCIENTIFIC NAME	COMMON NAME	HEIGHT	SPREAD	BLOOM SEASON	COLOR
Cercis canadensis	Redbud	15′–20′	12′–15′	Early Spring	Magenta
Cornus florida	Dogwood	12′–15′	10′–12′	Early Spring	White
Ilex decidua	Possumhaw	12′–15′	12′–15′	Fall, Winter	Red
Ilex vomitoria	Yaupon	12′–15′	12′–15′	Fall, Winter	Red
Lagerstroemia indica	Crape Myrtle	15′–20′	10′–12′	Summer	Many
Malus angustifolia	Crab Apple	15′–20′	15′–20′	Spring	Pink
Punica granatum	Pomegranate	12′–15′	6′–8′	Summer	Orange
Pyrus calleryana	Callery Pear	30′–35′	15′–20′	Spring	White
Vitex Agnus-castus	Vitex	12′–15′	10′–12′	Summer	Lavender
Prunus mexicana	Mexican Plum	12′–15′	12′–15′	Early Spring	White

FLOWERING SHRUBS

Flowering shrubs were an important part of early gardens in Texas and the Gulf South. In addition to the color and permanence they lend, several species bring fragrance to the garden. Used as specimens or in masses, flowering shrubs are useful plants for the modern or period landscape. The following list includes a sampling of flowering shrubs adapted to our area.

FLOWERING SHRUBS					
SCIENTIFIC NAME	COMMON NAME	HEIGHT	SPREAD	BLOOM SEASON	COLOR
Chaenomeles speciosa	Flowering Quince	5'–6'	4'–5'	Early Spring	Many
Callicarpa americana	Beautyberry	5'–7'	5'–6'	Summer, Fall	Purple
Hydrangea macrophylla	Hydrangea	4'–5'	3'–4'	Spring, Summer	Blue, Pink
Leucophyllum frutescens	Cenizo	3'–6'	3'–4'	Summer	Lavender
Lonicera fragrantissima	Winter Honeysuckle	6'–7'	5'–6'	Winter	Creamy
Michelia Figo	Banana Shrub	6'–8'	5'–6'	Spring	Creamy
Osmanthus fragrans	Sweet Olive	5'–10'	4'–6'	Winter, Spring	White
Prunus glandulosa	Flowering Almond	4'–5'	3'–4'	Spring	Pink
Spiraea thunbergii	Baby's Breath Spiraea	5'–6'	5'–6'	Late Winter	White
Spiraea Vanhouttei	Bridal Wreath Spiraea	5'–6'	5'–6'	Spring	White

VINES

Vines are an essential ingredient for cottage gardens. They add a dimension to the landscape unlike that of any other plants. Rambling roses, though not true vines, were favorite climbers in early Texas and Gulf South gardens. The following were also frequently present and provide considerable effect with little effort.

VINES			
SCIENTIFIC NAME	COMMON NAME	BLOOM SEASON	COLOR
Campsis radicans 'Mme. Galen'	Trumpet Creeper	Spring, Summer	Orange
Gelsemium sempervirens	Carolina Jessamine	Spring, Fall	Yellow
Lonicera sempervirens	Coral Honeysuckle	Spring	Coral
Wisteria sinensis	Chinese Wisteria	Spring	Purple
Vitis spp.	Grapes	Summer	Fruit

APPENDIX

The following list of mail order nurseries and plant societies is included to assist you in locating plants included in the text that may be unavailable locally. Some of the nurseries offer beautiful and interestingly written catalogs for which there is sometimes a small charge. It is suggested that when corresponding with nurseries or plant societies you enclose a stamped, self-addressed envelope. Some of the plant societies will gladly send a list of commercial sources for the plants they represent. This list is by no means complete, but is included to assist you in furthering your special gardening interests.

Mail Order Sources for Bulbs

California Gardens
18552 Erwin Street
Reseda, California 91335
(818) 344-4856
(Bulbs, succulents)

The Daffodil Mart
Route 3, Box 794
Gloucester, Virginia 23061
(804) 693-3966

Gladside Gardens
61 Main Street
Northfield, Massachusetts 01360

J.L. Hudson, Seedsman
P.O. Box 1058
Redwood City, California 94064

Kelly's Plant World
10266 East Princeton
Sanger, California 93657
(209) 294-7676
(Crinums, cannas, irises, daylilies, hymenocallis, etc.)

John D. Lyon, Inc.
143 Alewife Brook Parkway
Cambridge, Massachusetts 02140
(617) 876-3705

McClure and Zimmerman
1422 West Thorndale
Chicago, Illinois 60660
(312) 989-0557
(Bulbs, corms, tubers of many species)

Grant E. Mitsch Novelty Daffodils
P.O. Box 218
Hubbard, Oregon 97032
(503) 651-2742

Pine Heights Nursery
Pepper Street
Elerton Hills, Queensland 4053
Australia
(07) 353 2761

Shields Horticultural Gardens
P.O. Box 92
Westfield, Indiana 46074
(317) 896-3925, evenings and weekends

Anthony J. Skittone
1415 Eucalyptus Street
San Francisco, California 94132
(415) 753-3332

Ty Ty Plantation
Box 159
Ty Ty, Georgia 31795
(912) 382-0404

Mail Order Plant and Seed Sources for Perennials

Andre Viette Farm and Nursery
Route 1, Box 16
Fisherville, Virginia 22939
(vegetatively propagated perennials)

Antique Rose Emporium
Route 5, Box 143
Brenham, Texas 77833
(cottage garden perennials and old garden roses)

Country Garden
Route 2
Crivitz, Wisconsin 54114

The Fragrant Path
P.O. Box 328
Fort Calhoun, Nebraska 68023
(Seed of cottage garden and fragrant plants)

Harris Seeds
961 Lyell Avenue
Rochester, New York 14606

Heirloom Gardens
P.O. Box 138
Guerneville, California 95446

Holbrook Farm and Nursery
Route 2, Box 223-B
Fletcher, North Carolina 28732
(704) 891-7790
(Plants of many perennials)

Douglas W. King Company
P.O. Box 200320
San Antonio, Texas 78220
(Seed of native ornamental grasses)

Lamb Nurseries
101 East Sharp Avenue
Spokane, Washington 99292
(Less common perennials)

Louisiana Nursery
Route 7, Box 43 (Hwy. 182)
Opelousas, Louisiana 70570
(318) 948-3696 or 942-6404
(Daylilies, magnolias, many others)

Park Seed Company
P.O. Box 31
Greenwood, South Carolina 29648

Plants of the Southwest
1570 Pacheco Street
Santa Fe, New Mexico 87501
(Specializes in native grasses and wildflowers)

Sweet Springs Perennial Growers
2065 Ferndale Road
Arroyo Grande, California 93420

Sunnyslope Gardens
8638 Huntington Drive
San Gabriel, California 91775
(Specializes in chrysanthemums)

Thompson and Morgan
P.O. Box 1308
Jackson, New Jersey 08527

Turner Seed Company
Route 1, Box 292
Breckenridge, Texas 76024
(817) 559-2065
(Seed of native grasses)

Wayside Gardens
Hodges, South Carolina 29695

We-Du Nurseries
Route 5, Box 724
Marion, North Carolina 28752
(Specializes in southeastern U.S. natives)

White Flower Farm
Litchfield, Connecticut 06759
(wide assortment of perennial plants)

Wildseed, Inc.
P.O. Box 308
Eagle Lake, Texas 77434
(713) 578-7800
(Seed of annual and perennial wildflowers and grasses)

Woodlanders, Inc.
1128 Colleton Avenue
Aiken, South Carolina 29801
(Specializes in southeastern U.S. native plants)

Yucca Do Nursery
Peckerwood Gardens
P.O. Box 655
Waller, Texas 77484
(409) 829-6363
(Mail order list of unusual perennials, trees, shrubs. Appointment requested to visit gardens.)

Sources for Old Garden Roses

Antique Rose Emporium
Route 5, Box 143
Brenham, Texas 77833

Heritage Rose Gardens
16831 Mitchell Creek Road
Fort Bragg, California 95437

Pickering Nurseries
670 Kingston Road
Pickering, Ontario L1V 1A6
Canada

Roses of Yesterday and Today
802 Brown's Valley Road
Watsonville, California 95076

Plant Societies

American Daffodil Society
Miss Leslie E. Anderson, Executive Director
Route 3, 2302 Byhalia Road
Hernando, Mississippi 38632

American Hemerocallis Society
Mr. B.F. Ater
3803 Greystone Drive
Austin, Texas 78731
(publish extensive source lists)

American Hibiscus Society
Sue J. Schloss, Executive Secretary
P.O. Drawer 5430
Pompano Beach, Florida 33064

American Horticultural Society
Box #0105
Mount Vernon, Virginia 22121

The American Hosta Society
Mrs. Joe M. Langdon
5605 11th Avenue South
Birmingham, Alabama 35222

The American Iris Society
Mrs. Larry D. Stayer, Secretary
7414 East 60th Street
Tulsa, Oklahoma 74145

American Plant Life Society
Dr. Thomas W. Whitaker
P.O. Box 150
La Jolla, California 92038
(Primarily Amaryllides)

American Rock Garden Society
Norman Singer
Norfolk Road
South Sandisfield, Massachusetts 01255

The American Rose Society
P.O. Box 30,000
Shreveport, Louisiana 71130

Bulletin of American Garden History
P.O. Box 397-A, Planetarium Station
New York, New York 10024

The Cactus and Succulent Society of America
Miss Virginia F. Martin
2631 Fairgreen Avenue
Acadia, California 91006

Bev Dobson's Roseletter & Combined Rose List
215 Harriman Road
Irvington, New York 10533

The Herb Society of America
2 Independence Court
Concord, Massachusetts 01742

The Heritage Rose Foundation
Charles A. Walker, Jr.
1512 Gorman Street
Raleigh, North Carolina 27606

Heritage Roses Group
Mitzi VanSant, South Central U.S. Editor
810 East 30th Street
Austin, Texas 78705

National Chrysanthemum Society, Inc.
B.L. Markham
2612 Beverly Boulevard
Roanoke, Virginia 24015

North American Lily Society, Inc.
Dorothy B. Schaefer, Executive Secretary
Box 476
Waukee, Iowa 50263

Old Texas Rose Newsletter
Mrs. Margaret P. Sharpe
9426 Kerrwood
Houston, Texas 77080

The Royal Horticultural Society
Vincent Square
London SW1P 2PE
England

Seed Savers Exchange
Route 3, Box 239
Decorah, Iowa 52101

Southern Garden History Society
Old Salem, Inc.
Drawer F, Salem Station
Winston-Salem, North Carolina 27108

The Yellow Rose
Joe M. Woodard
8636 Sans Souci Drive
Dallas, Texas 75238

BIBLIOGRAPHY

Affleck, Thomas. "Recommended rose varieties for the South." (November 1856) found in the Louisiana and Lower Mississippi Valley Collections. LSU Libraries, Louisiana State University, Baton Rouge, La.

Affleck, Thomas. *Southern Rural Almanac.* (1860) found in the Louisiana and Lower Mississippi Valley Collections. LSU Libraries, Louisiana State University, Baton Rouge, La.

Ajilvsgi, Geyata. *Wild Flowers of the Big Thicket, East Texas and Western Louisiana.* College Station: Texas A&M University Press, 1979.

Bailey, Liberty Hyde, and Ethel Joe Bailey. *Hortus Third.* New York: MacMillian Publishing Co., 1976.

Bowles, E.A. *The Narcissus.* London: Waterstone & Co., Ltd., 1985.

Britschneider, Emilio. *History of European Botanical Discoveries in China.* Leipzig: Unversandter Nachbuch, Koehler's Antiquorium, 1935.

Bryan, James Perry, ed. *Mary Austin Holley: The Texas Diary, 1835–1838.* Austin: University of Texas Press, 1965.

de Zavala, Lorenzo. Correspondence, Archives, E.C. Barker Texas History Center, University of Texas, Austin.

de Zavala, Adina. "In Grandmother's Old Garden Where the Rose Reigned as Queen." *San Antonio Express*, September 2, 1934.

de Zavala, Adina. "Memories of Grandmother's Garden." *The Dallas Morning News*, December 16, 1934.

Doell, M. Christine Klim. *Gardens of the Gilded Age.* New York: Syracuse University Press, 1986.

Downing, Andrew Jackson. *The Architecture of Country Houses.* New York: Dover Press, 1969.

Downing, Andrew Jackson, ed. *The Horticultural and Journal of Rural Art and Rural Taste.* Vol. 4.

Earle, Alice Morse. *Old Time Gardens.* New York: MacMillian Company, 1902.

Earle, Alice Morse. "Old Time Flower Gardens." *Scribner's Magazine.* Vol. 20 (1896) pp. 161–178.

Fortune, Robert. "A Letter from Robert Fortune." Vol. 6 of *Journal of the Royal Horticulture Society.* 1851.

Gerdts, William H. *Down Garden Paths: The Floral Environment in American Art.* New Jersey Association of University Presses, 1983.

Griffiths, Trevor. *My World of Old Roses.* London: Whitcoulis Publishers, Christchurch, 1983.

Harkness, Jack. *Roses.* London: J.M. Dent & Sons, Ltd., 1978.

Harper, Pamela, and Frederick McGourty. *Perennials: How to Select, Grow and Enjoy.* Tucson: H.P. Books, 1985.

Hill, Madelene, and Gwen Barclay with Jean Hardy. *Southern Herb Growing.* Fredericksburg, Texas: Shearer Publishing Co., 1987.

Jekyll, Gertrude. *Wood and Garden.* London: Langmans, Green & Co., 1899. Reprint. Salem, N.H.: The Ayer Company, 1983.

Jekyll, Gertrude. *Colour Schemes for the Flower Garden.* London: Country Life, Ltd., Salem, N.H.: The Ayer Company, 1983.

Jekyll, Gertrude. *Wall and Water Gardens.* London: Country Life, 1901. Reprint. Salem, N.H.: The Ayer Company, 1983.

Jekyll, Gertrude, and Edward Mawley. *Roses for English Gardens.* London: Country Life, 1922. Reprint. Woodridge, Suffolk: Baron Publishing Co.

Jones, Beatrix. "The Garden As A Picture." *Scribner's Magazine.* Vol. 42 (1907) pp. 2–11.

Keays, Ethelyn Emery. *Old Roses.* 1935. Reprint. New York: Earl M. Coleman Publishing, 1978.

Lawrence, Elizabeth. *A Southern Garden.* rev. ed. Chapel Hill, N.C.: University of North Carolina Press, 1984.

Lawrence, Elizabeth. *Gardening for Love, The Market Bulletins.* Durham, N.C.: Duke University Press, 1986.

Metz, Mary Claire. *A Flora of Bexar Co., Texas.* Washington: Catholic University of America Press, 1934.

Nokes, Jill. *How to Grow Native Plants of Texas and the Southwest.* Austin: Texas Monthly Press, 1986.

Odenwald, Neil, and James Turner. *Identification, Selection and Use of Southern Plants.* Baton Rouge, La.: Claitors Publishing Division, 1987.

River Oaks Garden Club. *A Garden Book for Houston and the Gulf Coast.* Houston: Pacesetter Press, 1975.

Robinson, William. *The English Flower Garden.* 15th ed. London: Publisher, 1933. Reprint. New York: The Amaryllis Press, 1984.

Scruggs, Mrs. Gross R., and Margaret Ann Scruggs. *Gardening in the South and West.* Garden City, N.Y.: Doubleday & Co., Inc., 1949.

Sibley, Marilyn McAdams. *Travelers in Texas: 1761–1860.* Austin: University of Texas Press, 1967.

Simmons, Adelma Grenier. *The Silver Garden.* Tolland, Conn.: The Clinton Press.

Simmons, Adelma Grenier. *The World of Rosemary.* Tolland, Conn.: The Clinton Press.

Sperry, Neil. *The Complete Guide to Texas Gardening*. Dallas: Taylor Publishing Co., 1982.

Steen, Ralph W., and Frances Donecker. *Texas: Our Heritage*. Austin: Steck Vaughn Co., 1962.

Steen, Nancy. *The Charm of Old Roses*. Washington: Milldale Press, Inc., 1987.

Steitz, Quentin. *Decorating with Texas Naturals*. Austin: University of Texas Press, 1987.

Thomas, Graham Stuart. *Shrub Roses of Today*. rev. ed. London: J.M. Dent & Sons, Ltd., 1980.

Thomas, Graham Stuart. *The Old Shrub Roses*. rev. ed. London: J.M. Dent & Sons, Ltd., 1980.

Wasowski, Sally, and Julie Ryan. *Landscaping with Native Texas Plants*. Austin: Texas Monthly Press, 1985.

Wills, Mary Motz, and Howard S. Irwin. *Roadside Flowers of Texas*. Austin: University of Texas Press, 1969.

Index